Beyond Behavior Management

Beyond Behavior Management

The Six Life Skills Children Need to Thrive in Today's World

Jenna Bilmes

Redleaf Press
St. Paul, Minnesota
www.redleafpress.org

Published by Redleaf Press
a division of Resources for Child Caring
10 Yorkton Court
St. Paul, MN 55117
Visit us online at www.redleafpress.org.

Cover designed by Amy Kirkpatrick
Interior typeset in Adobe Minion, Scala Sans, and Triplex Sans
and designed by Dorie McClelland

Library of Congress Cataloging-in-Publication Data
Bilmes, Jenna, 1948-
Beyond behavior management : the six life skills children need to thrive in today's world / Jenna Bilmes.
p. cm.
Includes bibliographical references and index.
ISBN 1-929610-53-X (pbk. : alk. paper)
1. Classroom management. 2. Social skills in children--Study and teaching. I. Title.
LB3013.B54 2004
371.102'4--dc22
2004014238

Manufactured in the United States of America
11 10 09 08 07 06 05 04 1 2 3 4 5 6 7 8

For the children
and those entrusted with their care.

Acknowledgments

As I typed out this manuscript, so many names and faces passed before me—the children who taught me to look beneath the surface and the teachers who taught me their art, the new understanding from one training session and the new connection that was made at another. The book that you now hold is the collected wisdom of those hundreds of folks and dozens of presenters who have crossed my path and left their marks on my personal and professional life. I feel so honored to have been given the opportunity to gather that wisdom in this one volume, which I now pass on to you in their names.

A number of individuals, however, have altered my life path over the past thirty years and this book never would have happened without them. Y'all know who you are, but just for the record, I'd like to thank you one more time here:

- Sharon, who first got me to wonder how her one hug worked better than my ten time outs
- Isela and Lori, who hung in there for better and for worse and made possible the impossible
- Susan, who taught me that if you watch carefully enough and listen quietly enough, children will let you know what's in their hearts
- Mindy, Bev, Jen, Keith, Tyler, and John, who, because they trusted that I had something to teach, gave me unbelievable opportunities to learn
- Dr. Tara and Dr. Marcy, who brought their own knowledge and wisdom to the table and were never too busy to teach me what they knew
- The incredibly gifted and dedicated staff at FACES of Crisis Nursery, who have tried, fine-tuned, and endorsed virtually every idea in this book
- Those of you who asked for this book to be written; Redleaf Press, which made this book possible; and my editor, Beth, who did her magic to make it right
- The kids I work with every day, who amaze me with their complexity, diversity, and hope
- My ever tolerant family, who put up with my unavailability and all-nighters
- My buddy MR, who pushed me snitty by snitty, never doubting that I could do this

—Thank you to all
Jenna Bilmes

Contents

Introduction

Until Lizbeth entered my life, I believed I was a wonderful teacher. But it turned out that years of experience and my college degree were no match for this five-year-old. She threw paint on the windows and turned a favorite tape into a twisted mass of ribbon. She was fluent in the vilest profanity, and during a tantrum she head-butted me hard enough to crack a rib. Lizbeth was first to arrive in the morning, last to leave in the afternoon, and the only one not absent with chicken pox.

That year with Lizbeth was painful. But more importantly, that year I started on a journey that was to change the way I taught forever.

Lizbeth crossed my path after I had a few years of experience with children. By then I had learned classroom management from teachers with far more experience than I had. I gave my kids clear limits and time outs. They received praise when they behaved and stern words combined with "the look" when they did not. I saw, I tried, I conquered. It was the year of stickers, a student-of-the-week phase, and gold tokens for good nappers. With each management technique, I gained more and more control over the children in my care.

In my opinion, Lizbeth was a stubborn, spoiled, headstrong girl who needed to learn that she wasn't the boss of the universe, and I was determined to be the one to teach her that lesson. I reached deep into my bag of tricks and techniques in an effort to control and manage her. When she crashed a bike, I made her lose outside time. She demolished the class gingerbread house, so I forced her to sit in the time-out chair until she apologized to the other children. When she bombarded an innocent boy with her infamous profanity, I took away her right to go on the zoo trip. As she escalated her behavior, I escalated the consequences. But Lizbeth only became more disruptive and defiant.

When my bag of tricks was exhausted, I looked for others to blame. How could I be expected to fix a child whose mother wasn't willing to work with us? Look at the neighborhood she was free to roam at all hours of the day and night. And every time I sent her to the office, the director would give her a hug and a chat and would promptly return her to my room. I didn't send her down there for a hug! I wanted that girl to have the fear of God put into her. I wanted blood!

This child brought out the worst in me, time and time again. I became consumed with mean-spirited battles of will with a five-year-old that left me frustrated and discouraged. I had allowed Lizbeth's behavior to turn me into somebody I didn't like very much. It was time to look within myself, not only to examine my relationship with Lizbeth, but to rethink my entire approach to discipline and guidance. What were my goals for kids, anyhow? And did my current strategies help children reach those goals?

I had a pretty good idea of the beliefs and skills I wanted my kids to have. They should know how to have a friend and be a friend, and they should be able to solve conflicts with words rather than force. I wanted them to know right from wrong and to "be good" because that is what people do, rather than behaving so that they could get a reward or avoid a punishment.

But if that is what I believed, then why was I doing what I was doing? How were children to learn compassion when I told them to ignore their friend in the time-out chair who wept for his mommy? How could they practice conflict resolution when I was so quick to jump in as both judge and jury to solve all their problems? How were children learning to "be good" for good's sake when I was bribing them with rewards? Why did I make it my job to manage children's behavior? Shouldn't I focus instead on ways to give them the guidance and practice they needed to manage their own behavior?

One day in a workshop, a group of teachers listed all the strategies we used to teach children language and literacy. Lo and behold, time out wasn't on the list. Neither was the loss of recess, exclusion from the group, or guilt. Instead, we teamed reading-challenged children with other children in the class who could read. We gave them extra one-on-one practice, and we made sure they never felt inadequate. We gave them messages that there was nothing wrong with them and that we would all work together as a team to support them. Punishment was out of the question! If we punished them, wouldn't the child avoid reading or feel stupid and different from the rest of the children?

If we didn't make children feel bad to help them learn how to read, why, then, did we try to make children feel bad to help them act good?

The clouds cleared and the sun rose and I had my moment of epiphany. I heard the Big Message: The way most of us instinctively react to misbehavior is the least effective way to help children develop good behavior.

I probably should have felt good about this revelation, but I didn't. I knew I had to change my old practices, but I had no idea what to put in their place. I didn't even know anymore what my role was supposed to be in a child's life.

When I first taught two-year-olds, one of the more experienced teachers told me to try to distract children who cried when their parents left them. "Bring them to the window to watch the birds," she said. "If that doesn't work, just ignore them. They'll stop after a few minutes."

And then I had the privilege of working with Sharon. English, with long, wild hair and a tattered Laura Ashley dress, she was a combination Pied Piper and Mary Poppins to the fourteen kids in her care. I watched as she knelt down by a distressed child. "Oh you poor dear," she cooed. "You miss your mommy, don't you?" I expected the child to scream even louder, but instead the child began to calm down. "I sometimes miss my mommy too," Sharon continued. "Me too," the child said as the sobs stopped. "I like to look out the window when I feel sad," Sharon said. "Come, let's look together."

What a lesson for me! What a lesson to the child! And what a lesson to the other children in the class! In one brief moment, Sharon modeled compassion, empathy, and emotional management skills to all of us. In all of her interactions with children, she made herself the child's ally, not the child's enemy.

I began to think of different supervisors I had worked under. Florence was a nightmare. As soon as she would come near me, my stomach would tighten and I would avoid all eye contact in the hope that she would pass me by. Her exchanges with me were inevitably a list of things I was doing wrong and how she wanted them changed. Now and then she would throw me a bone with a "Good job" comment, which would roll off my back as I would await the ax to fall.

Sienna, on the other hand, was a born motivator. She worked with each of us as a mentor and a colleague. She would share her observations and solicit our input as we worked together strategizing how to make our school a better place.

I began to wonder how the children in my class saw me. Was I Florence, micromanaging their every move and pushing them to think of themselves as part of a problem? Or was I Sienna, respecting children and empowering them to be part of the solution?

I began to imitate new techniques I observed from my gifted mentors, often with no understanding of the theory behind the practice. All I cared about was that these new practices worked better than the management techniques I had learned before. Not only did my children with challenges improve, but also the atmosphere of community, acceptance, and cooperation flourished for all children in the classroom.

It has been fourteen years since I put a child in time out or handed out a sticker. Still a classroom teacher, I have also led workshops for hundreds of fellow teachers in the theory and practice of effective and humane guidance for young children. These generous educators have shared their own experiences and discoveries with me, and I pass along the wisdom I have collected.

I invite you to explore the theories and practices that can turn you and your children around. Help an unreachable, unteachable Lizbeth begin to connect with and care about others. Model compassion and caring for children so they know that the classroom is a safe place. Allow children to see you as their guide and ally as they learn to develop friendships, manage emotions, and resolve problems. Transform your classroom into the place you always imagined it could be.

I wish I could tell you that this journey is a simple one, but I can't. If guiding young children's behavior were an easy procedure, principals' offices would not be hosting a steady stream of children sent by teachers for being unmanageable. Parents, teachers, and the court systems would not be pulling out their hair trying to figure it all out, and you probably wouldn't be picking up this book today. The truth is that there simply isn't a step-by-step method that fits all situations or all children.

The good news is that each of us has a wealth of life experiences and wisdom within us. We can draw upon that knowledge to guide our thinking in effective ways to help kids on the path to becoming responsible, happy, and productive citizens.

As you tap into your personal wisdom, you will find yourself validating many of your current practices. Your effective strategies will become much clearer. At the same time, you'll start to understand why other strategies have not produced the results you were seeking. You won't find cookbook approach to "discipline" here. Instead, you will gain new understandings and some fresh approaches to weave into the art of your teaching.

1

The Six Life Skills

The journey from childhood to adulthood is a long one. There are many paths a child might take, each one leading to a unique future. As a teacher, you have the opportunity to guide children along their path for a short distance. To be successful as a guide, however, you need a clear vision of your destination. Only when you know where you are going can you make wise decisions about which roads to take.

Take an imaginary trip into the future for a few moments. Imagine that you are meeting up with your students again when they are in their early twenties. What do you hope to see?

Think for a moment or two about your hopes for the children you work with. Jot down a list of what you'd wish for them when they are young adults.

Your work with children helps to guide them into the future. This is especially true when we consider the issue of children's behavior. How we behave with children today models skills and gives them social and emotional choices they will use for the rest of their lives. Once you have a clear vision of where you are heading, it's far easier to find the road that will lead you to your destination. As we continue to explore the factors that influence children's behavior choices, keep your destination map in mind. Begin to envision what the road that leads to your goals will look like.

Beliefs and Skills

Children are born with no preconceptions about the world. It's only through their interactions with people and the environment that they begin to develop beliefs about how the world works. Loving people, plentiful food, and a peaceful environment surrounds one child. Another is born into a life of scarcity, surrounded by hunger, loneliness, pain, and fear. Reality for each of these children is different. The first child experiences life as a safe and happy adventure while for the second, every new experience carries the threat of harm and trauma. These experiences form the child's understanding of how the world works. A young child's beliefs about how the world works has a big influence on how that child approaches life at school. Will past experiences set the child up to look at school as an exciting adventure filled with potential new friends? Or, like Lizbeth, will that child come into school believing that the world is an unpredictable place full of people out to harm her?

Each child also brings to school a set of unique skills, traditions, and customs, which they have learned by watching and listening to the people around them. Some of these may come from socially unskilled models or from the media. Children may have had the fortune to learn from others who are socially competent. Some of this training is intentional, such as when a grandmother prompts her grandchild to say, "Thank you." Some of it is unintentional, as when children pick up skills and habits by paying attention to what works to get their needs met. Some children learn that smiles get attention while others learn that whining or tantrums work to get what they need.

Home Culture/School Culture

Our interpretation of children's behavior is based on our own, very personal philosophy of "right and wrong." These deeply ingrained beliefs evolve from the cultural norms with which we were raised. Don't confuse "cultural norms" with ethnicity. Culture encompasses more than that. It includes where we grew up, our socioeconomic status, our gender, our education, and many other variables. Because these cultural norms are so deeply ingrained, they become invisible to us. They are just the way things are done.

To do our best work with other people's children, it is essential that we start to clarify our own cultural assumptions and the beliefs of the families with which we work. The better we understand the cultural beliefs of our families, the better we can provide a culturally responsive classroom.

One way of thinking about cultural differences is to envision a spectrum, with *independence* at one end and *interdependence* at the other. Cultural ways of doing things lie along this spectrum. For example, many child-raising practices of white middle-class American families are designed to encourage children to be as independent as possible as soon as possible. It isn't "good" or "bad" to be at one end or the other of the spectrum, or to be in the middle. But teachers and parents whose child-raising practices are at different points along the spectrum may find themselves in conflict.

Let's see how a teacher at each end of the spectrum might interpret the same child's behavior. Notice how the same behavior might be interpreted as "good" or "bad" depending on the teacher's cultural background.

WHEN A CHILD . . .	A TEACHER FOCUSED ON *INDEPENDENCE* MIGHT SAY . . .	A TEACHER FOCUSED ON *INTERDEPENDENCE* MIGHT SAY . . .
Asks for help to put on her shoes	"You're a big girl. You can do it by yourself. Keep trying." (independence)	"Who can help Lotus with her shoes? She's having a hard time by herself." (helpfulness)
Won't share stickers she brought from home	"Robin doesn't need to share. Those are her stickers from home." (ownership)	"Robin, if you're going to bring stickers to school, you really need to share with your friends." (sharing)
Says, "Look, didn't I wash these paintbrushes good?"	"You sure did!" (child as an individual)	"You did your part to help keep our room clean." (child as part of the group)
Calls out an idea or thought during story time	"You're right, Pedro! This cat looks just like the cat from *Cat in the Hat!*" (oral expression)	"When I am reading, you need to be quiet. Raise your hand if you want to speak or wait until the end of the story." (listening to authority)
Spills milk while serving himself at snack	"You poured your own milk. Good for you!" (praise to promote self-esteem)	"Go clean up the milk you spilled." (criticism to correct behavior)

Like teachers, families'cultures place them somewhere along this spectrum. A culturally responsive early childhood classroom will support the child's home culture as well as introduce the child to a spectrum of other beliefs.

The activities, scripts, and interventions in this book can be used to support children and families whose cultural ways come from anywhere on a spectrum of independence to interdependence. They are designed to help teachers meet goals like these:

- Recognize children both as individuals and as members of the group.
- Promote both independence and interdependence.
- Work with children to balance assertion with respect for authority.
- Help children recognize their areas of strength and strategize how to work on their challenges.

If you find that a strategy isn't working or that a parent disapproves of a particular strategy, look deeper to see if the reason might be a cultural clash. If it is, either modify the activity or simply try another one instead.

The Six Life Skills

For children to negotiate the world successfully, they need to develop six strengths which grow out of positive beliefs about the world around them and culturally appropriate social skills. The six essential strengths are

- Attachment—"I have a grown-up who cherishes me and keeps me safe."
- Affiliation—"I can have a friend and be a friend."
- Self-regulation—"I can manage my strong emotions and am in control of my behavior."
- Initiative—"I am constantly growing and changing and learning new things."
- Problem solving—"I can solve problems and resolve conflicts."
- Respect—"I have unique gifts and challenges and so do others."

The way teachers approach guidance and discipline can either help children develop the strengths they need to have productive and purposeful lives or hold them back.

Attachment—"I have a grown-up who cherishes me and keeps me safe."

Reflect for a moment on your own experiences, and think about the people who have affected your life. Was it a grandmother or a teacher? Was it a coach? What were the qualities of those personal relationships? Did you feel safe with that person? Did you feel valued? How did that person earn your respect?

To be successful in school and in life, children must believe there is an adult they can count on to nurture them and keep them safe. They need a vision of adults as valuable resources who can guide and support them through their journey of growth and development. Children who have no need for or trust in adults, resist when teachers try to help them navigate their worlds. Once teachers establish warm and mutually respectful relationships with children, children become open to being influenced and guided. Often the fastest course to get a child back on track is to build up the relationship between the adult and the child.

The idea that personal relationship is vital is the most puzzling and, at the same time, the most exciting part of guiding young children. When you strengthen your relationship with a child, you earn the possibility of influencing her development. Only when you heal your relationships with difficult children can you help them heal their behavior. Attachment is the single most important place to start the healing when you are faced with a child with challenges. It is the most essential and most basic of all the strengths. The first step in working with a challenging child is to examine your personal relationship with that child and to find ways to strengthen that relationship.

Adults instinctively express pleasure with children who are behaving appropriately. It's also natural to express displeasure with children who are off track. We assume that all children want our approval and that they will change behavior that gets our disapproval. When our pleasure and disapproval fail to work, we look for "stronger" ways to express approval and displeasure, such as reward and punishment systems. However, children who are not attached place little value in our feedback. When we escalate our guidance attempts by using techniques such as rewards and punishments, we often push children even further away. Instead of drawing children closer and increasing their attachment, we erode our relationships with them. They place less value on our approval or disapproval, and the whole cycle continues.

The importance of personal attachment was driven home to me years ago by a very wise supervisor when I was teaching a particularly challenging child. My laundry list of offenses that PJ had committed was miles long and my efforts to control his behavior went nowhere. Time outs, stickers, sharp words, and lost recesses meant nothing to this child. As I grew more frustrated, he grew more defiant and disruptive. In frustration, I went to my supervisor for tips on what else I could do to manage his behavior. When she told me to start a daily journal on him, I expected her to tell me to keep track of his offenses. But that wasn't her goal at all. Instead, she told me to write down ten positive things about PJ every day. The notion was laughable. I was sure I could barely find one positive thing a day about this defiant and unlikable child, much less ten.

It was almost impossible that first day for me to come up with ten positive things to say about PJ. But each day it became easier. I never shared my list with anyone, not my supervisor and not PJ. But remarkably, the more positive things I began to write down, the more compliant PJ seemed to become. By the end of the week, it was clear that we had turned our ugly relationship around and began to actually enjoy each other. The exercise of looking at PJ through new eyes of appreciation was the trigger I needed to begin to bond with him. As I focused more on his positive and lovable traits, he felt that love and acceptance and began to draw closer to me in return. This is an example of the magic of attachment.

Affiliation—"I can have a friend and be a friend."

We want children to become happy and productive members of society. One of the stepping-stones toward this goal is for children to identify themselves as members of a larger group. For young children in our care, that translates into being an important and useful member of the classroom community. Many children need help to make the step from thinking the world revolves around them to identifying themselves as part of a larger group.

Children who value being community members have a vested interest in the overall well-being of the group and are motivated to learn and apply empathy, social skills, and conflict resolution. Children who possess basic friendship skills get along well with their peers. They know how to enter a group without triggering conflict, and they know how to "play car races." They sing along with others during circle time and pass the instruments around the circle when the signal is given.

Children may feel alienated from the classroom community for a number of reasons: cultural differences, ability differences, physical differences, or because other members of the classroom community have not drawn them in. They often exhibit problematic behavior. Some may strike out at other children or become agitated, cry and fuss, or fall into a tantrum. Other children might begin to withdraw and play more and more often by themselves. When you have a child in your class who lacks "entry to play" skills, how might that child try to join in with children who are building a tall block tower? More often than not, they will knock the tower over, which is their inept way of saying, "Can I play too?" Without appropriate play themes, these children might toss baby dolls across the room instead of feeding them and putting them down to nap or they might crash bikes into the fence instead of playing gas station. Children who don't know how to take turns or share might hoard all the glue at the art table or have a tantrum when another child has the job of line leader.

Children who feel alienated from their peers may be on a serious path to destruction. Some of these children internalize their feelings of isolation and end up being suicidal as adolescents. In fact, statistics released in 2002 revealed suicide as the third leading cause of death among U.S. teens age fifteen to nineteen (National Center for Injury Prevention and Control 2001). While some children internalize their isolation, others may externalize their feelings and become aggressive or may strike back. The Columbine disaster is one example of how a group of alienated young adults chose to express their isolation.

An alienated child is a potentially dangerous child. An affiliated child is on a healthy path to success in school and in life. Help children connect with their peers and to see themselves as a valued and essential part of their classroom community.

Self-Regulation—"I can manage my strong emotions and am in control of my behavior."

One of the most troubling challenges for early childhood teachers is the child who lacks emotional self-management skills. These children might hit before they think, can't wait for a turn, or cry and have tantrums easily. Teachers might observe that these kids seem to be controlled by their emotions, much as newborns are. When newborns are hungry, they cry. When they are colicky, they kick their legs and scream. When they sense a nipple, they root and latch on. No thought goes into this behavior. Newborns feel and then do. Children who lack emotional self-management skills appear to behave in a similar way.

Managing emotions is a very complex skill:

- Children must have a basic understanding that actions have consequences, both positive and negative.
- Children need to know what kinds of behavior are culturally acceptable. Can boys cry? Can girls play with action toys? Is hitting okay?
- Children need an awareness that they, not their feelings, control their behavior and that they have the power to manage their emotions.

Children learn about emotions from the people around them. When adults manage their own anger and frustration, they are teaching children emotional self-management skills. The way adults guide and support children with their emotions sends strong messages to children about ways to express and manage feelings and behavior.

Some children struggle with transitions and change because they are unaware that feelings fluctuate and that their emotions don't have to control their behavior. For example, when such children are contentedly playing at the water table, they might feel frightened by being asked to move on to another activity, which requires them to leave their comfort zone. This kind of transition is threatening to their sense of well-being. A child might feel similarly uncomfortable when the room has been rearranged or when there is a new parent-helper in the classroom. Children may express these feelings in very different ways: one child might call out of turn or talk during quiet times; another might hit or call names or use profanity when asked to move out of her comfort zone; another might cry easily or collapse into a tantrum over a relatively minor obstacle, or perhaps even one that is invisible to the teacher. It's important to remember that even if you don't understand what is wrong or why the child has such strong feelings, the feelings are real to the child.

Model and teach emotional self-management skills to impulsive and emotionally overwhelmed children. Help them develop the foundations they need to eventually manage strong emotions on their own.

Initiative—"I am constantly growing and changing and learning new things."

Safari concentrates on putting together a new puzzle, trying one piece after another to find the special one she is looking for. Javonne tests what will happen when she pours water down a funnel into an empty bottle. Adrian asks his teacher how to write "I love you, Mama," and Manny sits at the table with the teacher learning how to hold scissors so they will cut better. All of these children are showing initiative.

When a child lacks initiative, they may choose the same activity day after day or quit an activity as soon as they encounter the first challenge. Children may be verbal about their lack of initiative. They might say things such as, "I can't do it," "I don't want to try that," and "This is too hard for me." You may notice that they don't look forward to events in the future.

Help children build initiative by modeling your own initiative and by paying careful attention to your interactions with children. What you say and what you do when you interact with a child who is struggling with a challenge influences how that child will react to the next challenge. Gain an understanding of which factors build or tear down initiative so you can weave initiative-building strategies into the daily life of the classroom.

Problem Solving—"I can solve problems and resolve conflicts."

Problems and conflicts are part of everyday life. Teachers can help children understand this and can also arm children with confidence that problems can be resolved. Children who believe that problems can be solved will be able to cope with the ups and downs of daily life better than children who don't.

Problems can overwhelm some children, as a result of temperament or life experiences. A simple challenge, such as being unable to put on a shoe, can feel like the end of the world. Spilled milk or a conflict over the red swing can be so overwhelming that a child feels no choice other than to strike out with fists or hurtful words. Some children become so overwhelmed by what appears to be an uncontrollable situation that they withdraw into a corner or fall apart weeping or screaming. Children who have a long history of being punished when they have problems or conflicts with others often get out of the habit of thinking of strategies to resolve problems and become resigned to just paying for the misdemeanor.

Help children understand that problems and conflicts are a natural and expected part of daily life. Model your own strength in the face of adversity to help children understand that they have within themselves the ability to work through these challenging situations. While few people find problems and conflicts pleasurable, children can learn to see these obstacles as manageable.

Children need to learn the skills of problem solving in the same way that they need to learn the skills to get dressed. Think of all the little steps children need to practice and perfect to put on a pair of pants. They have to find the front of the pants, coordinate putting in one leg at a time, pull the pants up over their hips, and learn how to work the fastenings. What is so easy for adults takes time and practice for children to master. When we realize the many skills children need to solve problems on their own, we can understand why problem solving is so challenging for young children and why they need so much support.

Respect—"I have unique gifts and challenges, and so do others."

Almost every preschool activity book includes an activity called "I Am Special." However, developing a respect for oneself and others is far more than that. "I Am Special" guides children inward toward an egocentric view, but it is equally important to turn children's attention outward. Help children focus on recognizing and celebrating the unique gifts that each individual brings to the group. At the same time, we want children to appreciate that everyone has their own challenges. When children learn to respect their own uniqueness and the uniqueness of others, they can begin to appreciate how powerful they can be when they join in with others to complete a project or a task. Help children value interdependence as much as they value independence.

What Can Teachers Do?

Children come to early childhood classrooms with a whole range of skills and personalities. Some children are beginning to read while others have no previous experience with books. Some children are social butterflies who draw peers to them like bees to a flower. Other children are content to play alone. Some children are well on their way to developing the six strengths, and others have barely begun.

What steps can a teacher take to help individual children reach their destination of social and emotional competency? What role does a teacher play in guiding children along that path?

As you read through the six strengths, specific children may have popped into your mind. Reflect now on those children you know or have worked with. Think of a child who has the six strengths. How does she behave? Think of a child who lacks many of these strengths. What kinds of behavior do you see from him? If you are like many other teachers, your own evidence shows that children who have these six strengths tend to do well in life, while those who don't have these strengths tend to struggle more.

When children present us with challenging behavior, we are in a hurry to stop that behavior as fast as possible. The problem is, though, that behavior is just a symptom of an underlying problem. Focus on stopping the symptom and you might not eliminate the problem. Perhaps you will get the child to stop biting, but now the same underlying problem will be expressed with new symptoms such as tantrums or withdrawal.

To understand this better, imagine that you have had chronic, severe headaches. You have tried a few aspirin and other over-the-counter painkillers to address the symptom, but nothing has eliminated the headaches. What would be your next step? You might go to your family doctor. The doctor would gather information from you about your symptoms and about what you had tried so far. Next, the doctor would schedule a number of tests to diagnose the underlying problem. Perhaps the problem is low blood sugar or migraines or a vision issue or stress or a brain tumor. Each of these problems would require a different approach to eliminate the headaches.

The same is true with children's behavior. Perhaps the tantrums are a result of stress, or maybe they are a learned behavior, or they might be due to limited language or few self-regulation skills. Maybe the child doesn't know how to solve problems or maybe the child uses tantrums to get a need met. Until you figure out the underlying problem, you can't figure out the best way to address the symptom.

Build the Six Life Skills

The most effective way to help a kid change a problem behavior is not to address the behavior itself, but instead to address the strengths that underlie the behavior. Every time we intervene with a misbehaving child, here is the first question we should ask ourselves: Am I helping this child to build the six strengths, or am I moving this child even further in the wrong direction?

If the response or intervention moves a child further away from building the six underlying strengths, how can we expect more positive behavior?

When you have questions about interventions or strategies you are using or thinking of using, always ask yourself "Will using this strategy help build or weaken the six strengths this child needs to thrive in today's world?"

Attachment

Will the strategy move the child to see you as a supportive and loving ally or as an opponent who works against them? Will the strategy help the child feel safe and secure or add a layer of fear and apprehension?

Affiliation

Will the strategy build ties, friendships, bonds, and a team or family feeling? Or will the strategy single this child out as somewhat unappealing, unacceptable, and deficient? Will the strategy move the child to be more a part of the group or will the child feel more apart from the group?

Self-regulation

Does the strategy validate children's feelings and reassure them that the whole range of human emotions is acceptable? Will the strategy help the child understand that feelings change over time? Does the strategy model self-regulation on the part of the adult?

Initiative

Does the intervention promote the idea that we are all growing, changing, and learning, or does it leave the child feeling like a failure before he's even five years old? Does it leave the child feeling hopeful or hopeless, empowered or powerless?

Problem Solving

Does the intervention help children understand that all problems can be solved? Does it promote the belief that "might makes right" or does it encourage working to find the best solutions for all parties involved?

Respect

Does the intervention help the child build self-respect? Did the interaction help the child strengthen respect for others? Was the child demeaned in the eyes of peers?

Sphere of Influence

While we would love to be able to control the behavior of children in our care, the reality is that compliance is voluntary. While we might be able to influence Little Johnny, ultimately he is the only one who can directly control his behavior, just as we are the only ones who can control ours. And while we may have concerns about the neighborhood he lives in, we can't change his home environment.

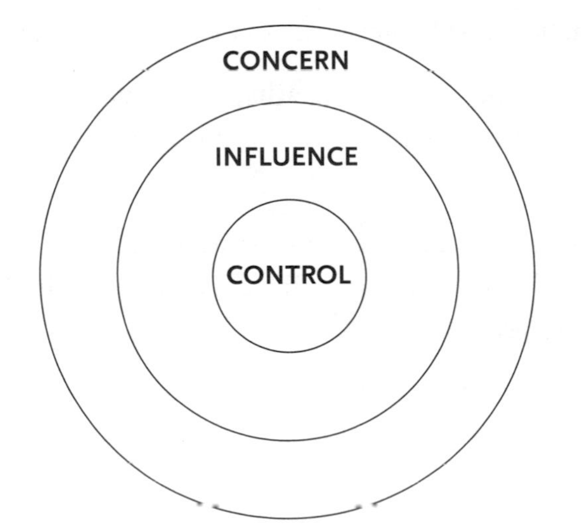

How then can you control Little Johnny and the rest of the class? You can't. Attempts to control the class or make a child behave will only be an exercise in frustration. The only person you can control is you. The better question is how to expand your sphere of influence so that you can help the class function better and help Little Johnny make better choices. There are many strategies under your control that will expand your sphere of influence over the children in your care:

- Strengthen your personal relationship with children and their families.
- Learn new guidance techniques, attend workshops, read books, and consult colleagues.
- Make a plan to help all the children develop the beliefs and skills they need to manage their own behavior.

All these strategies are within your control. You will never have control over Little Johnny's bedtime or the discipline choices of his family, but by working to build bridges of trust and respect, you can expand your sphere of influence and begin to work with them as a team.

Be clear about those things over which you have direct control, those you might influence, and those about which you may have concerns but no control. Remembering the limits of your control will help you invest your time and energies wisely when you make plans on how best to approach children's behavior and social-emotional growth.

With an awareness of our sphere of control, what is our overall plan to empower children to manage their own behavior?

Our Behavior Plan

Our plan is to help each child develop positive beliefs about how the world works and learn the social and emotional skills they need to succeed in school and in life.

- We will provide a supportive and nurturing environment that meets children's needs physically, emotionally, socially, and cognitively so that children feel cherished and safe.
- We will commit to providing interactions and experiences that help children develop the strengths of attachment, affiliation, self-regulation, initiative, problem solving, and respect.
- We will design specific intervention programs and support for children who need additional help in developing the strengths they need for success in today's world.

- We will bring in outside resources as necessary to help all children in our program reach social and emotional competency when we have exhausted our own resources.

Discussion/Reflection Questions

1. What are your long-term goals for the children in your class? Twenty years from now, what kind of personal qualities would you like to see in them?
2. Are there any connections between the six strengths and what you want for children? Describe them.
3. Look at each of the six strengths from a parent's point of view. How might a parent who values *independence* describe each of the six skills? How might a parent who values *interdependence* describe each of the six skills?

Exercises

1. Take a closer look at a challenging child in your group. Which of the six strengths are they lacking? What is the relationship between the behavior that is driving you crazy and that strength or strengths? Which strengths is the child already developing?
2. Looking either at that same child or another challenging child in your group, explore whether the behavior that bothers you might be a cultural difference in expectations between school and home. Might you value independence while the family emphasizes interdependence? Might you expect more interdependence while the family guides the child toward more independence? How can you find out what the family's expectations are?

Reflection/Journal Assignment

Think of yourself in relation to the six strengths. How have these strengths helped you to get to where you are today? Are you still working to develop one or more of these strengths? If so, how has lacking a strength had an impact on your life?

Resources

Brooks, Robert, and Sam Goldstein. 2001. *Raising resilient children.* Chicago: Contemporary Books.

Cesarone, Bernard, ed. 1999. *Resilience guide: A collection of resources on resilience in children and families.* Champaign, IL: ERIC Clearinghouse on Elementary and Early Childhood Education.

Divinyi, Joyce E. 1997. *Good kids, difficult behavior: A guide to what works and what doesn't.* Peachtree City, GA: The Wellness Connection.

Dreikurs, Rudolf, and Vicki Solz. 1964. *Children: The challenge.* New York: Duell.

Greenspan, Stanley I., and Serena Wieder. 1998. *The child with special needs: Encouraging intellectual and emotional growth.* Cambridge, MA: Perseus Publishing.

Katz, Lilian G., and Diane E. McClellan. 1997. *Fostering children's social competence: The teacher's role.* NAEYC Research into Practice series, vol. 8. Washington, DC: National Association for the Education of Young Children.

Marshall, Hermine H. 2001. Cultural influences on the development of self-concept: Updating our thinking. *Young Children* (November): 19–22.

National Center for Injury Prevention and Control. 2001. *Injury fact book 2001–2002.* Atlanta: Centers for Disease Control and Prevention.

Nelson, Jane, Lynn Lott, and H. Stephen Glenn. 2000. *Positive discipline in the classroom: Developing mutual respect, cooperation, and responsibility in your classroom.* 3rd ed. Roseville, CA: Prima Publishing.

Perry, Bruce Duncan. n.d. Keep the cool in school: Promoting nonviolent behavior in children. http://teacher.scholastic.com/professional/bruceperry/cool.htm.

Tobin, L. 1991. *What do you do with a child like this? Inside the lives of troubled children.* Duluth: Whole Person Associates

Trumbull, Elise, Carrie Rothstein-Fisch, and Patricia M. Greenfield. 2000. Bridging cultures in our schools: New approaches that work. A WestEd Knowledge Brief. http://www.wested.org/online_pubs/bridging/part4.shtml

Weinstein, Carol. 2003. Culturally responsive classroom management: Awareness into action. *Theory into Practice* 42, no. 4 (Autumn): 269–76.

Werner, Emmy. 1993. Risk, resilience, and recovery: Perspectives from the Kauai Longitudinal Study. *Development and Psychopathology* 5 (Fall): 503–15.

York, Stacey. 2003. *Roots and wings: Affirming culture in early childhood programs.* St. Paul: Redleaf Press.

2

Effective Teaching Strategies

As a teacher, you already have many of the skills to help children develop the strengths they need for success in school and in life. Let's begin by reviewing what you already know about how best to teach young children. In the chart below, list five or more typical discipline and guidance techniques in the left column.

TYPICAL DISCIPLINE AND GUIDANCE TECHNIQUES	TEACHING RHYMING WORDS
______________________	______________________
______________________	______________________
______________________	______________________
______________________	______________________
______________________	______________________

Now imagine for a moment that you have decided to teach the children in your group about rhyming words. For two or three weeks you have used many of the strategies that you know from experience will help children learn the concept of rhymes. You read poems and do finger plays. You read predictable rhyming books and play rhyming games. And after that time, most of the children in the class can tell you that *hat* rhymes with *cat.* But Bev and Jennifer are still in the dark. After another week of activities and songs, Bev catches on, but Jennifer still doesn't understand. In the column at the right, list at least five things you would do to help Jennifer.

Did your right column include most of the strategies you listed in the left column?

Probably not. As you look over the column on the left, you might notice that many of those strategies would not help a child learn a new skill such as rhyming. Those strategies might even discourage a child from learning at all! The reasons that you wouldn't use those techniques to teach Jennifer rhyming are the same reasons those techniques won't teach children appropriate social or emotional skills. They're not effective teaching strategies.

What Is an Effective Teaching Strategy?

Responding to troubling behavior is difficult, and we want that behavior to stop immediately. When individual children do things to hurt others or to disrupt the peace of the classroom, we sometimes feel like striking back and making that child "pay" for the pain and chaos they have created. We have the mistaken belief that making the child feel bad is the fastest road to making the child act good.

Years ago teachers tried to use many of those techniques to teach reading or math. When my mother was a child, teachers sat children in the corner with a dunce cap or they rapped a child across the knuckles with a ruler if they lagged in reading. We listen to those stories now and say "Tsk, tsk, how primitive." Yet when a child is struggling socially, we still have him wear a version of a dunce cap—only now we call the dunce chair a time-out chair and we have replaced the dunce cap with names written on the board. Our public, shaming techniques flaunt the child's social or emotional challenges to her peers and to anyone else who walks into the classroom.

Maybe you have tried your best to teach a child a certain social skill, but still the child repeats the undesirable behavior. What do you do then?

Think again about a literacy problem such as rhyming. What if you had taught the skill in all the ways you know how and the child still didn't get it? Most teachers say that they would refer the child out to find out if some developmental or organic problem was preventing the child from learning. And that is exactly what you should do for social or emotional issues as well. Once you have tried all the techniques you know, it's time to tap into the wider circle of your professional support team for help. You assume something else might be going on with the child that another specialist might spot.

Punishment

"But what if I have taught the right behavior and I know they have learned it, and they still purposely misbehave? Isn't punishment appropriate then?" Many, many teachers have questions like these. Let's think about why children might not be using the skills we are pretty sure they have, and what might be effective to help them.

Have you ever made a New Year's resolution? Have you ever kept one? You're an adult, you're highly motivated, you know exactly what you are supposed to do, and by Valentine's Day you find yourself slipping back to old patterns. Think of a child who has learned at home to print his name in all uppercase letters. We invest a lot of time to teach children how to print their names in upper- and lowercase letters. Do they still print their names in all caps frequently? Many do. They know the new behavior, they know what is expected, and they are highly motivated to be successful. Yet they still revert back to old habits. The same happens with social and emotional skills. We can teach children how to stand in line and practice many times, but when they are excited or under stress, they go back to their old behavior of pushing and hitting. For all of us, it takes lots of practice to change old patterns until the new behavior becomes so automatic that it becomes part of who we are.

So often we teach the child a skill and immediately throw him back into the problem situation and expect him to "perform." Maybe he is splashing others at the water table where we have used a kind but firm technique to teach that splashing others is out of bounds at school. The child seems to have clearly understood our guidance and has agreed to keep the others dry from now on. A minute later, there he is again, splashing his buddy. What is happening here?

Here is an example from an adult's life experience: Imagine for a moment that your best friend is a recovering alcoholic, celebrating her third week sober. You have gone with her to a holiday party where alcohol is being served. Would you leave your best friend alone at the beckoning champagne table for half an hour while you make a phone call? When our friends or relatives are struggling to break an addiction or a sweet tooth, we stay sensitive to their vulnerability as they work to establish new habits. We support them in situations when temptation hovers. We surely don't intentionally put temptation in their path.

Extend the same care and courtesy to the children in your care. When a child is struggling to learn not to push in line, have her be your partner so you can support her early attempts. If a child is learning to share toys, stay close by with him in the block area and at the water table. When a child is practicing the new skill of conflict resolution, gently reinforce the process rather than sending the child back alone to "use your words." Don't expect more from a young child than you would expect from yourself or a loved one.

But won't punishing children help them to pay attention? Won't knowing there's a consequence for misbehavior motivate them to remember the behavior we have spent so much energy to teach them? Often this punishment debate is a sticky issue for adults. It seems to make sense to punish children or give them consequences for misbehavior now, since that is what we do later on in adult society. If adults speed, they get a speeding ticket. Shouldn't children learn now that bad behavior gets punished?

On the surface, it seems to make a lot of sense to give children consequences. After all, isn't it important for them to learn that if they continue challenging behavior as adults that they will get adult consequences?

Shift your thinking again to literacy. What are some of the consequences in the adult world for being functionally illiterate? Less income? Fewer choices about the kind of work you do? Lower standards of living? If functionally illiterate adults suffer those consequences, wouldn't it make sense to give negative consequences now to a child who never pays attention at book time? Should we give that child the old broken desk in the drafty dark corner of the classroom? Should we give the child half portions at lunch and explain, "Here you go. Illiterate people don't earn enough money for a lot of food. And no more desserts at school since only literate people can afford them."

Most teachers would read the above paragraph with horror that I even suggested such treatment of a child who is not interested in books. It seems absurd to punish a young child for not liking to read. It is just as crazy to punish children for being socially or emotionally illiterate. We should do everything in our power while these children are still young to give them skills so they can avoid having that kind of life later.

Punishing children doesn't help them to develop the strengths they'll need to thrive in today's world. Punishment, and other negative and hurtful strategies, do nothing to move children along the road to learning life skills. In fact, they knock children off the road to social and emotional competency. Teachers should do their best to teach children the skills they need and help children build the strengths they require for success in school and in life. Teachers who follow this path will be instrumental in guiding children to reach their social and emotional goals.

Rewards

Do we want to raise children who make behavior choices based on bribes and rewards? Do we want to motivate children to say "What will I get if I clean up the room?" or "How much will you pay me to get an 'A' in math?" Rewards and punishments are the flip side of the same coin. While a reward feels like a reward, lack of a reward feels like a punishment.

Rewards change behavior in the short term, but what is the long-term cost of using such a strategy? Do we really want to raise kids who behave only when they think they will be rewarded?

Teachers are bigger than little kids and have a wealth of goodies, whether it is stickers, praise, recess, or tokens, that they can use to get their own way. As the adults in charge, teachers have the power to give or withhold the goodies. The downside of these techniques is that we are not modeling the kinds of behavior we want to see the children imitate. On the contrary, the use of rewards models the very behavior we want children to stop! Instead of helping children appreciate that success in life depends upon maintaining healthy relationships, we model for children the promise of bribes and the threat of pain to navigate relationships. How many times have you shuddered to hear such manipulations as "If you don't give me the bike, you can't come to my birthday party," or "If you give me the truck, I'll be your best friend." Where do you think children learned them?

Surely we don't want to begin modeling this kind of manipulation during a child's most vulnerable years. Instead, help children build their own internal motivations and moral compasses so they can make positive choices in life.

Blame or Moving Forward

Most of us respond to the finger of blame with excuses or rationalizations. Blame also goes hand in hand with an attempt by the blamer to somehow make the other pay for what they did. Instead, an approach of defining and solving problems is based on making a better future.

Problem solving may involve making amends or fixing what went wrong. It may involve looking at the original source of the problem and developing strategies to prevent the problem from happening again in the future. While the focus of blame is to punish and look to the past, a focus on problem solving is to plan for a better future.

There is a difference between consequences, which are designed to have children pay for a misdemeanor, and making amends, which is designed to help repair an error or an injury. Making amends is a life skill, and an important lesson for children is "If you've messed it up, it becomes your responsibility to fix it up." When adults do something inappropriate, the social expectation is that they will make the situation right. If a child knocks over paint while running through the classroom, having her sit in a time-out chair isn't as effective as helping her take responsibility for the mess she created.

What amends can you think of for a child who has knocked paint off the shelf? If you are having trouble thinking of something, try to picture a staff room where a teacher has knocked paint off the shelf. What kind of behavior would we hope to see from an adult? Perhaps we would expect them to clean it up. Maybe if it is a special paint, they might work to replace it. We don't want to teach children that punishment erases the damage done. We want them to take responsibility and make it right.

When we focus our energies on blame and on trying to make children pay for their poor choices, children focus their energies on making excuses. When we focus our energies on problem solving, children are guided toward taking responsibility for their behavior choices. Here's how this might look in the classroom:

Blame

TEACHER: Adrian, I warned you about splashing water on the floor at the water table. Go find someplace else to play now.

ADRIAN: I didn't do it. Ja'Quan made me splash the water.

TEACHER: I'm not talking about Ja'Quan, I'm talking about you. I saw you doing it. Now walk away.

ADRIAN: *(Throws the cup in the water table, splashing again)* I hate this stupid school.

Problem Solving

TEACHER: Adrian, I see water on the floor by your feet at the water table. How are you going to take care of that?

ADRIAN: I didn't do it.

TEACHER: It doesn't matter who did it. But it's dangerous and needs cleaning up. What are your ideas to fix it?

ADRIAN: Ja'Quan and me can get the paper towels and wipe it up together.

TEACHER: That sounds like it might work. Try it out and see.

Make a conscious decision. Will you invest your energies in pointing the finger of blame and guilt, or will you encourage children to learn from their mistakes and guide them toward making a better future?

Making a Start

Where do we start when we try to figure out how best to respond to and support children in their growth and development? What characteristics make us effective guides for children? What kinds of environments will bring out the best in children?

Think for a few minutes about the best job you ever had. And also think about the worst job you ever had. Think about the workplace atmosphere; think about your supervisor. Fill in the chart on the next page with words and phrases that come to mind.

WORST JOB/WORST SUPERVISOR	BEST JOB/BEST SUPERVISOR
______________________	______________________
______________________	______________________
______________________	______________________
______________________	______________________
______________________	______________________

After you have filled the chart with your initial thoughts, ask yourself these follow-up questions:

- How did you feel in each situation when you made a mistake?
- How did you feel in each situation when you did a good job?
- How did you feel about going to work each day?
- When you reflect back to each of these situations, which emotions come to the surface?

Add your reflections to the bottom of each of the columns, then review your lists when they are completed. Think once again of what each job brought out in you, how you felt, and how well you worked. Now take a deep breath and try to figure out how your lists relate to working with young children.

When we reflect on our own histories, it becomes clear what kinds of leaders and what kinds of environments bring out the best in people. A quick reflection on what kind of leaders we are and what kinds of environments we have established for children often reveals cause for celebration as well as startling and disturbing revelations.

You may realize that you have many of the qualities you have admired in your own best supervisors. You may suddenly understand why many of your practices have been so successful.

You may also begin to understand why you struggle in other areas. This is not meant as an exercise in guilt. It is meant as a paradigm shift—a new way to look at an old situation. This new view may reveal many things that were hidden before. The first step in change is to be able to see the current situation objectively and identify any problem areas.

When I first did this exercise, I ran the gamut of emotions. Initially I was shocked. I had always viewed myself as an excellent and conscientious teacher. Suddenly, though, I saw many of my practices in a different light. Would I want to work for me? The answer was a firm no. Justification came next. I rationalized my practices by saying that adults are different than children, that in the workplace some of these children would be "fired," and that jobs and school are two different things. Even though a part of me understood that changes needed to be made, I felt defensive about my practices. I had learned and modeled my guidance practices from the best of the best. I have always tried to be a good and moral person who only wants the best for children. I couldn't accept the clear revelation that some things I was saying and doing with them were harmful.

When I entertained the notion of making some changes, my feelings moved on to panic and being overwhelmed. Where to start? How to do it? Would the children get out of control? What if it didn't work?

Understanding your definitions of quality leaders and environments will help you learn how to become the teacher you dream of being. Children respond to different leadership styles in the same ways we do. The same things that motivate us in the workplace motivate children in the school environment. The same qualities we admire in leaders in our own lives are the qualities that children respond to in the classroom community. Become a leader who fosters positive attitudes, behavior, and responses.

Would I want to work for me? That is the key question to ask yourself. The immutable law of nature is that we will reap what we sow. If your supervisor's behavior would motivate you to grow and change, if that supervisor's practice would excite you about doing your best work, if that environment would feel good and keep you coming back for more, then it will probably do the same for the children in your care.

What we teach children is directly linked to *how* we teach children. The values that a leader establishes for her organization become an integral part of the institutional culture itself. Leaders who model and practice honesty create institutions with honesty as a part of their culture. When leaders reward competition, the organizational atmosphere becomes competitive rather than cooperative. As you begin to think about your best approach to this monumental leadership role, stay aware that what we teach is directly linked to how we teach.

Institutional Culture

Like home and school, work environments have cultures. The institutional culture of a business can either support or undermine the people who work there. When we look at the lists that people generate about their best and worst job situations, we find common themes regardless of the industry in which they work. The lists for those who work in restaurants, offices, construction, and teaching are very similar. Lists about people's best work environments include items like adequate training opportunities, respect, teamwork, professionalism, empowerment, problem solving, and celebration of each person's contributions. It may surprise you to discover that these workplaces are also identified as the most productive and successful work environments. The time and energy that leaders invest in building supportive and healthy environments is not an interruption of business, but is in fact one of the cornerstones of a successful business.

WHEN LEADERS . . .	INSTEAD OF . . .	THEY ESTABLISH A CULTURE THAT VALUES . . .
Develop relationships	Putting mission and product before people; encouraging competition instead of teamwork	Attachment and affiliation
Think things over and respond thoughtfully and professionally	Reacting impulsively and in the heat of the moment	Self-regulation
Are proactive; acknowledge and resolve problems	Reacting every time something goes wrong, either ignoring problems or looking to place blame	Problem solving
Empower individuals and teams to make good decisions; encourage best work by focusing on intrinsic motivation	Micromanaging people; trying to control people by using rewards and reprimands	Initiative
Honor and recognize strengths and contributions of all	Focusing on challenges and deficits; publicly favoring some and speaking poorly of others	Respect

In the same way, the investment of time and energy in building a mutually respectful, proactive classroom atmosphere for children is not an interruption of the curriculum, but is the cornerstone of all positive growth and learning. It is just as important as beginning literacy and math; in fact, it makes teaching those things possible.

The specific answers of what to do, how to interact, and what kind of atmosphere and environment to set up lie within each teacher, and each teacher will have a somewhat different approach. Teaching is an art, not a science, and each teacher will express that art with her own distinctive style. At the heart, though, each teacher can discover certain guiding principles to guide his way, and for many of us, these guiding principles follow some general themes.

Develop relationships

WHEN LEADERS . . .	INSTEAD OF . . .	THEY ESTABLISH A CULTURE THAT VALUES . . .
Develop relationships	Putting mission and product before people; encouraging competition instead of teamwork	Attachment and affiliation

Good leaders know that the most powerful path to maximizing their impact and influence is to nurture healthy and respectful relationships and generate mutual respect. Investing in people expands their sphere of influence. Powerful leaders establish themselves as allies instead of opponents. As they lead their organization, they focus on relationships instead of on judgment.

Teachers can expand their spheres of influence in the same way as other organizational leaders:

- Develop a community based upon mutual respect.
- Establish yourself as each child's biggest ally and most loyal cheerleader.
- Keep your focus on maintaining healthy relationships while avoiding judgment.
- Expand your sphere of influence with a focus on relationships and the social and emotional climate of the classroom.

When in doubt about how to respond, reflect back on your favorite job and your favorite supervisor. Ask yourself "How would I like my own boss to handle this situation?"

The number one factor in children's development of positive beliefs and skills is the quality of the relationship between the child and the teaching staff. Children with easygoing temperaments, a quick smile, and well-developed social skills generally know how to engage adults and draw them close. On the other hand, children with difficult and challenging behavior do not bring out the best from most adults. It is very easy for our relationships to deteriorate quickly with these children. The result, unfortunately, is that the children who most need us to be emotionally attached are the same children who are most skilled at driving us away.

Learning a multitude of professional strategies, techniques, and interventions will help strengthen relationships with each of the unique personalities in your classrooms. When personal relationships have been damaged, you can use these strategies to begin repairing attachment, which is so necessary for the development of healthy beliefs and skills.

Think things over and respond thoughtfully and professionally

WHEN LEADERS . . .	INSTEAD OF . . .	THEY ESTABLISH A CULTURE THAT VALUES . . .
Think things over and respond thoughtfully and professionally	Reacting impulsively and in the heat of the moment	Self-regulation

When faced with children's behavior, two parts of us respond simultaneously—our impulsive, personal selves and our thoughtful, professional selves. The personal self often reacts from the feeling part of the brain, while the professional self reacts from the thinking portion of the brain.

To help clarify the difference between personal and professional responses, imagine that you are an emergency room nurse. The paramedics rush an accident victim in on a gurney, rattling off statistics, IV tubes swinging. As the first nurse on the scene, you pull back the sheets and see a devastating injury. The emotional, personal part of you initially retreats in horror—your eyes squeeze shut, your heart pounds, and your stomach gets tight. That is the feeling part of the brain reacting. However, you have a job to do. Immediately, you take a deep breath and move to the professional, thinking portion of the brain to give your best responses at the moment to save the patient.

Responding professionally to children requires a similar skill. The feeling part of you may be horrified, frustrated, repulsed, or hurt by a particular child's behavior at a particular moment. That human reaction is fine and to be expected. However, as a teacher, you have a job to do. You must move yourself from your personal feelings to your professional self. The thinking portion of your brain contains your long-term goals for the child, strategies you have tried and discarded, strategies waiting to be tested, your knowledge of beliefs and skills, the length of time until the next transition, and other situations that must be dealt with simultaneously. Your thinking brain can compute all the available information to come up with your best professional response for the moment.

For example, you might feel offended when a child picks food off her plate at snack and drops it on the floor. While your emotional self might say, "Pick that food up off the floor this instant and move to this table by yourself," your professional self might evaluate all the currently available information and say, "At school, when you don't want to eat you can say 'Miss Bev, I don't want to have snack.'"

Here's a strategy you might try to move from your impulsive, feeling self to your thoughtful, professional self: (a) stop, (b) take a step back physically, and (c) say to yourself, "What unusual behavior." Practice this response to give yourself the two seconds you need to move from the impulsive part of your brain to the thinking part of your brain. This strategy also allows you to assign the behavior back to the child where it belongs, instead of seeing children's behavior as a personal affront.

When you move yourself into that professional, thinking portion of your brain, you have switched into a problem-solving mode and have become a professional resource for the child. Isn't that part of what being a teacher is all about?

Acknowledge and resolve problems

WHEN LEADERS . . .	INSTEAD OF . . .	THEY ESTABLISH A CULTURE THAT VALUES . . .
Act proactively; acknowledge and resolve problems	Reacting every time something goes wrong, either ignoring problems or looking to place blame	Problem solving

Reacting to a problem or a behavior can be looked upon as rushing in to fix an emergency situation in process. For example, Tink bites Mack and an adult rushes over to deal with the situation.

Being proactive means attempting to prevent the problem from happening over and over. In this case, it might mean having Tink be your partner during transitions for the next few days to keep her close during a vulnerable time when she might strike out. At the same time, you would observe Tink to understand the underlying problem behind the biting so that you can address it.

To best understand the difference between being reactive and proactive when working with young children's behavior, imagine that suddenly the smoke detector goes off in your home. You rush everyone out and call the fire department, and they quickly arrive to put out the fire. They report to you that the fire began in the ceiling crawl space of the kitchen and that they were successful at putting it out. A few days later, the detector goes off again. Everyone is herded safely out of the house; the fire department arrives, puts out the fire, and reports to you that the fire started in the ceiling crawl space of the kitchen. The following week, the detector goes off again.

What is wrong with this story?

Putting out the fire is a reactive way of dealing with the problem. It is a crisis intervention technique. A proactive strategy would be to look for the source of the problem and address the cause so that the problem doesn't keep repeating itself. It doesn't matter how many times you put out that kitchen fire—until you find out *why* the fire gets started, you will continue to have the problem. Once you invest the time to hire an electrician to check out that crawl space and fix the problem, you will no longer have to waste your time calling the fire department.

Responding to children's behavior is very similar. Some problems seem to happen over and over again. Stormasia keeps hitting kids; Antwon always yells out at circle time; Patrick never participates at clean-up time. When children continue to repeat behavior regardless of the response, it's a sign that it is time to discover the source of the fire.

Empower and encourage

WHEN LEADERS . . .	INSTEAD OF . . .	THEY ESTABLISH A CULTURE THAT VALUES . . .
Empower individuals and teams to make good decisions; encourage best work by focusing on intrinsic motivation	Micromanaging people; trying to control people by using rewards and reprimands	Initiative

One of our goals for children is that they learn to take responsibility for their behavior. However, so many of the hand-me-down strategies that teachers use assign the bulk of responsibility to the adult, not the child. Even the common term *behavior management* spells out who takes the largest burden for controlling behavior—the teacher! Rather than learning more strategies to manage children's behavior, we might better reach our long-term goals by empowering children to manage their own behavior. It's not a matter of "doing *to*" children. Instead it's a matter of "doing *with*" children.

For example, when we say to a child, "I like the way you clean up toys," what we are really trying to do is to manipulate them to behave in a way to get our affection. Sometimes we try to get one child to behave by praising another; for example, getting JoJo to sit in circle by saying to the group, "I like the way Mike is sitting." Our praise to Mike may be well deserved. However, it becomes false praise when it's a tool to manipulate another child's behavior.

Instead, make it your goal to empower children to manage their own behavior.

When I was first learning how to guide young children's behavior from more experienced teachers, the core message was "reward behavior you want to see and punish behavior you don't want to see." This message is still implicitly and explicitly present in most of the ways we think about guiding children's behavior. Rewards and punishments do, indeed, cause rapid change in behavior for most children. However, the behavior changes will only last as long as the reward and punishment system is present. When individuals are *intrinsically* motivated, they make decisions based upon their internal values and beliefs. When they are *extrinsically* motivated, they make decisions based on external factors—what other people might think or do as a result of their behavior or the promise of reward or the fear of punishment.

Think for a moment of someone you admire and respect. What motivates that person to do the things for which you admire them? In all likelihood, it is not for the promise of reward or the fear of punishment. That person probably has some guiding principles of behavior, a moral compass, that they follow.

What's wrong with extrinsic motivation? Think about it a minute. As children grow and become adolescents and then adults, do you want them to make decisions based on what other people might think about them? Is that how you want them to handle peer pressure in high school? Do you want them to make the right decisions only as long as they are rewarded for them? Or do you want them to have an internal sense of what's right and wrong, a moral compass that they follow regardless of what others think or what the material rewards are for their decisions? Which makes them a stronger person?

When children grow to be adults, the moral police and the sticker lady don't trail them throughout the day. When adults do the dishes, bring soup to a sick friend, or show up for work on time, they don't get a gold star. We make those behavior choices because of an inner motivation to do what we know needs doing or what we feel is the right thing to do. Isn't that what we want for children?

Honor and recognize strengths and contributions of all

WHEN LEADERS . . .	INSTEAD OF . . .	THEY ESTABLISH A CULTURE THAT VALUES . . .
Honor and recognize strengths and contributions of all	Focusing on challenges and deficits; favoring some over others	Respect

The story of the two wolves has been passed around in many versions, although I have been unable to track down the original writer. One night, a wise grandfather sat his granddaughter on his knee to tell her the tale of the battle between two wolves that was going on inside himself.

"One wolf," the grandfather said, "is angry, resentful, jealous, hurtful, a quitter, a liar, greedy, and arrogant. The other wolf is filled with kindness, compassion, good intention, honesty, generosity, faith, and humility."

"Which one will win, Grandfather?" the girl asked.

He replied, "The winner is the one that gets fed."

Common sense seems to dictate that by constantly catching children who are off-task and reminding them to get back on track, we will change behavior for the better. Instead, we are often surprised when the behavior we are trying to change not only continues but becomes even more frequent! It doesn't seem to make sense until we reflect back on the lessons of the two wolves parable.

Recognition invites repetition. Children crave to be noticed and recognized. Early on they learn that smiles and gurgles will bring adult attention, which leads to even more smiling and gurgling from the baby.

In our interactions with children, the behavior that gets our focus, attention, and energy is what will grow and flourish. When we notice children's block structures, they make more block structures. When we comment on their skills on the climber, they climb more. And for many children, when we notice their off-task behavior, they increase their off-task behavior. Recognition invites repetition.

Think again of the story of PJ in chapter 1. When I focused on PJ's "flaws," things only got worse. Once I shifted my focus to PJ's strengths, the problem behavior began to recede and he began to flourish. The wolf that gets fed wins out in the end. Make sure you are feeding the right wolf.

Supportive Interactions, Classroom Culture, and Special Activities

Each of the next six chapters of this book focuses on building one of the six strengths. Within each chapter, activities and strategies are broken down into three categories: supportive interactions, classroom culture, and special activities. This order is deliberate. The most powerful impact we can have on children's behavior is through our daily, personal interactions. A classroom culture that supports and upholds the strengths is the next most powerful intervention. Our interactions and the classroom environment exist from the moment the child walks in the door until they leave at the end of the day. Invest the bulk of your energy in modifying interactions and the classroom culture.

Interactions and Relationships

Who we are and what we live—what we model for children—has the most powerful impact of any strategy on children. Our talk to children becomes their self-talk. Our expectations become their expectations. As an adult, you have the wisdom and experience needed to be a powerful influence on a child's life. Your interactions and interventions can help children become empowered citizens, committed to solving problems and making purposeful choices in the best interest of themselves and others.

Our daily interactions with children not only affect our personal relationships, but also model and set community norms for the entire classroom. The significance of adult modeling was brought home to me when my daughter, Tati, was a four-year-old in preschool. One of her favorite games to play at home with her dolls was a game she called "Christopher Vedra." She would set out a dozen dolls on the floor, each one lying on a baby blanket. Then she would announce, "Naptime! Everybody get quiet now." A moment later, she would begin to drag one of the baby blankets with baby across the floor saying sternly, "I told you to be quiet, Christopher Vedra. Now I have to move your mat." Another moment would pass and once again she would drag Christopher's mat to another area of the floor. This reprimand-and-move sequence would be repeated ten or fifteen times, each time more severely. Need I tell you that Christopher Vedra was a very active and challenging child in her class at school?

How often have you seen children playing teacher at school and heard your words come from their mouths? How many times have you watched children replay last night's domestic squabbles in the dramatic play area?

Sometimes what we are inadvertently doing at school is modeling exactly the behavior we are trying to stop. For instance, many teachers say to a crying child, "As soon as you are done crying, I will be happy to listen to your words." I learned that line from other teachers when I began working, and I must have used it a thousand times or more before I examined my behavior a bit more closely. When we say these words, what messages are we sending to the child in distress? And what messages are we sending to the rest of the class about socially appropriate ways to respond to people in distress? Twenty minutes later, when Isabel hits Jarred and Jarred is crying, we attempt to employ "Standard Teacher Script Number Two," which goes something like this: "Isabel, look at Jarred's face. How do you think he is feeling?" Isabel is most likely thinking, *As soon as he is done with that dang crying I'll listen to what he has to say.*

As we guide, support, and live with children, we can never lose sight that they are watching and listening to everything we do. To get children to say thank you, make sure you say thank you. To teach children to solve problems, make sure they see and hear you solve problems. To help children learn how to manage frustration, make sure you demonstrate your own anger management skills.

Look back again to the lists of qualities of your most and least favorite jobs. How many of the factors had to do with relationships and daily interactions? Was there an atmosphere of trust and respect? Was collegiality promoted or was there dog-eat-dog competition? Did administration establish an environment of all work and no play, or did the workplace include an element of joy and playfulness? Did you feel alone or did you feel like a part of a team?

As the leader of the classroom, you establish the standards for everyone in the room. The actions you take, the beliefs you have about individual children, and the learning environment you establish will be directly reflected in children's behavior and beliefs about themselves and each other.

Next to home, school is the biggest influence on young children. And next to the family, teachers are the biggest single influence on children. You have it within your power to make a significant impact on the beliefs and skills of the children in your care. And affecting beliefs in the right direction will result in the internal growth and development that children need to thrive in the classroom and in the larger world.

The Classroom Environment

The rituals and routines—the way of life you establish in your classroom—are a reflection of your philosophy and your leadership. Are there jobs for everyone in the classroom? Do you have a consistent daily schedule and a clear room arrangement? Do you have a routine to welcome new children and say good-bye to children who leave the program? The best way to help children learn the skills they need is to introduce and weave the skills regularly into many situations throughout the year.

Think about how you would like the children in your classroom to talk to each other. How would you like them to ask each other if they can play? How do you want them to share tools at the playdough table? What words would you like them to say if they accidentally hurt someone? Children learn what they live. Plan carefully how you will ask for a turn when you sit to work on a puzzle with a child or what you will say when you must interrupt a child's conversation.

Special activities help reinforce the lessons that children are getting from personal interactions and the classroom culture. They're a nice supplement, but by no means do they do the job on their own.

One Step at a Time

As you read the rest of this book, remember that growth and change involve a series of baby steps. Gradually, learn one new technique at a time—try it out and begin to weave it into your daily practice until you feel comfortable with it before you try another. Changing belief systems may be a revolution, but changing practice is an evolution. And similarly, it is important to remember that growth and change in children are also an evolution, not a revolution. Certainly, some strategic changes in practice have an impact on children and their behavior in immediate and dramatic ways. But true growth and change happen slowly over time, for us and for them.

What is the destination of our journey, then? As we have reflected on children that we know, we begin to see that those who are not armed with the six strengths struggle to survive from day to day. Their destination is mere survival. Our goal is for children to thrive. In our frustration or disappointment with a child's behavior, we need to learn to keep our focus on our long-term goals for the child rather than on the quick fix. Focus on reward and on its mirror side, punishment, produces fast yet temporary results. Focus on building relationships, self-regulation, problem solving, initiative, and respect for self and others helps children build the strengths they will need to thrive in school and in life.

As teachers of young children, it is important to keep our eye on the goal so that we don't get lost along the way. Help children learn to make good choices for themselves, for their communities, and for society as a whole.

Many children are unable to reach that destination alone. They need compassionate and clear-minded adults to help lead them along the path. Be that adult.

Discussion/Reflection Questions

1. What are some advantages and some disadvantages you have found in using punishments and rewards to manage children's behavior?
2. Discuss the quote "What we teach children is directly linked to how we teach children."
3. A Chinese proverb tells us "A child's life is like a piece of paper on which every person leaves a mark." How might a teacher's leadership style in the classroom have a long-lasting impact on a child's life?

Exercises

1. Increase your awareness of your personal interactions with children over the course of a day. What are some ways your current practices are helping children build the six strengths? What is one practice you are thinking of changing?
2. What kind of support do you need when you are making changes in your own life? How might you use this knowledge to support children in your classroom as they learn to develop the six strengths and change their own behaviors?

Reflection/Journal Assignment

Reflect on your favorite job or favorite supervisor, and describe your vision of the kind of classroom you would like to lead. What would the classroom feel like when you walked in the door each day? How would everyone in the classroom community interact with each other? How would successes be recognized? How would problems be solved? As the children's supervisor, how would you like them to see you?

Resources

Center on the Social and Emotional Foundations for Early Learning. University of Illinois at Urbana-Champaign. http://csefel.uiuc.edu.

Covey, Stephen R. 1989. *The seven habits of highly effective people: Powerful lessons in personal change.* New York: Simon and Schuster.

———. 1990. *Principle-centered leadership: Give a man a fish and you feed him for a day; Teach him how to fish and you feed him for a lifetime.* New York: Summit Books.

Devereux Foundation. 1999. *Classroom strategies to promote children's social and emotional development.* Lewisville, NC: Kaplan Press.

Divinyi, Joyce E. 1997. *Good kids, difficult behavior: A guide to what works and what doesn't.* Peachtree City, GA: The Wellness Connection.

Dodge, Diane Trister, and Laura J. Colker. 1988. *The Creative Curriculum.* 3rd ed. Washington DC: Teaching Strategies.

Greenspan, Stanley I., and Serena Wieder. 1998. *The child with special needs: Encouraging intellectual and emotional growth.* Cambridge, MA: Perseus Publishing.

Kaiser, Barbara, and Judy Sklar Rasminsky. 2003. *Challenging behavior in young children: Understanding, preventing, and responding effectly.* Boston: Allyn and Bacon.

Katz, Lilian G., and Diane E. McClellan. 1997. *Fostering children's social competence: The teacher's role.* NAEYC Research into Practice series, vol. 8. Washington, DC: National Association for the Education of Young Children.

Perry, Bruce Duncan. n.d. Keep the cool in school: Promoting nonviolent behavior in children. http://teacher.scholastic.com/professional/bruceperry/cool.htm.

Peters, Tom, and Nancy Austin. 1985. *A passion for excellence: The leadership difference.* New York: Random House.

Swift, Madelyn. 1999. *Discipline for life: Getting it right with children.* Southlake, TX: Childright.

Tobin, L. 1991. *What do you do with a child like this? Inside the lives of troubled children.* Duluth: Whole Person Associates.

Trumbull, Elise, Carrie Rothstein-Fisch, and Patricia M Greenfield. 2000. Bridging cultures in our schools: New approaches that work. A WestEd Knowledge Brief. http://www.wested.org/online_pubs/bridging/part4.shtml.

Weinstein, Carol. 2003. Culturally responsive classroom management: Awareness into action. *Theory into Practice* 42, no. 4 (Autumn): 269–76.

3

Attachment

"I have an adult who cherishes me and keeps me safe."

Juan Carlos held his shoe up to his teacher. "Did you need help?" she asked. He nodded yes and Ms. G sat down to help him put it on. "There you go," she said, and he ran off with a big grin on his face. When the librarian came into the room to read a book to the children, Juan Carlos hid behind Ms. G's leg. "Hey, baby," she said to him. "That's the Story Lady, remember? We saw her before. Come sit by me, and we'll listen to the book." Later in the day, Mrs. Morales came in to pick up her son. "Mama, mama, mama," Juan Carlos shouted as he ran up to her. "Let's get your things," she said. "Come," he answered, pulling her by her hand to fetch his things from his cubby.

Juan Carlos shows many signs of a child who has attached to a primary caretaker. He sees adults as potentially supportive and helpful. He is wary of strangers and goes to an adult he trusts to stay safe, and he is excited to be reunited with his primary caregiver at the end of the day.

What Does Attachment Look Like?

Young children need much more from adults than a peer playmate can provide. Don't confuse forming relationships with becoming a child's best friend. Adults have the maturity and resources to keep children safe and secure, and to provide food, shelter, and clothing. Adults are able to give children love, comfort, and a sense of belonging. Young children rely on adults to pass on information about how the world works and to teach them language and expectations.

When children have a healthy attachment to a primary caregiver, they do the following:

- Look to adults for love and affection
- Depend on adults for safety and security
- Seek out adults for conversation and play
- Accept adult's help and comfort

When Things Go Wrong

Children are survivors. When they don't have a consistent strong, caring, and supportive adult figure in their lives, they learn to be very self-sufficient. On the surface, teachers might appreciate the lack of neediness in these children, but the flip side of this independence is that these children often view adults as useless, irritants, or peers. They are unresponsive to adults, often ignore adult requests, and show no emotional response to adult praise or displeasure. They don't care to join in play or conversation with adults and almost never go to an adult for help or comfort.

What are some signs that you may be working with a child like this? Read the following stories. Do these children remind you of any children in your program?

Sullivan's mother picked him up after school. "Hi, Donna," the teacher greeted. "Sullivan, your mom is here." Sullivan looked up briefly, glanced at his mother, and then returned to his play. "Sullivan, let's get going. I'm in a hurry," called Donna. Sullivan shuffled over to his cubby, grabbed his backpack, and followed his mother down the hallway. If this behavior is consistent, Sullivan's lack of response to reuniting with his mother at the end of the day might be a sign that he lacks typical attachment to his primary caregiver.

Keylon had scratches on his legs from climbing a tree in the park and a scab on his knee from falling off the scooter at school. He was a constant whirlwind who loved to roughhouse. His favorite activity during outside time was to challenge his buddies with feats of strength and speed. Emily, his teacher, had been having many challenges with Keylon. He ran up the climbing structure when she called the children to come inside, he clowned around at group time, and he often responded to her requests with "You're not the boss of me."

"He rarely even says hello to me. This kid is a boy's boy. All he cares about are his friends," Emily said. "He's been in time out more times than I can count for sassing me, but he only seems to get worse. The kid just wants nothing to do with me."

Children like Sullivan and Keylon who don't have a strong attachment to a significant adult might ignore adults. Oddly, though, these same children might seem very comfortable and friendly with total strangers.

"Frieda is such a friendly child," said the teacher. "She just jumps onto anyone who comes into the classroom. She gloms right on to the volunteers, the substitutes, visiting parents—it doesn't matter who walks into the room. Right away they become her best friend."

Frieda's behavior looks friendly and healthy, but actually, it is anything but that. Healthy preschool children become very close to trusted and familiar adults. Children who are not strongly attached to a primary caregiver sometimes demonstrate this by attaching to many adults without discrimination. Attached children take the time to get to know people first. Children with a history of attachment issues don't discriminate between adults they know and trust and total strangers.

"Hey, Case, what's up? You look really angry about something," Ms. F asked. "I didn't do nothing," Case answered, looking down at the floor. "I didn't say you did anything wrong. I just saw your face, and I wonder if I can help you with something," Ms. F said. "'I didn't do nothing,' I said," Case repeated, and he moved off to the loft to be alone. Children like Case don't expect a supportive response from adults for their strong emotions, and Case has learned to keep his feelings to himself, dealing with them the best he can.

Similarly, Mahika took a tumble in the yard and skinned her knee. She hid under the play structure to poke at it in privacy. It wasn't until naptime that Mahika's teacher saw the hole in her pants and blood on her knee. Mahika doesn't think of going to the teacher for comfort or support.

Case and Mahika both need help to see adults as a source of comfort and guidance. They try their best to handle life by themselves, but children don't have the skills, knowledge, and wisdom to take care of themselves in the many challenging situations they will find themselves in. Help children like these understand early on that you are somebody that they can come to for help, support, guidance, and comfort.

Culture

Sometimes a problem in the bonding between a teacher and a child can be traced back to a difference in cultural expectations regarding relationship.

- Some cultures regard a child making eye contact during redirection as a sign of respect. Other cultures see that as a sign of disrespect.
- Some cultures find a child's frequent requests for assistance to be clingy behavior. Other cultures consider it as a sign that the child trusts adults to nurture and care for them.
- Some cultures admire a child who always wants to know the reason why, while others expect children to obey without question.

Don't be too quick to jump to conclusions about children's behavior, especially when teaching a diverse population or a group of children who are mostly culturally different from you. (Remember, too, that in this sense cultural differences include such things as socioeconomic class, coming from a rural or urban background, even coming from a different region of the country.) Young children reflect the culture in which they were raised. When you are surprised by children's behavior in the classroom, don't first assume there's a problem with the child. Dig a bit deeper and communicate with families to uncover any possible cultural conflicts that may exist. Often it is fine to do things differently at home and at school, but help both the child and their family understand what the expectation at school will be, without invalidating the child's home culture.

Use Affection to Strengthen Relationships

What teachers do when they respond to children is important, but how we do it is often what makes the difference between a helpful and hurtful technique. For example, what message is Kataryn getting from the teacher in the following scene?

Early in the day, Kataryn hit Stormasia when Stormy wouldn't let her use the red swing. Ms. R helped the girls solve the problem, and things seemed to go fine until they went inside and Kataryn purposely got paint on Yvonne's dress. "Kataryn, that's enough. If you keep on bothering kids, you'll work at the round table by yourself. Kids who can't play nice, play alone." Not five minutes passed before Kataryn pushed Marquis into the wall. "That's it, Kataryn. I've had enough of you this morning. You just sit your self at that round table and think about being nice to our friends." "Kataryn's always bad," Adrian told a visitor later in the day. "Ms. R always makes her sit by herself 'cause she's not nobody's friend."

Now compare it to this version. What message are Kataryn and the other children getting in this scene?

Early in the day, Kataryn hit Stormasia when Stormy wouldn't let her use the red swing. Ms. R helped the girls problem solve and things seemed to go fine until they went inside and Kataryn purposely got paint on Yvonne's dress. "Kataryn, something seems to be bothering you today. Do you want to talk to me about what's wrong this morning?" "Nothin' is wrong. Yvonne got in my way," Kataryn answered. Not five minutes passed before Kataryn pushed Marquis into the wall. "Oh sweetie. You're just having a hard time managing yourself this morning. I need to keep you and the other kids safe. I'm afraid you're hurting others today, and I'm also scared somebody might hurt you back," Ms. R said, getting down to Kataryn's level and pulling her in for a hug. "Come stay over here by me, now, so we can all stay safe here. Maybe later we will find some time to talk more. Right now, let's find something close to me so that if you feel like you need to bother others, I'll be right here to help you." "Ms. R helps kids here," Adrian told the visitor. "She's teaching Kataryn how to play nice with the kids."

When the teacher in the second scenario pulled Kataryn away from her peers, she made it clear to everyone that she liked Kataryn, but at the same time intended to keep them all safe. Her attitude and language toward Kataryn during the episode did not alienate the child either from herself or from the others in the classroom.

For children to relax and learn, they first need to know that there will be an adult around who will take care of their basic needs. They need to feel sure that they will be fed, cleaned, and kept warm. They have to know that they will be kept safe and secure. They need to feel loved and cherished, and they need to feel like they belong.

Making love and affection contingent upon "good behavior" may seem to make sense on the surface. If children crave attachment to significant adults, wouldn't they behave better in order to get that love? In fact, the opposite is true. Children cooperate more with adults who accept them unconditionally. Early learning for children is relationship based. The way in which teachers go about guiding children can strengthen or undermine the relationships between the teacher and the children, and between children and their peers, even when their actions look similar on the surface. Children are more responsive to corrective guidance when they are feeling safe and secure in the relationship, rather than defensive and uneasy. Treating children with love and affection regardless of their behavior makes a teacher's job easier.

Supportive Interactions

When all goes well in a child's early development, he will identify one or more adults who will nurture and cherish him. The language and daily interactions we have with children set the tone for the kind of relationship we have with them. Our careful choice of language can help children view us as a valuable mentor rather than an opponent. Language that helps children feel safe and supported promotes positive emotional growth and development.

Healthy and productive relationships with children are based on many of the same factors you listed about your own favorite supervisor in chapter 1. When our language with children lets them know that they are seen and understood, we begin to increase our sphere of influence.

Get to Know Children Well

It's one thing to be civil and kind to children, but quite another to develop genuine affection for individual children. True affection grows over time as we learn the endearing qualities of another. Some kids have personalities that are easy and quick to know. Other children may be more private or may have personality qualities that rub us the wrong way. Discover their more lovable characteristics before you get overwhelmed by their challenges and fall into unhealthy relationships.

Learn about children by talking to families and by observing children both at home and in the classroom. Who is this child?

Home Visits

Some schools have policies allowing teachers to make home visits early in the year. Home visits are a good opportunity to learn about children, their families, and their neighborhoods. If you can visit the child's bedroom, ask the child to show you her favorite toys and books. Make sure to take notes to refer to later for lesson plans and progress reports. If your school doesn't make home visits, gather information from the families at other times. Talk to families during enrollment to find out information they would like to share about their child. Chat with families briefly at drop-off and pick-up times to fill in your picture of this child. Make sure you discover the answer to questions like these:

- What does the child like to be called?
- Who lives in the household? How does the child refer to each of these people?
- What does the child enjoy doing? What is she good at?
- What are the family's goals for their child this year? What are their goals for the child's future?
- How does the child let people know he is sad, scared, or frustrated?
- What does the family do to help their child calm down when she is upset?

You may find that families have very different beliefs from your own about child-rearing. Your own cultural background might lead you to believe that the parents are babying their four-year-old. Perhaps you believe the parents are too harsh or too sarcastic when dealing with their child. Maybe when you ask a parent what the child is good at, they appear uncomfortable with the question. Make these conversations with families a time to explore differences in cultural expectations and beliefs about children. Approach these differences with an "aha!" as you gain insight into a child's behavior. What you might have seen as passive might really be respecting authority. What you might have perceived as low self-esteem might really be a family emphasis on community instead of individual glory.

Review the exercise you did in chapter 1 where you defined long-term goals for children. Compare your goals with the family's goals for their child. Do your goals lead more toward fostering the child's independence? Do the family's goals lean more toward interdependence? Is it vice versa? Or are you coming from a similar orientation? As you work with other people's children, stay conscious that your strategies must respect and support the family's goals for their child at the same time that you prepare children to be successful in a mainstream school setting.

Observation

Observe children closely in the program over several weeks before you make too many conclusions about them. Ask yourself questions about children's learning styles, interests, talents, and preferred play styles as well as their challenges. You may find the "Getting to Know You" form in the appendix to be a useful tool for gathering information about individual children. Use this information as you plan both daily activities for the class and specific interventions for individual children.

Learning style

Different children have different learning styles, and most children have two or three preferred ways that they learn best. Some kids can sit for an hour looking at a book about puppies. Others have their hands all over things on the science table. Still others are constantly in motion. Observe children over a period of time to identify their preferred ways of learning. Here's one way of thinking about children's learning styles:

SEEING	Learns best when he can see what he is learning. Likes photos, pictures, posters, books, and watching puppet shows and dramatic plays. Loses interest when activities are "talk heavy," but focuses when there is something to look at.
DOING	Learns best from hands-on activities, playacting, opportunities to practice, journal writing, experience charts, and field trips. Enjoys getting actively involved in special projects.
TOUCHING	Learns best by touching things such as artifacts and books. Likes to make things. Finds it hard to "look with no touching."
MOVING	Learns best through dramatic play, puppets, dance and movement, and learning centers. Doesn't sit still for more than a few minutes.

CHATTING	Learns best with discussions, buddy work, group work, and scripts. Finds it hard to keep quiet.
WORKING WITH OTHERS	Learns best working with a partner, in a small group, or in larger groups. Most often finds others to work with.
EXPLORING ALONE	Learns best when she can explore by herself or with an adult partner. Goes off often to work alone.
INDIVIDUAL CULTURES, INTERESTS, AND CHALLENGES	Consider culture, family, language, and individual abilities or challenges that influence the best learning situations for children.

Interests and talents

What does this child like to play? What kinds of books engage this child? Does she know the name of every dinosaur? Is he interested in bugs? Can she speak another language? Is this child great at large-motor activities, singing, dancing, or drawing?

Play level

How does each child play most comfortably? Alone, next to others, with one other child, or in small groups of children? Does this child do well in large group activities?

Build Nurturing into the Classroom Culture

Weave nurturing moments into the daily life of the classroom. Nurturing moments don't require the same sort of daily and weekly planning that projects and special events do. Nurturing moments are just "the way things are done here." Teachers can consciously build nurturing time into the regular schedule. Because children have so little control over their worlds, they are dependent on their adult caregivers to provide for their other basic life needs. Even as adults, we often show others that we care by paying attention to their basic needs.

When we make sure to focus our daily practices to accommodate children's needs, we help them feel comfortable and connected. At the same time, we model essential life skills for living peacefully and in community with others.

Get Close

So much to do, so little time. Sometimes, just by tweaking things we already do, we can greatly enrich our relationships with individual children. Instead of calling to children across the room, move close to the child, get down to their eye level, and speak quietly enough that only you and the child hear what is being said.

INSTEAD OF . . .	TRY . . .
Calling across the room, "Lavone, is this your coat on the floor?"	Bringing the coat over to Lavone, squatting down, and gently saying, "Lavone, is this your coat? Put it in your cubby to keep it clean."
Calling across the room, "Frederick, did you wash your hands after you went potty?"	Walking over to Frederick, squatting down, taking his hands in yours, and gently saying, "Frederick, your hands are dry. I think you might have forgotten to wash. Scoot back in there and clean them up real quick."

Greetings and Farewells

Remind children of your personal connections every day by individually greeting each child. Some teachers do this as the children enter the classroom; others do it at morning meeting time. What words should you use?

Reflect on your own experiences of being a guest in a friend's home or greeting guests in your own home. What are some of the ways we help others feel comfortable? Record some of your personal reflections below. How might you adapt these words and gestures to greet children in your classroom?

WITH MY FRIENDS . . .	WITH THE CHILDREN IN MY CLASS . . .
"Hi. I'm so glad you could come over."	"Hi. I'm so glad you came to school today."
______________________________	______________________________
______________________________	______________________________
______________________________	______________________________
______________________________	______________________________

Departures are another important time of the day to connect personally with children. Good-byes help everyone feel a sense of closure and anticipation to reconnect the next day. Imagine how empty and "unfinished" you would feel if when you left a gathering at a friend's house, nobody acknowledged that you were leaving! Again, in the chart below, write down some things that you might hear when you leave a gathering or some things you say or do when friends leave your house. How might you adapt these words and gestures to the children in your classroom?

WITH MY FRIENDS . . .	WITH THE CHILDREN IN MY CLASS . . .
I had fun today. Let's get together again next week.	I had fun with you today. I can't wait for tomorrow.
I know a wonderful place for coffee.	We've got some fun things to do the next time you come.
______________________	______________________
______________________	______________________
______________________	______________________

Greetings and good-byes not only help children make easier transitions to and from the classroom, but teach children important life skills for building and maintaining important relationships. Make sure to learn how to greet and say good-bye to all the children and families in their home languages.

Give Children Opportunities to Talk and Play with Adults

The best environments for young children provide ample time for small group and individual activities. Center-based classrooms provide children with learning tailored to young children's learning styles and, at the same time, free up adults to interact with children individually or in small groups.

Some teachers make the mistake of limiting their involvement with children to teacher-directed large-group activities. They use center time to catch up on paperwork, planning, or cleaning tasks. Center time is a wonderful opportunity, however, to connect with children individually for conversation or play.

Limit large group time to once or twice a day for only fifteen minutes or so. Make sure the bulk of your time is invested in working and interacting in groups small enough to have frequent and meaningful interactions with individuals.

Play with Children

One of the best investments of time you can make with children is to play with them on a regular basis. Five minutes of one-on-one play daily can do more to improve a child's behavior in a week than most other interventions can do in a year.

Many teachers find that center time is the best opportunity to find five uninterrupted minutes to play. To make the most of the time, imagine yourself as another child in your class who has very good play skills. Remember that when children play blocks with each other, nobody ever says, "How many rectangles did you use to build that farm?" That's a teacher script. When playing with children to build connections, let the child lead the play and allow yourself to join in.

INSTEAD OF SAYING . . .	TRY . . .
"How many rectangles did you use to build that farm?"	"How can I play?"
"Let's match up the mommy animals and the baby animals."	"Here's some food for the cows. Eat, cows."
"Oh no. Elephants don't belong in a farm. Where do elephants go?"	"Oh no. My chicken is scared of the elephant. He's running to try to get under the fence."

Sportscasting

Some children are not ready to let anyone else play with them. A beginning step is to keep them aware that although they won't play with you, you still see them and appreciate their play and their thoughts.

Begin to connect with these children by using a technique called "sportscasting." When you sportscast, imagine yourself as an announcer at the Olympics, reporting on an athlete at an event. Speak aloud and report just what you see. Remember that sportscasters don't interview athletes during the event!

INSTEAD OF SAYING . . .	TRY . . .
"What do you think will happen if you pour the water into the funnel?"	"Lulu is picking up the large bottle of water. It looks like she's going to pour it into the funnel."
"The boat is upside down. Turn it over and see how it works."	"Stephano has the boat upside down and is riding it in the water. He let go and the boat went right down to the bottom. Now he's picking it up. He turned it over. He let go. It is staying on top this time."
"What color is that water?"	"Tito has a pitcher of red water. He's filling little cups. Now he's filling the big cup."

Keep Children Safe

Children seek out and need reliable adults who keep them emotionally and physically safe and set predictable and clear limits. Safety is fundamental to attachment.

Be a Pillar of Safety

Children who feel unsafe often behave in unsafe ways. Safety and security are not "normal" for them; their status quo is risk and insecurity. Because they don't feel safe and secure, they have trouble recognizing when they do things that cause others to feel unsafe and insecure. What seems dangerous and scary to other children or even to adults just seems normal to them. Help children begin to identify you as their pillar of safety and security in the classroom.

WHEN	INSTEAD OF SAYING . . .	TRY . . .
Tyesha cries to you because Jaylyn hit her back	"That's what happens when you hurt. You get hurt back. See?"	"This is a safe place. Let's find a way to keep you safe and a way to keep Jaylyn safe."
Mazen uses profanity toward you	"Do you want to get kicked out of this school like you got kicked out of your last school?"	"Let's figure out words you can use here at school to tell me when you are angry with me."
Sovannary gets anxious during transitions and starts to toss things around the classroom	"Go sit over there by yourself in the thinking chair. I'm tired of you breaking our things."	"Sovannary, come on over here with me so I can help you feel safe."
Matthew bites Amina	"Nobody likes bad boys, Matthew."	"Let's get ice for Amina, and then you can stay by me so everyone stays safe here this morning."

Mean What You Say and Say What You Mean

Have you ever heard yourself saying something like this? "Mitchell never listens to me the first time I give him a warning. I always have to give him three chances before he stops."

It's not a kindness to give children three chances. It's confusing. Some children hear the first warning the way you intend it. They hear, "Stop going down the slide head first." Other children like Mitchell hear, "You can go down the slide three times head first. Then you will have to stop."

Here's another example. "Find a book and go to circle, Esme," the teacher said. "I don't want to read a book," Esme replied, as she wandered off to the home-living center to get a baby doll instead. "It's reading time, Esme. Go fetch a book," the teacher repeated. Esme ignored her and sat down at the little housekeeping table to feed her baby doll. "Last warning, Esme. Put down the doll and go get a book." Esme didn't even flinch. The teacher sighed and turned away to finish cleaning up the lunch table.

Although at first glance, we might think Esme feels a sense of power that she can do whatever she wants, in truth she feels unsafe and insecure. Deep inside, children know that they are children. They depend on kind but firm adults to run the show and keep them safe. Children who don't have this sense of safety and security compensate by trying to take over more control and power. Without an adult to depend on, they try to become their own adult. However, they know inside that they aren't ready for that kind of power, and they are terrified by the failure of the adults around them to take it on instead.

Help children feel safe and secure by being a person of your word. If you don't mean it, don't say it. If you choose to say it, commit to following through. When you decide to change your mind about what you said, make sure you let the child know. If you decide that Esme can get a doll instead of a book, don't leave her guessing. Say something like, "Okay. You can get a doll instead if you like."

Mean what you say and say what you mean. Don't leave room for children to misinterpret your intent. Earn children's respect and trust by being exquisitely consistent with your words and your actions.

Repair Breaks in Relationships

If a child does something to hurt a relationship with a caregiver or a peer, what kinds of strategies might you teach that child to help repair the damage? List three possibilities in the space below.

1. ______________________________

2. ______________________________

3. ______________________________

The strategies that we want children to use to repair weakened relationships are the very ones that we should use for those times we have mistakenly damaged our relationships with children. By modeling conciliatory behavior and words, we teach children that making that first move is a sign of strength, not weakness. We demonstrate that all of us sometimes act in haste or do and say thoughtless things when we are upset or stressed. And we show them that, with caring and effort, relationships can be repaired. Make a plan now for what you might say or do if you have said or done something to damage your relationship with a child. One example of what you might say is "I apologize for being so angry. Let's talk about it." Can you think of other examples?

1. ______________________________

2. ______________________________

3. ______________________________

Respond to Children's Emotions

The greatest gift we can give to others is to truly listen. And few things build bridges faster than being a good listener. As teachers, though, we are multitasking at such a frantic pace that we slip much faster into the "problem-solver mode" than the "listening mode." Listen carefully to children's words to hear whether they are asking for information or for emotional support.

Feelings comments

Is the child expressing an emotion such as frustration, disappointment, fear, hurt, or joy? When you hear a sentence that expresses a feeling, reflect the feeling back. Name the feeling in your answer. Let the child know that you are really listening, that you care, and that you will help her express her strong feelings.

YOU MIGHT WANT TO . . .	SOUNDS LIKE . . .
Ask how the child is feeling.	"Are you upset about that?"
Guess how the child is feeling.	"Your face and voice tell me you are very happy about your grandpa visiting you."
Mirror what you hear.	"So you tried to tie your shoes and you couldn't get it?"
Validate feelings.	"I can see why you feel frustrated."
Empathize.	"You must feel so frustrated."
Let the child know that her feelings are a reaction to a trigger.	"You got scared when the fire alarm went off, huh?"
Reassure the child that his reaction is normal.	"A lot of kids are scared of loud noises."

Beware of these less effective ways of responding to children's emotions.

WHEN YOU . . .	IT . . .
Gush with sympathy—"Oh, you poor little thing. How mean of Allegra to say that to you."	Promotes victim mentality.
Give advice—"Here, let me show you how to put the bead on the string."	Sends the message that the solution is more important than the feeling.
Use humor—"You big old angry bear you. Ha, ha, ha. Can you growl like a bear like this?"	Makes light of the child's strong emotions.
Reassure—"Oh, don't feel like that. He didn't really mean it. He was just angry with you."	Sends the message that the child shouldn't feel the way she does.

Information questions

Listen carefully to the words a child uses so that you can tell if they are expressing an emotion or simply asking for information. When a child uses the words *who, what, where, when, why,* and *how,* they are usually looking for information, not empathic responses.

WHEN A CHILD SAYS . . .	FEELING OR INFORMATION	TRY SAYING . . .
"Nobody will play with me."	Feeling	"You sound lonely to me."
"Where does this block go?"	Information	"Look on the shelf and find the shapes that match."
"I can't draw a horse."	Feeling	"You aren't happy with how your horse looks?"
"How many crackers can we take?"	Information	"The sign shows that you can take two crackers."

Give Children Help and Comfort

Some children come to your classroom with a history of seeing adults as hurtful instead of helpful. When children see adults as the enemy instead of the ally, they don't think of using adults for help or comfort.

Use a Magic Word: *Come*

Give children the gift of your physical support. When you see a child beginning to spin out of control, move over to him and take his hand. Gently say, "Come sit by me" or "Come hold my hand."

Use the word *come* in place of the word *go* when asking resistant children to do something.

INSTEAD OF SAYING . . .	APPROACH THE CHILD, TAKE HER HAND, AND GENTLY SAY . . .
"Go wash your hands."	"Come. Let's wash hands."
"Go put on your shoes before we go out."	"Come. Let's get your shoes."
"Sit down while you eat."	"Come. Let's sit down."

Help Fix Mistakes

Being a guide and mentor has nothing to do with being bossy and punitive. Being a guide and mentor involves establishing yourself as an unconditional support system, cheerleader, and safety net who also brings years of life wisdom and experience to share.

Think about your own experiences. You goofed big time. First week on the job in a new school, and you said the wrong thing to the wrong parent. By the next morning, she had already called your supervisor, and now you are being called into the office. What words do you want to hear? What words would help you feel that your supervisor had been there for you, to help you learn and to help you do your job? What would your dream supervisor say, and how would she say it?

When children have failed to live up to the expectations of their significant adults, they have many of those same feelings. Will the adult abandon them? Will the adult leave them feeling worse? Can the adult somehow help pull them through and motivate them to move on? Be a child's safe guide and mentor as they learn to navigate the world and recover from their mistakes. Use phrases like these to reassure children and help them move forward:

- We can fix this.
- I'll teach you what you need to know to do school.
- Let's figure out a way to solve this.
- It might be helpful (friendly, thoughtful) if you . . .
- Let me show you another way to . . .
- Let's practice the school way to . . .

Our interactions with troubled children show the rest of the class what our practice will be when dealing with troubled children. It's essential to draw the child in to be a part of the group rather than push the child out to be apart from the group. If we respond in a punitive way, other children will follow suit and also behave in punitive ways. If we respond as supportive mentors, we model the classroom standard: we all help each other in this classroom.

Bonding Activities

Integrate deliberate bonding activities into the daily programming. These activities guide all children as they learn to view adults as a source of comfort and strength. They are especially effective with children who have not learned to rely on or connect with adults. The following story shows how powerful these games can be with the children that teachers typically find most difficult.

To her astonishment, when Emily played "Tickle Bug" with Deion on his cot at rest time, Keylon called over to ask her to come do it with him. When Keylon's turn came around, the four-year-old giggled like a toddler and pleaded, "More, more." Within a few days of beginning baby games, Keylon started being more responsive to Emily and for the first time ran to greet her when he arrived at school.

Paradoxically, while kids like Keylon might shy away from playing four-year-old games with you, like Legos, they may be very willing to play baby games like "Tickle Bug." Children who have not had warm and playful experiences with adults as infants and toddlers are often starved for this adult-baby interaction. For some of these difficult children, this is the place to begin to rebuild relationships. Punishing kids who are not connected to adults only reinforces their belief that adults are useless. Over time, these children become more and more alienated and difficult. Instead, begin to find ways to bond with children like Keylon.

Baby Games

Baby games are warm and simple bonding games—the kind of games that you might play with an infant or toddler. Adults naturally play baby games with tiny ones to help build reciprocal and affectionate relationships. Use these guidelines to help make the activities successful:

- Teach the child to say or sign *more* when they want the activity repeated, which helps children develop the habit of initiating interactions with adults.
- Try to do the activity over and over until the child is finished. The more we practice a new skill, the more we learn.
- Do the activity exactly the same way each time you do it. Predictability helps the child feel safe and secure.
- Baby games are particularly effective to use if a child is having a bad day or is beginning to show signs of stress or falling apart.

Tickle Bug

1. Put one hand high in the air and begin to chant, "Here comes the Tickle Bug."
2. Slowly bring your hand lower and closer to the child while you continue the chant.
3. Gently tickle the child with one finger. Touch a neutral part of the child's body, such as his arm or his foot, if you are not comfortable tickling his belly.
4. When you tickle, say, "Tickle, tickle, tickle."
5. Try to do this until the child indicates that he is done.

Peekaboo

1. Put a small blanket or cloth over your head.
2. Chant, "Where's (your name)?" over and over.
3. When the child pulls the blanket off, say, "Here I am!"
4. Allow the child to put the blanket on their own head if they like. Change the chant to, "Where's (child's name)?" and "Here you are!" when you uncover them.

This Little Piggy

1. Take one of the child's hands in your own.
2. Taking each finger in turn, chant, "This little piggy went to market, this little piggy stayed home, this little piggy had roast beef, this little piggy had none." On the last finger, say your line with great anticipation, "And this little piggy went . . ."
3. Put you hand high in the air and as you bring it close to the child say, "Wee, wee, wee, wee, wee."
4. Tickle the child gently with one finger while saying, "All the way home."

One, Two, Three, Jump

1. Start with the child standing on a very low box or step.
2. Stand a few feet away with your arms outstretched to catch the child.
3. Say, "One, Two, Three, Jump," with great anticipation.
4. Catch the child in your arms and say, "Wheeeeee," while you swing or twirl her around gently.

Doubles

1. Sit on a swing, and seat the child on your lap facing you with his legs straddled around your body.
2. With one arm, hold him around his back.
3. Chant a singsong as you pump and swing together. Either sing a lullaby or make up a singsong, such as "Swing, swing, swinging together. Swing, swing, swinging together."
4. If you are not comfortable having a child on your lap, push the child on the swing from the front instead of behind. Push the child's feet. Sing and chant as above.

One, Two, Three, Whee

1. Sit in a chair and seat the child on your knees facing you.
2. Either hold the child from behind with both hands, or hold the child's forearms.
3. Bounce the child on your lap while you chant, "One, Two, Three."
4. On three, part your legs so that the child drops down a foot or two while you still hold onto her safely. Say, "Whee" in an excited tone of voice.

Bonding Games

Many children need predictable and structured activities to help them attach to their primary caretakers. Teachers have found the following three activities to be useful tools to help children develop these skills.

Follow these general tips for success:

- Present only one activity at a time—the same activity every day for one week. Rotate the three activities, one week at a time, all year long or as long as children are still interested.
- Initially, most children will want to participate. Over time, many children will be "done" with the activity, but a handful of children will still show interest. These are the children who need the activity the most. Keep offering it as long as any children still need it.
- Some teachers set up these activities outdoors. The teacher sitting at the table with the child also supervises a section of the play yard.
- Set up a waiting list for children who want to participate. That way, they can play someplace else while waiting their turn.
- Allow children to watch if they wish. But make sure to teach the guideline that the teacher will only be talking to the child at the activity table.
- Boys and girls both love all of these activities.
- Some teachers like to have these activities available for children to use independently or with each other. Remember, though, that when they are being used for attachment, they are teacher-child activities.
- Some children have trouble defining their body boundaries. Use universal precautions and clearly define that you will only put lotion or "nail paint" where you have said you will (lotion goes on hands; nail paint only on nails). Some children will beg for lotion or paint on arms, faces, or other body parts. To help children better define boundaries, make sure you stick to your predefined limit. This is particularly important for children who have been violated or who invade the body space of others.
- Teach families how to do these activities during parent meetings or in newsletters, and explain to families how these activities help children to feel safe and secure.

Lotion Table

1. Fill a basket with three or four small plastic bottles of lotion.
2. Invite the child to sit across from you to have lotion rubbed into their hands.
3. Open each bottle in turn, holding it up for the child to smell. Let the child choose the lotion they would like to use.
4. Pour a small portion of lotion onto your own hand, and rub it gently into the child's hand.
5. Either quietly sing a song to the child, or carry on a soft and gentle conversation.

Tips to remember:

- White lotion can be disturbing for children who have been victims of sexual abuse. Use universal precautions and shake a drop of food coloring into any bottles of white lotion you may have.
- When rubbing lotion into the child's hands, some teachers find it useful to think to themselves something such as, "This is such a precious baby." This self-talk helps to set a mood where attachment can flourish.
- Invite family participation by asking families to donate extra bottles of lotion they are not using at home.

Nail Painting

1. Use a regular, inexpensive watercolor paint set with a fine brush and a cup of water.
2. Invite the child to choose a paint color.
3. Engage the child in one-on-one conversation while you paint his nails.

Tips to remember:

- If you use the term *nail painting* rather than *nail polish,* some boys feel more freedom to participate.
- When painting children's nails, some teachers find it useful to imagine themselves as manicurists in a nail salon. This helps them to carry on respectful and interested chat with their "client." Most children, like adults, love the combination of physical grooming and casual, respectful chatting.
- Some teachers have children wash the nail paint off during the next transition. The paint comes off easily with regular soap and water.

Owie Table

1. Gather a supply of plain, inexpensive adhesive bandages, cotton balls, a washable red marking pen, an eyedropper and a cup of clear water, disposable rubber gloves, and a small plastic container for waste.
2. Invite the child over for you to attend to their pretend owie.
3. Ask the child where on their hand their owie is.
4. Put on the rubber gloves. Dab a small, red dot with the washable marker on the "injury." Using the eyedropper with water, drop a bit of water on the marker dot. The ink will dissolve and will look like blood.
5. Use the cotton ball to dab up the red water, and dispose of the cotton in the waste container.
6. Put an adhesive bandage on the "injury."
7. During the care of the injury, say something such as, "Sometimes kids get hurt here at school. Some hurts are on the inside and some are on the outside. When a kid gets hurt, they can come to a grown-up for help."

Tips to remember:

- For children to feel safe and secure at school, they need to know that adults will be in charge and will be responsive to their feelings of hurt, fear, and anxiety. This activity is very helpful for children who have had to take care of themselves and who haven't used adults much as helpers.
- Some teachers find it useful to limit children to one "owie" session a day. If some children want to repeat the play over and over, teachers can repeat the activity every day until children are done with it.

Discussion/Reflection Questions

1. In twenty years, when a child from your class reflects back, how would you like him to remember you?
2. What is the difference between teaching preschool and teaching twenty unique preschool-age children?
3. Consider a traditional one-size-fits-all, school- or centerwide discipline policy (for example, first offense gets a verbal warning, second offense pulls a card, third offense note is sent to parents, and so on). How do you think this would work for teaching social and emotional skills to young children? Do you think

it's important for children's development that their teachers respond exactly the same way to the same behavior, regardless of the situation or the underlying need of the children involved? Why or why not?

Exercises

1. Observe a challenging child in your classroom for at least one uninterrupted hour. Use the "Getting to Know You" form in the appendix to describe that child. Did you learn anything new that gives you insight into that child's behavior?
2. Choose one or two baby games and introduce them to one of your challenging children every day for a week. Did anything change?

Reflection/Journal Assignment

Nurturing moments help children feel safe and secure. They should be designed to meet the basic needs of children to send the message that adults take responsibility for the child's well-being and that adults will maintain predictability and order. How do you already meet the basic needs of children in your class? What other ideas might you try? As you read through the rest of this book, make sure to add to your chart any new ideas that come to you.

CHILDREN'S NEEDS	HOW I CAN MEET CHILDREN'S NEEDS THROUGHOUT THE DAY?
Physical needs: food, rest, exercise, toileting, grooming	
Safety needs: physical safety, emotional safety	
Belonging needs: love, affection, connections to others	
Self esteem needs: I matter, I am seen, I am valued, I am accepted	
Cognitive needs: materials and activities that are accessible to each individual child	

Resources

Bailey, Becky. 1996. *I love you rituals: Activities to build bonds and strengthen relationships with children.* Oviedo, FL: Loving Guidance.

Brooks, Robert, and Sam Goldstein. 2001. *Raising resilient children.* Chicago: Contemporary Books.

Covey, Stephen R. 1997. *The seven habits of highly effective families: Building a beautiful family culture in a turbulent world.* New York: Golden Books.

Devereux Foundation. 1999. *Classroom strategies to promote children's social and emotional development.* Lewisville, NC: Kaplan Press.

Dinkmeyer, Don, and Gary D. McKay. 1973. *Raising a responsible child: Practical steps to successful family relationships.* New York: Simon and Schuster.

Greenspan, Stanley I., and Serena Wieder. 1998. *The child with special needs: Encouraging intellectual and emotional growth.* Cambridge, MA: Perseus Publishing.

Gordon, Thomas. 1970. *P.E.T.: Parent effectiveness training: The tested new way to raise responsible children.* New York: Peter H. Wyden, Inc.

Kohl, Herbert. 1998. *The discipline of hope: Learning from a lifetime of teaching.* New York: Simon and Schuster.

Koplow, Lesley. 1996. *Unsmiling faces: How preschools can heal.* New York: Teachers College Press.

Marston, Stephanie. 1990. *The magic of encouragement: Nurturing your child's self-esteem.* New York: William Morrow and Company, Inc.

McClellan, Diane E., and Lilian G. Katz. 2001. Assessing young children's social competence. EDO-PS-01-2.

Mulligan, Sarah A., Kathleen Miller Green, Sandra L. Morris, Ted J. Maloney, Dana McMurray, and Tamara Kittelson-Alred. 1992. Welcoming all children: A closer look at inclusive child care. In *Integrated child care.* Tucson, AZ: Communication Skill Builders. http://www.usd.edu/cd/systemschange/wac/communication.htm.

Pollack, William. 1998. *Real boys: Rescuing our sons from the myths of boyhood.* New York: Henry Holt and Company.

Tobin, L. 1991. *What do you do with a child like this? Inside the lives of troubled children.* Duluth: Whole Person Associates.

York, Stacey. 2003. *Roots and wings: Affirming culture in early childhood programs.* St. Paul: Redleaf Press.

4

Affiliation

"I can have a friend and be a friend"

"My buddies, my buddies," Ryker called out as soon as his mother dropped him off at his classroom. He ran into the room airplane style, with his arms wide out and a huge smile on his face, soaring around the other children. "Weekends are so hard for him," his mother said to the teacher. "There are no other kids around, and he keeps asking me when it will be school again. All he can talk about are his friends Mikey and David." Ryker ran back to kiss his mother good-bye. "Miss Stephanie, can we play the farmer game again today, and can I be the dog again and David be the cheese again?" he asked his teacher.

What Does Affiliation Look Like?

Children with affiliation enjoy being around other children, develop one or more special friends, and begin to participate in teacher-directed group activities for short periods. One of the main tasks for preschool-age children is to learn how to develop friendships and connections with people outside of the home. As teachers, it is as much our responsibility to facilitate children's social development as it is to teach them colors or numbers. Children become affiliated in stages:

1. Solo play—Although infants and toddlers are very tuned-in and show curiosity about one another, they lack the skills they need to sustain meaningful peer play for more than a moment or two. Most of their play and exploration is done alone, even when they are in the middle of a room full of other children.

2. Adult-child play—As infants mature and develop relationships with their significant adults, they begin to also develop play skills with those adults. They may attempt to "talk" to their adults, will giggle at patty-cake, and will repeatedly toss a toy down from a stroller to have their grown-up fetch it for them.

3. Parallel play—When young children are first introduced to other children, they are very curious. They may observe the other child for long periods of time and will often try to touch and feel the other's face or clothing. They seem to regard each other more as playthings to explore than as potential play peers. Very young children still lack the language and skills needed for meaningful interactive play with peers, so while they will be happy to play side by side, they will have very little actual interaction.

4. Dyad play—Next, children will begin to play interactively with others and will identify somebody as their friend. For example, two children might race their bikes or build a zoo together from blocks.

5. Small group play—When three to five children are role-playing in the home-living area or when they are working together at the art table sharing materials, they are demonstrating that they can do small group work. To be successful at small group play, children must learn how to be included in play, how to take turns and share, and how to play common themes such as babies or building roads in the sand.

6. Large group play—Although most preschool children are unable to function in large groups without significant adult support and guidance, they can take the first step of identifying themselves as an important member of the classroom community.

Most preschool classrooms will have children who span the developmental stages of play, regardless of their chronological ages. Some are still working alone. Some are working next to, although not with, other children. Some have learned to play well with one other child, while others can be found in the dramatic play or block areas working cooperatively in small groups. You may even see a child who shows some skills with large groups. Sometimes we notice these children playing teachers with a group of his pretend students, looking and sounding a bit too much like ourselves!

When Things Go Wrong

Children have few problems playing and working at their current level of competency, but moving up the play-skills ladder can be challenging. It takes practice and, for some children, modeling, coaching, and direct instruction to master the skills they need to move up to the next level of play. As children begin to move to the next stage, they'll naturally encounter many challenges, struggles, and conflicts.

Many classroom problems can be traced back to conflicting play levels. When we look closely, we find that that we often ask children to function independently at a play level higher than their current skill level.

For example, Tatiana and Clay were given the buddy job of washing paintbrushes at the sink. Immediately, conflict broke out. Clay was trying hard to get Tatiana to share space at the sink, but Tatiana kept elbowing him out of the way and finally pushed him off the step stool he was trying to share with her. "Teacher," Clay complained. "Tatiana pushed me off the steps." "Tatiana, be nice to your friend. Move over and share the steps," the teacher instructed her. As soon as the teacher moved away, trouble broke out again as Tatiana grabbed the brushes out of Clay's hands. "Teacher," he yelled. This time, the teacher said, "Tatiana, pushing and grabbing are not nice. You've lost your chance to wash paintbrushes now. I want you to go sit down until the rest of us are done with our jobs." Tatiana threw herself on the floor crying and began to kick the step stool Clay was standing on. Eventually, the teacher carried her away to the time-out area to cool off.

This teacher wasn't aware that Tatiana was still at the solo-play level. Tatiana didn't have the skills she needed to work with a partner without adult support. She wasn't being mean or naughty; she was just put in a situation she couldn't manage alone. If the teacher had this information earlier, she might have either given Tatiana the job to do alone or could have stayed with the children to help them work together. She might also have worked with Tatiana at other times during the day to teach her sharing and turn taking—skills she was still missing. Before long, Tatiana would be able to do partner work without constant conflict and without needing so much intervention from the teachers.

When children are still at dyad play, small group areas like blocks or dramatic play can be a challenge for them. Because they don't know how to play easily with more than one child at a time, conflict can break out. For example, consider this story.

Zack and Adrian had been building together peacefully for ten minutes when Sean and Amy came over to join them. Zack said, "Adrian, don't play with those stupid kids. Let's hide so they can't find us." "I wanna keep doing blocks," Adrian said. Zack kicked down the structure they had been building and started tossing blocks around the area. A flying block hit Sean, Adrian began to suck his fingers and weep, and Amy struck Zack in the head saying, "You're the one who's stupid." "That's enough," Mr. F said, approaching the children. "The four of you pick up the mess and find another area to play where you won't fight." Amy immediately went to the water table and Adrian followed. Sean intentionally stepped on Zack's hand in response to being struck with the block; Mr. F returned just in time to prevent Zack from pummeling Sean with another block. "I hate that block area," Mr. F complained to his co-teacher later that day. "I think we need to close it down for a few months."

While closing down areas, such as dramatic play and blocks, might lead to a quieter room, that strategy also denies children the practice they need to work together in small groups. A closer observation would have revealed that Zack was at a dyad level of play. He didn't have the higher-level skills he needed to play in a group of three to five children. When Sean and Amy tried to enter the play, Zack's anxiety rose and he began a fight-or-flight strategy. Instead of closing down the block center, the teachers might have chosen to make sure an adult was always nearby to help less-skilled children to negotiate the area. If they found many children still at a dyad level of play, they might have divided the block area into two smaller "two-person" areas while they implemented other strategies into the daily program to help children build small group skills. As small group skills increased, bickering, name-calling, conflict, and aggression would decrease.

Other children at the dyad level of play might not be able to make sense of ongoing play and will avoid entering a play group altogether. "Kirsten is a loner child," Miss Felicia reported to her mother. "She'll either play alone or sometimes just with Maria. If Maria is playing doctor with the other girls, Kirsten complains there's nobody to play with. I try to get her to join the other girls, but she just runs to hide herself behind the sofa." Miss Felicia and her mother decided to stop pushing her to play with others and just let her be.

In fact, Kirsten was interested in playing with others, but had trouble understanding the play. She couldn't figure out what the kids were doing or how she could join in to be part of the group. Instead, she opted to be apart from the group. At the end of the year, Kirsten was no closer to being able to work in small groups than she had been in September. Closer observation might have revealed Kirsten's problem to her teachers. They might have joined Kirsten in small group activities and helped her figure out what the children were doing. They might have modeled language for her such as, "How can I play?" Gradually, Kirsten would have developed the skills she needed to figure out how to play in small groups without adult support.

One of the most frustrating times of the day in many classrooms is large group time, whether the activity is story, music and movement, or a class meeting or discussion. You might hear "Move," or "Stop touching me," or "You can't sit here," as children struggle to negotiate space. As they vie for your attention, some children will call out of turn or fight over who gets to sit next to you. Other children who can't yet control their impulses in large group settings will leave when they get bored, play with neighbors, talk during a story, or ignore directions. Some children will be so hungry for your interaction during large group that they cause continual disruption just so that they can get your attention! It's frustrating for teachers and children alike to have half of large group time focused on redirecting, reprimanding, and otherwise disciplining unruly children.

Imagine trying to include an eighteen-month-old in large group for story time! What behaviors might you expect to see? What strategies might you use if you had that eighteen-month-old for the day? You might expect that child to have a lot of trouble sitting still and paying attention quietly for the whole book. The child would probably get up and down many times, chatter to others, and try to come up and touch the book or turn the pages. Maybe she would just get bored after a few minutes and leave the group. You might try to hold that child on your lap or let her turn the pages. You might want to let her point to pictures in the book or to act out pieces of the story. When a preschool child is at a parallel or dyad stage of play, you will see many of these same behaviors and can use many of these same strategies.

Some children move through these stages of play with little adult assistance. Either through inborn temperaments, social observational skills, or watching others who are modeling behavior, they appear to effortlessly move from one stage to another. Others have more difficulty. Careful observation of children with challenges might reveal surprising insights. You might suddenly realize that rather than a discipline issue, you are seeing a developmental issue. These children need a great deal more help to move from one stage to the next. Once you understand the developmental play level of each child and the difficulty they are having transitioning to the next stage, you can accommodate children at each of the play levels, model and teach the language and behaviors of friendship, and make plans to scaffold children from one level to the next by using supportive interactions, an inclusive classroom culture, and special activities.

Friendship Skills

While children might want to work and play with their peers, many of them lack basic friendship skills. Friendship skills are not inborn. The desire to have a friend and be a friend may be inborn, but the skills needed to execute the desire are learned. When children don't know how to take turns, share space and things, or enter or exit play, the result is often chaos.

Each society and each culture develop their own norms for social skills. Miss Manners and Amy Vanderbilt are popular resources for adults who have questions about the right thing to do. We call that *etiquette*. "How should a wedding invitation be worded?" "What should I say to a friend who has just lost her father?" "What is the appropriate graduation gift to give to the son of a colleague?" The answers to these questions are not universal. They are different for different cultures. They change over time. And you may even have found that many of these "rules" are different depending on where you work or where you live.

Children also need a resource for information about the customs and traditions for interacting. Working and playing alongside others requires knowledge of social norms such as sharing, turn taking, and empathy.

Children who learn how to share and take turns, who begin to internalize that others have feelings and needs, move more smoothly through their daily lives than children who haven't yet learned these skills. Observe challenging children to see if they demonstrate these skills as they move throughout their classroom day. Identify missing social skills and mistaken behavior. Help relieve your problems and theirs by integrating a host of strategies into the daily program that model, coach, and teach culturally appropriate and effective social skills, norms, and customs.

Social Scripts—The Second Language of School

People use social scripts to interact with one another as they move through their day. These social scripts grease the wheels of human interactions.

For example, as you pass a colleague in the hallway, they might say "Hi! How are you?" What would be your answer to this? If you are like most folks, you might answer something like, "Fine. How are you?" This exchange is an example of a "greeting script" that many of us have learned for the workplace. The underlying meaning of this script is "Hello. I know and acknowledge you but I really don't want to begin a lengthy conversation with you. I merely want to acknowledge our relationship." What happens when you attempt this social script with somebody who doesn't know their lines? Imagine how you feel if the response to your greeting is something like this: "Oh my. You wouldn't believe what's going on in my life. My car is broken and James is coming down with something. I think it might be the flu." This is an example of one person using a social script that is not understood by the other. The misunderstanding can lead to annoyance or hurt feelings even when adults are involved. Imagine how much harder it is for children, who are just learning the social scripts of the world around them.

Successful adults and children constantly adjust their language and behavior to fit the social norms. When you are at the beach with your friends or family, you dress, talk, and behave differently than you do at work. Children who know and use the "Second Language of School" use socially appropriate language and socially acceptable strategies for navigating their day. When children are at the circus they are expected to follow different norms than when they are attending a religious service. Socially savvy people ask themselves questions like this one (perhaps unconsciously): "Where am I and what is the culture of this place?" The ability to move smoothly from situation to situation, adjusting language and behavior to conform to differing norms is being fluently bicultural. School is a little microculture with its own very specific language, norms, traditions, and guidelines. Teachers want kids to use their words, to behave and speak in friendly ways, and to refrain from profanity and name-calling. This language and these behaviors are the social scripting we have established as the standard for classroom culture.

Although these are ways that we do things at school, that is not the only way to "do things." At school, boys and girls often use different bathrooms. At home, family members probably use the same bathroom. At school children might be discouraged from roughhousing, while at home sibling wrestling may be condoned or even encouraged by families. A particular teacher might view eye contact as a sign of respect when reprimanding a child. At home, that same child might be taught to lower her eyes when an adult is redirecting her.

When you think about a child's behavior, remember that the child is coming to school with a set of social norms established in the home environment. Children begin by learning social scripts from their home. Perhaps their family has taught them to say thank you when they are given something. Maybe they were taught to lower their eyes as a sign of respect when they are reprimanded. Maybe adults in the home model that hitting is as a way to express frustration and displeasure.

Because children may be asked to use language and behavior at school that is different from that used at home, we might call the school standards the "second language of school." Part of your challenge is to help children become fluently bicultural so that they can shift seamlessly between the culture at home and the culture at school.

Knowledge of and skill in the social scripts used by peer groups is essential to the smooth relationships between members. Help children learn some standard social scripts used by their peers in the school setting. It is useful for children to have scripts for situations like these: greetings and good byes, apologies, entering play, rejecting play invitations kindly, and setting boundaries.

Play Sequences

Groups of children who play together on a regular basis establish informal rules for how play works. We call these loose patterns "play sequences." These play sequences are another form of social scripts.

Here's an example of a play sequence, and a child who hasn't picked up on it yet. Jake and Eric are playing car and garage in the block area again. Earlier this year, a few of the children in the class invented this game and it has been very popular for weeks.

They have made some ramps and are using one of the rectangle blocks as a garage door that they swing open and closed as they drive cars in and out. Damiano is new to the class. He's been watching the play. He loves to play cars and moves over to where the other two are playing. Damiano picks up a truck and starts to crash it into the block structure. "We're playing garage," says Jake. "Don't crash it down." Damiano has never played garage before. His previous experiences playing with toy cars have been to crash them into things. He continues to smash his car into the structure. "Get out of here, Damiano," Eric says. "Teacher, teacher, Damiano is wrecking our game," he calls out. The teacher comes over. "Damiano, you have to play nice in the blocks or you need to choose another area to play." Damiano's face falls. He throws down the car and storms off, kicking the blocks as he leaves.

Damiano entered the situation feeling like a part of the classroom community. He had the desire to enter the play, but lacked the knowledge about how to "play garage." Doing the best he knew how with the play themes he had, he failed at his attempt to join in. What Damiano needed at that moment was a perceptive teacher to note the play theme he was missing. The teacher could have then sat for a moment to teach him how to "play garage" or could have guided one of the other children to model the play for Damiano. Armed with this knowledge, Damiano might have been able to join into the ongoing play, strengthening his feelings of belonging at the same time. Instead, the situation ended with Damiano doubting his affiliation to the group and still lacking the play theme he needed to enter the play next time.

When children avoid play with others or are unsuccessful at play with others, observe carefully to see if they need some instruction on common play themes or language.

Always keep in mind that a major goal for a challenging child is to help him become a member of the class community more and more, every day. Be wary of any strategy or intervention that allows that child to drift further from the others.

Supportive Interactions

Children first learn play skills and a vocabulary for friendship by the way adults speak to and play with them. Children learn what they live. "Do what I say, not what I do" does not work with young children.

Help children learn to play by joining in the play yourself; model and coach how to speak to and play with others. What you say is what you'll hear. What you do is what you'll see.

Moving from Solo and Parallel Play to Dyad Play

When you play alongside children who are not yet interacting with other children, emphasize basic friendship concepts. Help them develop an understanding of what friendly behavior looks and sounds like. Focus their attention on the friendly overtures of others. Teach them the value of friendship and the basic friendship skills of turn taking, sharing, and using friendly language.

Comment on Friendly Behavior

Many teachers tell children, "We are all friends in our class." This is a myth, and children know it. Even young children have preferred playmates and friends. However, you can establish a more honest (and achievable) classroom norm by saying, "We all have friendly behavior in our classroom." When you enforce friendly behavior rather than artificial friendships, children develop skills that will serve them for life. So many times, we are required to interact with people who we would not choose as friends—maybe on a church committee, or as a member of the school council, or at work. Whether we are friends or not, we are still expected to maintain civil and friendly behaviors toward each other.

Telling children to "Be nice," or "Be friends," is akin to you being told tomorrow to "Speak Turkish." Instead of those vague directions, help children develop an understanding of friendly behavior with your daily language, commenting when you see it. For example, you might say:

- "I see two kids working together."
- "You guys look like you are having fun playing superheroes together."
- "Did the two of you set that table together?"

Name Friendly Actions

When children become aware of how their words and behaviors affect others, they can begin to evaluate what kinds of behavior will work to make friends. When they grab a toy away, they can look at their friend's face and discover that grabbing is not a good strategy to maintain a friendship. When they help a friend find their missing shoe, they can see the smile on their friend's face and discover that helping is a good friendship skill. Help children develop this awareness with a simple sentence template such as "You (action) so that (impact). That was friendly." Here are some examples:

- "You moved over so that Emilia could sit down. That was friendly."
- "You got off the bike to give Stephan a turn. That was friendly."
- "You found Dexter's car in the yard and gave it back to him. Look how happy he is now. That was friendly."

Eventually, you will notice that a child is familiar with various ways that friends speak and behave. At that point, you can begin to prompt her to come up with her own solutions.

INSTEAD OF SAYING . . .	TRY . . .
"Give Amit some of the blocks."	"Find a way for Amit to play blocks."
"Stacy needs a doll too. Paul, give her one of yours."	"Find a way for Stacy to play babies with you."
"Stanley, move over so Albert can sit at circle."	"Let's make room for Albert." (Then just wait.)
"LeBron, Abby is crying because her mama just left. Can you paint with her at the easel please?"	"Abby feels sad because her mama just left. How can we help her feel better?"

Notice Friendly Overtures

Some children are not aware that others are making friendly overtures. They need some help to recognize the friendly behavior of others. Support these children by giving them descriptive feedback when you see someone acting in a friendly manner toward them. Use a pattern such as "I saw (child's name and action). He was being friendly to you." For example:

- "I saw Raymond share his cookie with you. He was being friendly to you."
- "I saw CJ give you a turn with the easel. She was being friendly to you."

Use Peers as Resources

Help children learn that friendship is something worth working for. As you interact and speak with children throughout the day, help them view their peers as valuable resources for help and for pleasure.

WHEN YOU SAY . . .	THE CHILD LEARNS . . .
"____knows how to____. Go ask him/her." For example, "Brandon knows how to open the jar. Go ask him for help."	Peers are valuable resources.
"That was a heavy table. It was good to have two kids work together to move it."	Sometimes it takes more than one person to reach a goal.
"I saw you guys playing catch outside. It's good to have another kid to play with."	Interacting with others can be fun.

Model Taking Turns and Sharing

As children begin to play with others, they need to learn the skills of taking turns and sharing. However it is that you want children to behave, make sure you model that behavior in your interactions with children. As you play with children, remember that they see and hear everything you do. If Daija grabs markers with both hands and plops them on her paper, and we react by grabbing them back and saying sharply, "You can't take all the markers. Put those back!" we have just demonstrated to the others that grabbing and harsh words are a part of our classroom culture. Instead, if we say "Daija, I want to share the markers too. Please put them in the middle so I can share them with you," we have demonstrated an alternative way that our class handles conflict. Which method would you like to see the kids use? Look for opportunities to teach the language of turn sharing and turn taking as you play with children. Make comments like these:

- "Jeremiah, can I use the blue marker when you are done?"
- "My turn?"
- "Let's play 'My Turn Your Turn.'"
- "Can I have it when you're done?"
- "Let's play blocks together."
- "Let's play two-people water table."

Teach children "My Turn, Your Turn"

1. Take a stack of unit blocks and sit at a small table.
2. Invite one child at a time to play with you.
3. Build a tower of blocks by taking turns adding a block to the structure.
4. As you take turns, chant "My turn, your turn," and encourage the child to join the chant. Let other children observe the play. They will learn by watching, and you will save time teaching the skill to others.

As children become skilled at taking turns in the game, allow two children to do the activity together while you observe and continue to coach the "My Turn, Your Turn" chant. Eventually, children will be able to take turns without direct adult guidance. If problems develop, remind children that it is a "My Turn, Your Turn" activity.

Teach children turn-taking language

- Sometimes a child doesn't want to play with others or take turns. Teach children to say, "I want to play alone right now," and make sure others understand what that means.
- Children might worry that if they give somebody a turn with a toy, they might lose it for good. Teach children to say, "You can look at it if you give it right back."
- For children who grab from others to get a turn, teach language instead such as, "Thomas is using that. Ask him for a turn. Say, 'Can I have a turn when you are done?'"

Moving from Dyad Play to Small Group Play

Moving from working and playing with one friend to working with a small group of children is no small task. The social skills required to navigate multiple relationships at once can be challenging. Think of yourself sitting and sharing an intimate lunch with a close friend. Suddenly, a mutual acquaintance comes to the table and asks if she can join you. Do you sometimes feel like Little Johnny who says, "Go away. We're busy"? Clearly, the dynamics of a group of three or four people is quite different than what goes on between two close friends. And so it is with children.

Entering Play

Francie sees some children building a tall structure in the block area. If she doesn't yet have the skills and language to join in the play, what might she do? How might she attempt to join in? Most likely, she will knock down the tower, push in, or grab blocks. It's not enough to tell her, "Go over there, and use your words." Many children haven't yet learned the words to say. If she knew them, she probably would have used them.

As you play with children, model scripts and skills they need to join in ongoing play with others. A useful beginning script to enter play is "How can I play?" The chance of a child being excluded is less likely when a child asks *how* rather than "Can I play?" "How can I play?" invites the other children to be creative and come up with a way to integrate the new child. This is especially likely to happen if you have modeled appropriate responses to "How can I play?" in your own play with children.

When you are teaching a child how to integrate himself into ongoing play, invite the child to come with you as you model the words and strategies.

1. Invite the child to join you as you enter the play. For example, invite Ezekial to come with you to help with the block structure that a few other kids are building.
2. Say to the children already there, "Hi. How can we play?"

Joining the Play Theme

Successful players join into ongoing play themes. Whenever you model joining ongoing play, help the child figure out how to join in rather than changing the play theme. Don't go into a group that is playing doctor and suggest that they play bathing babies!

1. Invite the child to come with you as you attempt to join ongoing play.
2. Ask the small group of children what they are playing and tell them that you like to play that game. For example, say, "What are you playing?" If they say they are building a rocket ship, say, "I like to build."
3. Ask the group if you can use your idea of how to play. For example, say, "I'm gonna get all the big blocks for you, okay?" or "I'm gonna build a road that goes to your spaceship."
4. Coach individual children who have trouble joining in by suggesting an appropriate role for them. For example, say, "Ezekial, how about you start building the road, and I'll get you blocks."

Exiting Play

Children who don't know the language to exit play might decide to throw toys or tear down the work of other children when they are done playing. As you play with them, model a simple two-step routine such as this:

1. Put the toys down.
2. Say "Bye," and walk away.

Moving from Small Group Play to Large Group Activities

Adults have a unique role when they participate in large group play with children. When they participate in parallel play, or dyad play, or play in small groups, adults can most often allow the children to lead the play. They can sit back to model participation and gently coach children who need help with their play skills. Because most preschool children are very unskilled at managing large groups, it falls to the teacher to be the leader of the group as well as being a participant. As the leader of the group activity, it will be you who decides the purpose of gathering the group together, you who guides assigning roles to the children, and you who must keep gently directing children back to the activity at hand.

For example, think of joining a small group in the block area. If during ongoing play, one of the children proposes tearing down the castle and building a farm instead and the others agree, the agenda can quickly change. Your role in that play would be to act as one of the child participants to model appropriate negotiation and compromise skills. On the other hand, think about one of the large group activities you might be leading. Your role in that activity would lean more toward keeping the group on task to follow the existing agenda. Do you see the difference? In the first instance, you are a participant, while in the second, you have the added responsibility of being the group leader. Even in those cases when you might have individual children lead parts of a large group activity, they are acting in an apprentice role under your direct guidance and supervision.

Here are ways to be an effective role model and leader for large group activities:

1. Make sure the agenda or plan is clearly communicated to the group.
2. Ensure that every group member is included in the activity, and accommodate any special needs individuals might have.
3. Gently redirect individuals back to the task at hand when the group strays too far off course.
4. Recognize each individual's contribution to the group effort.

Perhaps you are in a setting where all the children will move as a group from the classroom to the school library. As the leader of this large group activity, you might want to take these steps:

1. Say something such as, "We are all going to go to see Ms. Alexander in the library now so she can read us a new book about bugs. Remember, at school we need to walk down the hallway in a quiet line. Justin, you are line leader so you can go to the front of the line."
2. Integrate other children individually or in small groups. For example, "If your name starts with the letter B you can get in line. If you are wearing red pants you

can get in line." Make sure to accommodate the special needs of individuals. If Priscilla and Austin have trouble walking down the hallway quietly in line, invite them to join you or another adult, or assign them a special job. "Pricilla and Austin, please come to the front of the line and help carry the book bin back to the library for us."

3. As you walk down to the library, gently redirect children to stay in line and be quiet. For example, if the children are getting too noisy stop and whisper in an exaggerated manner something like, "Let's see if we can be so quiet that even the little mice can't hear us. Can you move your feet oh-so-quiet? Can you make your mouths oh-so-quiet? Let's see if we can get all the way to the library and not even wake up one little mouse. Let's go."
4. As the children enter the library, recognize each child's contribution. "Justin, you led us all safely to the library. You are a good leader. Pricilla and Austin, you carried that whole box of books together down here. That was good partnership. Wanda and Freddy, you were so quiet walking down here. Mason, Luis, Jan, Tabby—you stayed right in line."

Support Play through the Classroom Culture

Since children develop at their own pace, classrooms are likely to have children at all stages of play development from solo through large group skill levels. Supportive classrooms will have spaces and places that support each level of play with opportunities for children to grow to the next. The classroom culture will also have established rituals and routines, a common social language, and an atmosphere of respect for developmental differences.

Support Solo and Parallel Play

Help children feel comfortable during the program day by providing time, space, and activities for children who choose to work alone or with one special friend. These opportunities allow children to practice friendship skills at their own pace. Think of setting up a few cozy areas that are set off to the side of more busy and active areas. Plan a few simple and predictable activities specifically for partners. These simple partner activities can be risk-free opportunities to practice working with others. Remember that even when children work alone or with one special partner, they will observe and learn from nearby children at work and at play in small groups.

One-Person Play Areas

All the people and action in a preschool room can easily overwhelm children who are still playing alone or next to others. Make sure to include options for them throughout the classroom where they can participate but still be alone. For example, if you offer a collage art activity at a table set with four spaces, you might want to invite a child to use the same materials at a smaller table off to the side a bit.

In the block area, you might want to put a hula hoop on the floor to define a child's space. Masking tape can be used in the same way to define space. Make sure that all of the children in the room know that when a child chooses to use one of these one-person areas that their space and privacy should be respected.

You might say something like, "Sometimes, children like to play all by themselves and that's okay. When a child plays in our one-person play spots, remember that we don't talk to them and we don't touch their stuff. That's called *private time.*" These one-person play areas should be an open option for any child in the room who feels a need or desire for some solitary time.

Side-by-Side Areas

When children are at the stage of parallel play, they don't actually interact with each other during the activity. It's important, then, to make sure that each child has their own set of supplies to do the work. For example, give each child their own blob of play-dough and their own set of playdough tools. When they move on to dyad play, they will be able to begin to negotiate sharing materials. Trying to get children to share materials when they are still at parallel play might result in grabbing and hurting.

Set up some areas where they can work side by side with the same materials. For example, you can put two tubs in the water table or set two easels side by side in the art area. Just as with one-person activity spots, you might want to set up a smaller table for just two children for special activities, such as collages or cooking.

Sharing Group Supplies

Introduce the concept of sharing by having children pass out community supplies to peers. It is easier for most children to "share" things they are not currently using. Introducing sharing this way now helps children get ready for dyad play with others later.

- Have them pass out paper or markers for a large group activity of some sort.
- Let them help you set the table for snack or lunch by passing out plates or cups.
- Have them pass out scarves for a dancing activity.

Support Dyad Play

Some of the children in your group will be ready for dyad play, or playing with one other child. Dyad play is very different from being able to play peacefully in a group of three to five children. In dyad play, there is only one relationship to manage and a minimum of negotiation over space and materials. Giving children plenty of opportunity for dyad play will prepare them for the more hectic and involved play with three to five children that comes later.

Two-Person Areas

Encourage children to practice dyad play by making sure that there are some materials and centers that are more fun to do with two people than alone.

- Include big blocks, rocking boats, wagons, bikes and trailers, and computer buddies.
- Put small tables that fit only two children in various centers around the room, such as table toys or the snack area.

Rejecting Play Invitations

As children move from playing alone to playing with others, there will be times that they still want to work or play alone. Often children will say things such as "You're not our friend," or "Go away," or "We don't like her, do we?" when a new child attempts to join play. Give children the language they need to graciously reject an invitation to play. Here are two suggestions: "Not now, maybe later," or "No, thanks." When you teach this script, make sure you also let children know that it is all right for children to want to work by themselves sometimes—it isn't meant to be a permanent rejection of friendship.

Partner Work

While some children seem to effortlessly morph from solo players to dyad players, other children benefit from a more deliberate and structured approach. Teachers can set up buddy activities with specific guidelines to help these children make the transition. The best way to teach buddies how to work together is to model the kind of behavior you want to see. You can do this by first being the child's partner and later inviting another child to take your place in the dyad. Make sure you stay with the two children long enough to help them work smoothly with each other. Here are some partner activities that teachers have found useful in their classrooms.

- Create buddy back rubbers. Teach children how to rub or pat the backs of their peers at rest time. Make sure to model appropriate social skills, such as where it is appropriate to touch another person, to ask first if they would like their back rubbed, to stop when the child requests, and how much pressure is appropriate to use. Some teachers assign the job of back rubber to children who don't nap or need less rest time than the others. You can also assign back rubbing as a rotating job so that everyone has a turn.

- Pair children to push each other on the swings or pull each other in the wagons.
- Assign two children to do a heavy job such as moving a table or carrying a large container of balls or blocks.

Peer Mentors

Young children are very egocentric. They see the whole world in relation to how it affects them. Most young children appreciate the value of adults. After all, adults are the ones who feed them, bathe them, take them out for fast food, and read them books. Dyad play requires that children begin to see their own peers as valuable resources as well. Encourage children in your group to share their talents and strengths with each other.

- Each one teach one: Buddy up children to help each other learn new skills such as pumping on the swing or finding their name card.
- Seek out child mentors on an ongoing basis. When a child says, "I don't know what to do with my painting," try saying, "Go ask around and find a kid who can help you." If this seems overwhelming to the child, try directing them to a specific child who has the information they need and the social skills to share it. Say something like, "You know, I bet Peng knows what to do with paintings—ask her."
- When a child is struggling at a particular time of the day, such as snack or cleanup, help them find a child mentor to partner with. Kids can often learn from peers easier than they can learn from adults.

Thank-You Notes

Along with guiding children to view each other as valuable resources goes teaching children the obligation of expressing thanks. A verbal thanks is one strategy to model and teach. Many teachers also find writing thank-you notes useful for this purpose—and a valuable addition to their literacy program as well.

1. Keep a supply of note cards or small sheets of colored paper in the writing center, along with an illustrated list of class members.
2. Model and encourage writing thank-you notes for expressions of kindness. Adults should remember to write notes to individual children frequently.
3. Make sure to also write thank-you notes to guests and the school's support staff on a regular basis.

Buddy Jobs

Smooth dyad play requires a delicate dance where the partners shift from being the leader to being the follower. Help children learn this skill with the structure of buddy jobs.

Instead of assigning classroom jobs to individual children, assign them to buddy pairs. Children can be paired up to do classroom jobs in a way that each child has a chance to be an "expert" as well as a "trainee." Learning how to be both a leader and a follower are useful skills not only for school, but for work, families, and adult life as well.

1. You will need to create one job for each buddy pair, so divide the total number of children in the room by two.
2. On a big piece of posterboard, print the classroom jobs down the left side of the page. Use photos or clip art to illustrate each job. Draw horizontal lines between each job to help the children read the chart. Put two tabs of the loop side of Velcro next to each job, leaving enough room to put one child's photo on each spot (see below). You can use a pocket chart instead of Velcro if you have one the right size.
3. Make 2 by 2 prints of each child's photo, and label with their names. Cover each one with Con-Tact paper to make them durable. Put a tab of Velcro (hook side) on the back of each photo.
4. Pair up children so two children are assigned to each job. Put the children's photos next to the job on the job chart.
5. For the first week only, you will need to teach one child in each pair how to do that job. You might begin the year by adding only one or two jobs every day so that you have time to train the children.
6. The child who knows how to do the job is now the "expert." Their partner is the "trainee." As children do their job for the week, the expert coaches and trains their partner.
7. At the end of the week, move all the experts to new jobs. They become the trainees, and the children who were trainees now become the experts.
8. Each week, continue by moving the current expert to a new job.

Here's a sample of what this kind of job chart might look like:

JOB		
Water plants	Chester	Tyrone
Feed hamster	Melinda	Joseph
Push in chairs	Ephraim	Daphne
Straighten book corner	Tyler	Kelsey

We Wish You Well

Help children expand their personal worlds to include concern for the well-being of others. One simple way to practice this in the daily classroom routine is to acknowledge children who are absent each day.

One teacher developed the following daily routine for her children:

1. During group time, look around to see who is absent that day.
2. As a group, sing "We Wish You Well" from Becky Bailey (sing to the tune of "Farmer in the Dell": We wish you well, we wish you well, all through the day today, we wish you well.)
3. For each absent adult or child, have one child "write" a "Wish You Well"note to that person, and put it in their cubby.

Support Small Group Play

Many preschool children are at the stage of small group play, and most early childhood classrooms are already set up to encourage groups of three to five children to work together. Some young children struggle to enter small group play because they are unfamiliar with what and how the children are playing. These children need adult support and intervention to learn how to play games such as "House" or "Building an Airport."

Small Group Play Areas

Here are some ideas for setting up space in your classroom so that small groups can practice working and playing together.

- Many classrooms use the dramatic play and block areas for small group activities. Some teachers choose to limit the number of children who can use the area at any one time. You can put up a graphic showing how many children can use the area, a pocket chart with limited slots for children to put their name cards, hooks where children can hang their symbol, or Velcro tabs where children can hang their photos.

- Art tables can be set up to accommodate four children who must share common supplies. Use chairs to define how many children can participate at an activity table. Teach the group to use the number of chairs to figure out if there is space for them at the table. Say something like, "Uh, oh, Choua. All the chairs are filled up at playdough. Let's find something to do until a chair is empty," or "I don't know, Patrick. Let's see if there is an empty chair at the cutting table. Yep, there are two chairs empty. That means there is room for you to work there now."
- Mealtime is another opportunity for four children to interact as a small group. Seat adults at tables with children who need help working together as a small group.

Some teachers also pull small groups of children out for teacher directed work during center time.

You Can't Say You Can't Play Areas

Design one or two spaces in the room as "You Can't Say You Can't Play" areas where children can practice inclusion skills. These areas have no limit for the number of children who can play there, and are not private play spaces. They are open to the entire classroom community, in the same way a public park or shopping mall might be. The job of the children already in the center is to find a way to integrate new children into the group activity. You might find the chant, "Find a way for (child's name) to play" helpful when reminding children of the guideline.

It's important that the "You Can't Say You Can't Play" areas be interesting and attractive to most of the children in the group, so that there is an incentive for children to stay in that area and include others instead of just leaving the area for another.

For example, if Oscar complains to you that the children in home living won't let him play, you can remind the group of the cultural norm for that activity:

1. Go with Oscar back to home living, and have him ask again to be included in the play.
2. If the children say something like, "We don't want Oscar here," you can remind them of the norm by saying, "Remember, this is a 'You Can't Say You Can't Play' area. That means that you need to find a way that Oscar can play."
3. If children include Oscar in the play, say something such as, "You figured out a way for Oscar to play. That was friendly."

4. If the children refuse to allow Oscar into the play, remind them that their choice is to let him play, or they can leave the area and find another place to play. "This is a 'You Can't Say You Can't Play' area. Your choice is to find a way for Oscar to play or find another area to work in. Which will you choose?"

What if you find that when given a choice of including a specific child or leaving the area, the children choose to leave the area? Wouldn't that be humiliating to the child who tried to join the activity?

As with all strategies in this book and with recommendations from others, sometimes they work the way you want them to, and sometimes they don't. Sometimes you can tweak a strategy or "go in the back door" to get around resistance. For example, if you find a particular child is always abandoned in the "You Can't Say You Can't Play" area, try these ideas:

- If the children leave, say, "Okay. Oscar and I will finish building the fire station together," and join in the play. Most likely, the appeal of playing with a teacher will override the appeal of leaving the area. If children change their minds and choose to stay, have them now ask Oscar how they can play. Prompting Oscar to make an inclusive response will increase his chances of being included next time.

- Another strategy for a child who is usually excluded would be to invite that child to be your first partner for a special project. For example, if you are adding potting soil and seeds to the sensory table, invite Becker to be the first child at the activity. Let other children know that if they would like to join Becker, they can ask him how they can play. Again, if needed, coach Becker to make an inclusive response.

- A variation on this strategy is to become involved in a desirable activity with an excluded child, such as shooting baskets during outdoor time. When other children want to join the play, have them ask the first child how they can play. Remain with the group long enough after the other children join in to make sure the play is working smoothly.

- When children begin to include the previously excluded child, make sure to give them positive reflective feedback such as, "Masha, I saw you found a way for Hope to play wagons with you and Tessa. That was very friendly."

Teacher-Invented Play Themes

Some children might come to your class with very limited play skills. To play successfully with each other, children need some basic, compatible play themes. A child who has come from a harsh or abusive home life might not understand the nurturing play of other "mommies" and "daddies" in the home living area. Their idea of play might be to fling kitchen items against the wall while shouting, "Shut up or I'll punch you." They might treat the baby dolls roughly or punitively and use profanity with them. Teachers may find this play offensive, and peers might be frightened by what they are seeing and hearing.

Begin to teach these children more successful play themes with teacher-invented scenarios. Make sure these games include very scripted and clear guidelines for interaction. Include some sharing and turn taking. When children participate in teacher-invented games, they don't have to figure out what to do. Everything is predictable and nothing needs to be "invented." Children who find success in these very prescribed "games" gain a sense of social competence that carries over into the rest of the program day. Invent simple play themes and teach them to all the children in the group. For example, you might invent the game called "Car Wash."

1. Invite children to the block center to play "Car Wash" with you.
2. Work together with the children to build a car wash building out of blocks.
3. Model the play by taking a car and saying something such as, "Oh no. My car is full of mud. I need to go to the car wash!" Drive your car to the structure, pretend to spray water on the car (with all the sound effects, of course), and as you drive out of the wash say something like, "All clean."
4. Drive your car through the "mud area" again and get your car dirty. Repeat the sequence.
5. Other children will pick up cars of their own to follow in your play. Some children more skilled at play might suggest that they take on the role of "washing lady." Others might modify the scripts. However, the basic theme of the play should stay consistent.

Other ideas for teacher-invented play themes are post office, doctor's office, feeding the baby, shopping, shoe store, and cooking supper. Consider using the bike area outdoors for play themes like car wash. Use your climbing structure for themes such as "Fire Rescue" or "Save the Cat in the Tree." Whatever the theme, keep it simple and make sure to include some basic, simple scripts. Three steps are enough.

Three-Step Play Sequences

Children learn some games like "Duck-Duck-Goose" from older children and adults. Other games just seem to evolve naturally and vary depending on the group. For instance, a group of children might invent a game of "Daddy-Baby." The routine might include changing the diaper, feeding the baby, and then putting the baby in the shopping cart to go shopping. You might see these invented games anywhere in the program. On the swings, they might be "pumping to the sky." At the water table, children might be "making tornadoes."

Observe challenging children over a period of play sessions to determine if they understand the basic play routines that children have established. Often when children have trouble figuring out the established play themes, trouble breaks out. Children playing "tornadoes" might physically or verbally push out a child who is not "playing right." They might say things like, "Logan can't play with us. He's stupid."

When you identify a child having trouble figuring out the play sequences, help children understand ongoing play themes with "Three-Step Play Sequence" books.

1. Make a blank book with a front cover and three blank pages.
2. Observe the children at play and figure out the three main steps. Look for the *trigger*, the *action*, and the *closure*. For example, in one class, ambulance play looked like this:

   - Trigger—"Help, help!" calls one child.
   - Action—Ambulance players run to the child and give aid.
   - Closure—"All done. We fixed her," says one of the ambulance people.

3. Help your target child integrate into the existing play. Take photos of that child for each of the three steps. Mount the photos in the book. On each page, print the simple step. On the cover, put the name of the play, such as "Ambulance." This book, for example, might say, "Help, help!" under the picture on the first page. The second page might say, "Run and help the kid." The third page might say, "All done. We fixed her."
4. Teach the child how to play by reading and rereading the book as often as the child wants. Keep the book in the class library for all the children to read.

Family-Style Dining

Family-style dining helps to build strong bonds in the classroom community and provides opportunities for adults to model how to eat in a group. In family-style dining, food is placed on the table in community bowls and is passed around the table. Each child and adult serves himself or herself a portion.

You can model appropriate mealtime manners by asking for a dish to be passed and by being attentive to the needs of others. When somebody drops or spills something, model how you would handle this with a table of adult friends.

Comments like "Oops. Let me help you," or "Oh dear, would you like a new plate?" help children learn social scripting that they will need for success in school and in life.

Adults can also lead mealtime conversations. These conversations should be similar to those that you would have with your own friends. Talk about upcoming plans, common memories, likes and dislikes, movies, books, and music.

Build Whole Group Identity

We focus so much on helping young children develop independence that we sometimes forget about interdependence. We want to encourage children to zip their own pants and clean up after themselves. But at the same time, success in school and in life requires that children also learn to develop community skills. They need to learn to work in pairs and in groups; they need to develop empathy and helping skills; and they need to begin to understand how to figure out a group's culture and expectations.

Balancing self and community, or independence and interdependence, is a tricky proposition for children and adults alike. It is not nearly as simple as it might sound. As adults, we may be asked to work on a committee with people who we would not choose as friends. We may be neighbors with families who are quite different from ourselves. We may have to work on a large project with a variety of people. It takes years of practice to figure out how to work well with others without losing the best of ourselves.

One area of the room might be used for a teacher-directed, large group activity once or twice a day. You could conduct large group morning meetings or large group music or story times. Often, furniture is moved for these times of the day so that all the children can fit comfortably in the space.

"I'm a Jumping Cactus kid," Efrain proudly announces to his father after the first day of school. "What's that?" asks his dad. "That means that we all yell 'Go, go, go' at the end of circle," Efrain explained. From the very first day, Efrain begins to identify himself as part of a community that has a distinct set of rituals and customs. Rituals and routines during the day help everyone in the class feel a sense of connection and belonging.

Morning Meetings

Personal greetings and good-byes are important bridge builders with individual children, and so are group meeting times. Meetings are useful for the whole group to use rituals to symbolically reconnect as a community, to greet those who are present and to think of those who are absent, or to pass on information about the day.

Have a regular routine for morning meetings to help children feel safe and secure. Here is one possible routine:

1. Sing a greeting song that includes the name of each child that is present.
2. Sing a song such as "We Wish You Well" (see p. 82) to absent members to let them know the class is thinking of them.
3. Preview special activities for the day.
4. Play a transition game.

Some teachers read a story in the morning; other teachers talk about an ongoing project or unit of study. Some teachers use the same schedule all year, and others begin with a shorter schedule early in the year and add more topics as the year goes on. However you chose to do your meeting, it is most important to follow the same routine day after day. This helps children anticipate what will happen in meeting. The meeting itself is apt to be challenging to many of the children in the class; knowing what will happen and about how long it will last helps everyone be less anxious. Think of yourself in an unfamiliar situation that you know will challenge you, surrounded by other people. Knowing what is coming and how long you have to endure it would help, wouldn't it? It's the same for children.

Welcome New Community Members

The more you have worked to establish community norms and common language, the more important it is to work with the children to establish a routine for welcoming new members. Think about what new children and adults would need to know. Where would they keep their things? How would they learn the routines? How would they be introduced to others?

Who will show them where things are, how to enter play, how to play games like shoe store? Here are some ideas:

- Make sure to visually include new children right away. Have a labeled cubby ready for them. Add their name cards and photos to appropriate areas of the room such as the sign-in sheets and job boards.
- Pair the child up with different partners throughout the day. Guide the child-mentors to explain traditional routines, rituals, and scripts to the new child. Make sure the new child has a partner for any transition times, since these moments can be most confusing to new members.
- At group time, have children review standard classroom procedures. For example, say, "Gordon is new to our class and he probably doesn't know about cleanup time. Who here can tell Gordon one of our cleanup time rules?"

Say Good-bye to Members during the School Year

Help children feel safe and secure by establishing rituals and routines for saying good-bye to staff or children who leave the group during the year. Remember that children are very egocentric and they interpret life through a "How will this affect me?" lens. If a child should leave your group without a farewell ceremony of some sort, many children will feel uneasy and might make up all sorts of wild fantasies about why the child is no longer with the group. Increased anxiety might show up as clingy behavior, aggression, destruction, or contrary behavior.

Work as a class to make a good-bye ritual for members who have to leave during the year. Here are some ideas:

- Have a simple good-bye party for a departing member.
- Set up a writing center with paper and markers so that children can "write" good-bye notes.
- Put together a blank book for the child who is leaving. Let the child paste in extra pictures you have of the class and then dictate captions for the photos. Invite children to "sign" the memory book if they like.
- Make up a good-bye and wish-you-well ceremony to do as a large group activity. This might include a song or a chant. Maybe each child can share a good memory of the parting child.
- Have the class present the child or adult who is leaving with one of the big books that they have made during the year.
- If you know the last day in advance, make a countdown calendar and mark off the days at the morning meeting.
- Sometimes members leave without notice. Explain to the group what you know about the departure and include a memory activity. For example, at center time that day you might set up a "We Remember (name)" table. Put a photo of the child or adult on a large piece of paper. Invite children to dictate their memory or sign their name on the poster. Mount the finished work on the wall.

Classroom Jobs

Community members all pitch in to support the community. There are many jobs to do and each member is needed to make sure everything gets done to support the group. Help children take group ownership of the classroom with class jobs for everyone. Think about using sophisticated titles for your class jobs. These terms help children make the connection between what they do in the classroom and job functions in the adult world. Here are twenty-three suggestions put together by teachers at a recent conference:

Paramedic (help with first aid)

Door holder (holds door open while class walks through)

Banker (collects lunch money, book orders)

Toy detective (find homes for stray toy pieces)

Housekeeper (sweeps or uses carpet sweeper)

Gardener (waters plants)

Audio visual technician (turns CD player on and off)

Transition person (rings chime to get children's attention)

Zookeeper (feeds pets)

Usher (puts out sit-upons or cushions)

Host (puts out name cards for lunch)

Wish You Well Kid (writes "We Wish You Well" notes for absent children)

Back rubber (rubs backs at rest time)

Computer technician (turns computer on and off)

Coat zipper (zips coats)

Busboy or busgirl (cleans tables after meals and snacks)

Room inspector (checks all centers after cleanup)

Story reader ("reads" a favorite book to other children)

Mail sorter (puts notes that go home in cubbies)

Greeter (greets guests)

Librarian (keeps library in order)

Light bulb keeper (turns lights on and off)

Hygienist (hands out toothbrushes)

If you have more than twenty-three children in the group, make some of the jobs two-person jobs or use the buddy job system described earlier.

Saying Good-bye

Teachers spend so much time at the beginning of the year helping children to develop friendships and a sense of community. But often, little time is spent at the end of the year learning how to say good-bye. Just as young children often need help learning how to form friendships and community bonds, they also need help to say good-bye at the end of the school year. Good-byes can be painful and scary. When children become aware that they will be moving on, they might begin to worry. Children who don't know how to say good-bye might behave much like the children who had trouble forming friendships at the beginning of the school year. They might hit or name-call or hide under the table. They might act younger in the hopes that they won't be old enough to move on. Often children will sabotage friendships and connections with peers and adults to ease the pain of parting.

Forming strong bonds and learning to say good-bye as we move on to new adventures is an emotional skill that will serve children for life. Saying good-bye at the end of the classroom year is a beginning step to saying good-bye to an old house or a disintegrating blanket. Learning parting skills also prepares children for a dying pet, a move, a divorce, or the death of a loved one.

Like other social and emotional skills, learning to say good-bye doesn't happen from one activity or one project. Plan on introducing good-bye lessons at least a month before the end of the school year or even earlier if children are beginning to show symptoms of "good-bye anxiety."

As important as forming the community is at the start of the year, saying good-bye is at least as important. The better job we have done to form a cohesive community, the more the members need to bring closure when the members of the community part ways.

- Have children draw a picture about what they think will be the same next year or what they think will be different. Bind these pictures into a "Same and Different" book to keep in the classroom collection. Read and reread the story as needed for the group and for individual children.
- Fill balloons with helium, and print one child's name on each balloon. Have a ceremonial balloon release. To protect wildlife, use only 100 percent latex balloons; don't attach them to one another; and don't release any balloons with ribbons, string, or plastic plugs attached.
- Distribute class-made big books to children if you have enough to give one to each child.

Expect Large Group Challenges

Trying to include children who are at the parallel play and dyad play stages in large group activities is frustrating for the teacher, the child, and the other children in the group. Without special accommodations or support, these children will quickly become fussy, noisy, distracted, and disruptive. Repeated reminders and threats to attend to the large group activity only serve to frustrate and discourage everyone. At the same time, some children in the group are ready for large group activities. How then can large group activities be conducted while meeting the developmental needs of all the children in the group?

Model and Coach

If you are in a two-teacher classroom, while one teacher is conducting large group, the other teacher can sit near one or more children who are still learning large group skills. That teacher can model group skills and help coach the charges to keep them on track. For example, "Hunter, I can't hear the story when you talk to your friends. Please be quiet for a few more minutes," or "Mason, look at the bear in the story. What do you think will happen next?"

Identify Peer Mentors

Help a child who is struggling with large group skills identify somebody who knows how to do the activity. Encourage them to match the other child when they are off-task. For example, Shastina has identified Viranda as a kid who knows how to do story time. Before group time starts, say, "Shastina, remember to check what Viranda is doing if you are not sure what to do when we read our book." You might even seat Shastina next to her model and ask Viranda to help Shastina.

Use Front-Row Seating

Seat children who are not ready for large group directly in front of the teacher with their backs to most of the other children. Many children in this situation will have the illusion that they are in a smaller group and will have an easier time.

Assign Special Tasks

Give a special job to a child who is still learning large group skills. They can turn the pages in a book, pass out materials, or hold the props.

Dismiss Children Early

Start large group time with all the children together. After the first short activity, tell children who are still learning large group skills that they are free to work in quiet centers. Over time, those children will be able to stay longer and longer.

Divide the Group

Break large group time into two smaller groups. In classes with two teachers, each one can lead one of the groups. In classes with one teacher, one group can be at large group while the other is at a center time activity, and then the groups can switch. Some teachers like to divide groups randomly; others like to have one group for children proficient at group skills and the other group for children who are still mastering group skills.

Teach Group Skills Explicitly

During center time, pull over a small group of children who are learning group skills. Help them figure out how to stay in their own body space, how to ignore distractions, and so on. You can find many ideas on activities in the chapter about self-regulation (see p. 105).

Make Large Group Optional

Make large group time an optional activity instead of a mandatory activity. Allow children to come and go as they wish.

Friendship Activities

Children's development of affiliation comes from your personal interactions with the children and the group culture that you have established for the classroom. From time to time, however, you might want to supplement the curriculum with some special activities to promote friendship skills.

Help Children Learn Dyad Play

Help children develop an understanding that some activities need two people. For children who are just beginning dyad work, consider having one of the adults in the room be the child's partner. However, as children become more skilled at working with others, your role will become one of facilitator instead of participator.

Buddy Art

1. Have each child draw a picture with a black marker. Have children exchange drawings and color in their buddy's picture with colored markers or watercolors.
2. Have children do body tracings for each other.
3. Put two children at one easel with one piece of paper and two brushes.

Author and Illustrator

1. Have one child dictate a story and have the buddy illustrate it.
2. Have one child draw a picture and the other child dictate the story.

Friend Books

Children who are learning dyad play find it helpful to see photos of themselves playing with others. Most children are visual learners, and they like to look at books and pictures as they are learning new skills or integrating new information.

1. Take pictures of children playing with each other.
2. Allow children to mount the pictures in blank books.
3. Take their dictation of who they were playing with and what they were doing.
4. Put the finished books in the class library, read the books at group time or when children request them, and lend the books to families to read at home.

Buddy Play Pictures

Children form a vision of themselves from the messages that they get from the outside world. Post photos of children playing with others in various areas of the room so they can see evidence of themselves having a friend and being a friend.

1. Take pictures of children playing together during the day.
2. Enlarge and mount the pictures on posterboard or construction paper.
3. Have the children in the picture give dictation about what they were doing.
4. Hang the pictures on the wall at children's eye level in a "We Are Friends" display area or in centers.

Tea Party

Tea party is a predictable, sequenced activity to teach pairs of children how to take turns and share. Both boys and girls alike are drawn to the ceremonial feeling of taking tea. Use a small, inexpensive breakable (not plastic; china or glass) tea set, a tablecloth, real food, and tongs to add to the special feeling of the activity and help children focus on the play sequences. Many teachers keep a waiting list for children who want to play. As soon as one child finishes, the next child on the list is called. Because children are so interested in this play, they will usually participate even if it is without a "best friend." This encourages children to interact with new friends and helps children who have previously been rejected to be able to play successfully with others. Some teachers model the activity by being the "tea partner" for the first few days that the activity is put out. After children have learned how to "do tea," they begin to work as child-child partners.

1. Gather a child-sized ceramic tea set, a basket with very small snack items such as broken graham crackers, a pair of tongs, a container of watered-down juice, a

container of disinfectant bleach solution, an absorptive tablecloth, and a small table with two chairs. Keep the snack food small and low-key and the "tea" (a juice/water combination) very dilute. This activity is not a snack. It is a chance for children to learn to control their behavior and interact with a partner. The tablecloth not only adds ambiance, but also absorbs spills to keep the area neater.

2. Invite two children to sit together at "tea."
3. Instruct children on how the game is played using the following guidelines:

    - Children take turns using the tongs to serve themselves one piece of snack food, which they place on their "cake plate," and pouring themselves "tea" from the ceramic pitcher into their teacup.
    - Children can serve themselves more food or drink when they have finished the portion on their plates. Children must use the tongs and may serve themselves only one piece at a time.
    - Children can be quiet or talk to each other, but may not carry on conversations with others outside of the game.
    - When one of the children is done playing, they should give their dishes to the teacher for her to dip into the disinfectant solution. The teacher will reset the table for the next child.
    - Rinse the cloth in the disinfectant solution at the end of the session, and hang it to dry for the next session.

Help Children Notice Friendliness

Supplement your personal interactions with children and support the classroom culture with additional friendship-forming activities.

Helping Hands Tree

Help children move from focusing only on themselves to focusing on the interactions of others in the classroom. When children are guided to focus on others' friendly behaviors, they begin to build up a repertoire of friendly behaviors that they can draw upon in their own interactions.

1. Draw a large tree on bulletin board paper or mount a real tree branch in a bucket of plaster of paris.

2. Cut out hand shapes from paper in various colors.
3. Have children identify when they have observed another child's helpful act, and record the event on the hand. For example, "Hazel helped Lola turn on the water in the bathroom."
4. Help the child who observed the act attach the hand to the tree.
5. Periodically, read from the hands at a group meeting. Then pass out the hands for children to take home.
6. It is important that all children be represented on the tree. If some children are not represented, observe those children and find examples of their helpfulness to add to the collection.

Random Acts of Kindness Board

This is similar to the "Helping Hands Tree" above. Instead of just focusing on helpful acts, however, children are guided to recognize any kind act in the classroom community.

1. Have children observe each other for acts of kindness.
2. Record the acts on self-adhesive notes. For example, "Amity let Kiyoshi have the doll with the long hair."
3. Help the child who observed the act attach the note to the board.
4. Read the notes, and distribute as in the previous activity.
5. Again, make sure every member of the community is represented on the board.

All About Us Book

When we help children learn about each other, we open the door to forge new friendships. Children will learn about each other in informal ways throughout the year. But teachers can also help everyone get to know each other early in the year by sharing some of the information they get during home visits or enrollment interviews. Put the results of a survey into a Big Book for the children and their families to share.

1. Print out answers to questions such as, who lives in your house, what is your favorite food, what is your favorite thing to play, and what are you good at?
2. Have children illustrate their page by drawing a picture.
3. Bind the pages together as a Big Book with posterboard front and back covers.
4. Read the book to children at group time.

5. On the top of the back page, write "Family Response Page." Circulate the book to a different family each night, and invite families to write comments.

6. Keep the book in the classroom library for children to look at and for adults to use as a reference and reminder.

Strengthen the Group Identity

Use activities such as the ones below to reinforce the group identity you have established through interactions with children and through the classroom culture.

Scrapbook

Shared history is one of the basic building blocks of community. Reflect often on common experiences to draw individuals together. Shared memories might encompass a whole range of emotionally charged moments. These moments might include celebrations, struggles, a joyful day at the park, or a sad day working through the death of a classroom pet. Sharing these moments is one way to create a shared history. Help children record these moments and pull them out from time to time for reflection and revisiting.

1. Get a photo album or three-ring binder.

2. Collect photos of special events, field trips, visitors, interesting projects, and so on.

3. Periodically, help children organize the pictures in the album and take dictation of their memories.

4. Keep the album in the class library or home living area.

Here is a powerful example of how one classroom teacher used her memory album.

Jazma had just finished reading the story "The Dead Bird" at morning meeting. "I remember when our worms died," said Jessica. "Yeah, they got too hot, didn't they?" added David. "They did get too hot, David. You're right," Jazma said. "At center time, if you like, you can come to the library corner with me and we'll look at the worm book we made." When meeting was over and the children were settled in for the morning, Jazma took out the class-made worm book and shared it with the children, who flowed in and out of the library center. They remembered the day they bought the worms and making a house for them. And they reflected on the Monday morning when they discovered the worms had died. They looked at the photos of the worm funeral and of the memorial worm sculptures that they made that week. While many of the memories were sad, the children were drawn together by the many "Remember whens."

Highlight of the Day

Help your children reflect and record experiences they have had, places they have visited together, and funny things that have happened. Don't only focus on special activities such as going on a field trip or having a snow play day. Help children recognize that every day is full of gifts and memories.

1. Assign a rotating job of deciding on the "Highlight of the Day."
2. Help the child find materials to illustrate the highlight, and take dictation to describe the action. In the beginning, you might have to help children notice that something special occurred during the day. Guide children to remember simple pleasures such as the bug they found outside, the new program for the computer, or a child's new haircut.
3. Post the highlight on the door for parents to see at pick-up.
4. Next morning, add the highlight to a binder collection that has all the highlights of the year. You can also post the highlights along the ceiling as a timeline of the year.

Photo Wall

Another strategy to build community and shared memories is to use your camera to record class history. Photos can be posted in centers or on a single, designated wall.

1. Collect photos of memorable events.
2. Help children mount photos on colored paper.
3. Take dictation from the children about their memories.
4. Post on a memory board or throughout the room.

Name the Class

Cohesive communities must establish common language, behaviors, and practices. Remember that children will have one set of norms and expectations at home and another set at school. Help children identify themselves as a community member by giving the class a name and by using this name often as you refer to routines and expectations. For example, say, "Sinker Dragons, come on inside and get ready for lunch," or "It's time for the Superstars to clean up the room to get ready for story." By using the group name, you will be cuing the children that they are expected to follow the group norm now rather than their individual desires.

1. Have the children suggest three or four names for the class.
2. Hold a group discussion on the names.
3. Help the children agree on a name. Sometimes it is helpful to suggest a combination of the two most popular names. One class came to agreement on Ballerina Dinosaurs.
4. Sometimes it may take three or four meetings before you can agree, but the time is worth it.

Class Pledge

Children need hundreds of repetitions and reminders to establish new habits and behaviors. One way to remind children of the group values is to design a class pledge that gets recited every morning during the first group meeting of the day. Some classrooms have used their class name and their classroom guiding principles to make a simple pledge or chant.

One teacher designed the following chant as her class pledge:

Superstars take care of themselves.

Superstars take care of others.

Superstars take care of the world.

Class-Made Big Books

Young children have trouble classifying objects two ways at once. For example, when they sort, they can often sort by size or by color but not by size and color at the same time. Likewise, young children often have trouble seeing themselves simultaneously as an individual and as a member of the classroom community. Sometimes a child may be so fearful of losing his sense of self that he resists blending in with others. This child might express this anxiety by singing the loudest or throwing the tambourine at music time. Assign each child one page to make for a class Big Book. Books like these give visual symbols that one can be an individual and still be a part of a group effort.

1. Gather large sheets of paper, one for each child in the group.
2. Have each child illustrate her page. Take dictation to narrate the contribution.
3. Bind the pages together with a front and back cover.
4. Print the name of the class somewhere on the front cover.
5. Use some of these ideas for Big Book: What We Do at School, My Family, When I Grow Up, I Can Help.

Class Puzzle

A class puzzle can help children visualize the community as a collection of individuals. For young children, the act of putting together a puzzle with a picture of the class gives them a symbolic way to understand how the community is made up of individuals.

1. Take a photo of the class, including adults and children.
2. Enlarge the photo to at least 8½ by 11, and mount on posterboard.
3. Cover with Con-Tact paper on both sides.
4. Cut into puzzle pieces using a template or free hand.
5. Store the pieces in a plastic sandwich bag or a small container, and add the puzzle to your collection.
6. Update your puzzle any time new children join the group.

Class Flag

A class flag, like a class name, is a concrete symbol of unity. The more visual and tangible cues and symbols you provide for children, the easier it is for children to grasp such intangible concepts as community. Kids need to see it and touch it in order to understand it . . . whatever "it" may be.

1. Use a piece of plain fabric or large posterboard.
2. Print the name of the class somewhere on the flag.
3. Have each child decorate the flag. You can use fabric paint to help each child put their handprint on the flag. Children can attach small photos of themselves or their family on the flag.
4. Adults are also part of the classroom community and should be represented the same way as the children
5. Make sure that the flag is updated when new children join the group.

Who's Missing?

Another visual tool to help children focus on the entire community is the large group game "Who's Missing?"

1. Have all the children close their eyes.
2. Quietly select one child and have him move to an area of the room where the others can't see him.
3. When the rest of the children open their eyes, have them try to figure out who is missing by looking to see who is still in the group.

Who Am I?

A variation on "Who's Missing" is "Who Am I?" This can be played in either a small or large group.

1. Have one child close her eyes.
2. Select another child to sit in a chair in the middle of the group. Put a sheet or light blanket over the child in the middle.
3. When the child opens her eyes, have her guess who is hidden under the sheet.
4. Have the child under the sheet say "Hello" or some other words if the child has trouble guessing who is under the sheet.
5. When the child has guessed, the one who was under the sheet will be the next one to close his eyes and guess.

Yearbooks

Help children reflect on the wonderful experiences and people they have met during the year. Just as bringing a toy for naptime was comforting to children early in the school year, taking home photos of their preschool year at the end of the year is comforting as they step out into new adventures.

1. Staple together some blank pages to make individual small books.
2. Gather photos that were taken of the class during the year. Add extra pictures if needed to make sure everyone is pictured multiple times.
3. Allow children to select pictures to glue in their books.
4. Some children might want to have friends "sign" their yearbooks.

Inclusive Versions of Traditional Games

Many traditional games for young children involve competition and elimination rather than cooperation and inclusion. When choosing games with the goal of encouraging affiliation, try to select cooperative and inclusive games. *Everybody Wins* by Jeffrey Sobel is a good resource for these games. Modify other games to make them cooperative and inclusive as well.

Farmer in the Dell

Tweak the game so that all of the children are chosen, and Cheese has lots of friends for the ending rather than standing alone. One way you can do this is to have Wife select a few children, the children each select Dog, and so on. On the last verse, after the rat takes the cheese, sing, "The cheese stands with friends, the cheese stands with friends. Hi ho the cheerio, the cheese stands with friends."

Musical Chairs

Eliminate chairs, not kids. At first, children will scoot over to share chairs. As more chairs are eliminated, children will begin to sit on each other's laps. Remind the children during the game that "We only win when everyone wins." Instead of the typical sounds of, "I was here first," and "Ha, ha, you're out," you will hear "Come here and share with me," and "You can sit on my lap." Remember to have a celebratory cheer at the end of the game.

Discussion/Reflection Questions

1. Compare time *spent* dealing with children's behaviors with time *invested* in teaching children how to have a friend and be a friend. Keep track during a typical week at your program. How much time did you spend on each? As you invest more time in teaching children social skills, does the time you spend managing their behavior lessen?
2. Do you think lack of friendship skills might affect children's academic learning? If so, how? If not, why not?
3. How might you design an outdoor play area to accommodate children at each of the play stages: solo, parallel, dyad, small group, and large group?

Exercises

1. Observe a challenging child in your group. Pay attention to how well he functions alone, next to another child, interacting with another child, in small group situations, and in whole class activities. What is the highest level at which the child does well without adult support? Do you have new ideas about the underlying causes for the challenging behavior?
2. Conduct a physical survey of your classroom, and review your daily schedule. Does your program and your room support children at each of the stages of play development? How might you modify your environment and your daily program to better serve individual developmental levels?

Reflection/Journal Assignment

Reflect upon your language, tone of voice, and behavior as you guide and redirect children. Are you modeling what you would like the children to do and say as they interact with each other? Can you identify an area that might be valuable as a professional development goal?

Resources

Devereux Foundation. 1999. *Classroom strategies to promote children's social and emotional development.* Lewisville, NC: Kaplan Press.

Gestwicki, Carol. 1999. *Developmentally appropriate practice: Curriculum and development in early education.* Albany, NY: Delmar Publishers.

Heidemann, Sandra, and Deborah Hewitt. 1992. *Pathways to play: Developing play skills in young children.* St. Paul: Redleaf Press.

Hewitt, Deborah, and Sandra Heidemann. 1998. *The optimistic classroom: Creative ways to give children hope.* St. Paul: Redleaf Press.

Levin, Diane E. 1994. *Teaching young children in violent times, building a peaceable classroom: A preschool–grade three violence prevention and conflict resolution guide.* Cambridge, MA: Educators for Social Responsibility.

Nelson, Jane, Lynn Lott, and H. Stephen Glenn. 2000. *Positive discipline in the classroom: Developing mutual respect, cooperation, and responsibility in your classroom.* 3rd ed. Roseville, CA: Prima Publishing.

Paley, Vivian Gussin. 1992. *You can't say you can't play.* Cambridge, MA: Harvard University Press.

Sobel, Jeffrey. 1984. *Everybody wins: 393 noncompetitive games for young children.* New York: Walker & Co.

5

Self-Regulation

"I can manage my strong emotions and am in control of my behavior."

"Bye, Tata Mary. You come get me after naptime?" asked Mario. "Sí, Mijo. After nap," she agreed. "I don't want you to go, Tata," he said with tears in his eyes. "Come give me a hug, Mijo. You'll have fun today. You'll see." Mario felt a little sad when his Tata left, but soon ran off to join his friends at the climber. When the chime rang, he met up with his teacher at the door, went to the classroom, and sat right at circle for morning meeting without any prompting. Later in the morning, when Mario was helping set the table for snack, he spilled a pitcher of milk. "Ms. D," he called out. "The milk dumped out." "What happened, Mario," Ms. D asked. "I tried to do it faster, and I ran into the chair and the milk got all over," he explained. "I go get paper towels," he said as he bounced off.

What Does Self-Regulation Look Like?

Mario is well on his way to establishing the four basic building blocks of self-regulation:

- He is beginning to take ownership for the consequences of his actions. He's getting a sense of cause and effect and of how his behavior affects himself, others, and his environment.
- He understands limits and expectations. He's beginning to learn some guiding principles of behavior and knows that there are some things he is expected to do, whether he wants to or not.
- He's learning to manage his powerful emotions. He's learning that although all his feelings are okay, he has to think before he acts.
- He's figuring out time, space, and transitions, and he can move in a predictable way through his day. He is learning how to wait, how to share space, and how to deal with changes.

Isn't this exactly what we hope to see from all the children in our care?

When Things Go Wrong

With these skills, Mario has a relatively easy time moving through his school day. Not all the children in his classroom are at the same level. Some children in his group still behave impulsively and have no sense of limits. Others have trouble managing their emotions and quickly get overwhelmed. Still others don't pay much attention to the consequences of their behavior and seem oblivious to the trail of destruction they leave behind them.

When children have tantrums, hit others out of frustration, refuse to clean up after themselves, or can't wait for a turn, it is useful to take a closer look to see if they are missing one or more of the four basic building blocks of self-regulation.

Hannah swung a toy telephone and hit Rachel on the side of her head. Moments later when the teacher got there, Rachel was screaming with tears pouring down her face and Hannah was looking on, concerned yet bewildered. "Hannah hit me," Rachel sobbed as a bright red bruise began to appear on her cheek. The teacher gathered Rachel into her lap and pulled Hannah over. "Look at Rachel's face," she said. "Look what you did. How do you think she feels?" "Sor-ry," Hannah replied in a mechanical singsong voice. "Sorry's not enough, Hannah. You hurt your friend. Look at her face. Look what you did. That was so mean what you did. You could have poked her eye out. You made that bruise on her face." "I didn't do it," Hannah said. "We were playing and the telephone hurt her." "Yes you did hurt her. You were very bad to do that," the teacher said. Hannah said again, "The telephone hurt her. Can I go now?" "You can go sit down and think about what you did, young lady. You should be ashamed. What do you think your mother's going to say when she finds out?" the teacher replied.

Later the teacher told her director that this was typical behavior for Hannah. She would hurt somebody and immediately say sorry in that distant, insincere voice. When pushed, she would deny any responsibility for what she did. The more the teacher tried to make her feel bad for hurting kids, the more distant and blank Hannah's face would become.

Hannah is a clear example that making children feel bad does not help them act good. Instead of teaching responsibility for her actions, blame, shame, and guilt only served to put Hannah on the defensive. What the teacher found out later by observing Hannah as she moved through her day was that Hannah didn't yet understand cause and effect in general. She still didn't understand that her actions were what caused hurt and damage to other kids.

Hannah's teacher began to give Hannah reflective feedback many times a day in nonthreatening situations to help her become aware of how her behavior had consequences—"You wiped up the water and now the table is all dry"; "You put on your shoes and now you are ready to go outside"; "You let Jalessa sit by you and now she feels happy." When Hannah hurt others, her teacher took the role of guide and partner in reflecting upon the incident: "You hit Ivan and now he's hurt. He needs some help." After Ivan's needs were met, the teacher went back to Hannah. "You wanted the playdough so you hit Ivan. That hurt him. We need to keep kids safe here at school. Come, let's practice a safe way to get playdough so nobody gets hurt." The teacher took Hannah back to the activity table and the two of them role-played asking each other to share a piece of their playdough. In a few weeks, the teacher noticed that Hannah hit less often and when she did, she would be much more concerned and remorseful.

"Alvin, gather up all those animals, and put them back in the animal box," Emily prompted him at clean-up time. Alvin put a few animals in the box, but stopped when Emily walked away and continued to play with the toys. "Hurry up, kiddos. Let's finish cleaning and come to the carpet for story," Emily called out to the group. Settling in to begin the book, Emily glanced around the room and noticed Alvin still playing in the block area with the animals. "Hurry, Alvin. We're getting ready to start," she said. "I'm gonna play blocks," Alvin told her. "It's story time. You can play blocks later," Emily said. She loudly continued, for his benefit, "I like the way JuJu is ready for story. I like the way Jesus is ready for circle." Alvin ignored her. "Sandra, please go help Alvin," Emily finally asked her program assistant. When Sandra tried to help Alvin clean up, he told her, "You're not the boss of me, stupid," and stuck his tongue out at her. The assistant was furious, but held her temper. She quietly replied, "I'm going to tell Miss Emily what you just did. You're going to take home a sad face again today."

Alvin is a child who has no concept of limits and expectations. In his vision of how the world works, he can do whatever he wants whenever he wants. He can ignore adult requests and feels free to act and speak with disrespect when others annoy him. Alvin has a lot to learn about how the world really works, and unfortunately, sending him home with a "sad face" won't teach him those skills. In fact, that sad face is just a report card of sorts. While it's a message that the child doesn't follow limits and expectations, the report card itself doesn't teach the subject matter. Chances are that Alvin will be as defiant in June as he was in September.

Instead, the teachers might have made more progress by clarifying two or three guiding principles of behavior that are used in the classroom. They might have worked with Alvin by giving him feedback during times he was compliant so that he got attention and clarification of what the expectations really were. They might have taken a photo of Alvin cleaning up after center time and kept it posted in the area he used most. Seeing himself every day in that picture could have begun to help Alvin revise his self-image as a child who is compliant.

False Praise

What about using the phrase, "I like the way JuJu is behaving," as a way to motivate Alvin to act like JuJu? Before trying this strategy, reflect on what values you might be teaching Alvin and the rest of the group. You are modeling that

- It is okay to give false praise to someone (in this case JuJu) and to take advantage of her without her knowledge and consent.
- Rather than approaching others directly with dignity and respect (in this case Alvin), it's okay to manipulate others and to keep them guessing about your motives.

Instead, it's much more respectful and genuine to talk directly to Alvin about your concerns and to brainstorm with him how to resolve the problem.

Impulsive Actions

Grace ran out to the yard and looked for the red bike with the blue seat. Campbell got outside before her and was already riding around the yard on what the kids called "the good bike." Grace ran over and grabbed at the handlebars. "Get off, you stupid. That's mine." As Campbell tried to pull away from her, Grace pushed hard. Campbell and the bike both fell to the concrete. Her teacher, Isela, shook her head in frustration as she went to attend to the problem. "Grace, that's it for you. That was your last chance. No bikes for you the rest of the week." Grace immediately ran to another unused bike and tried to get on. "I said no," Isela told her, carrying her off kicking and screaming. "That child is so quick to grab things from others. She can tell me that grabbing is not all right and that we use words at school, but as soon as she gets out there in the action, she loses it."

Some children and adults fail to see the difference between *feelings* and *actions*. One of Grace's challenges was that she acted impulsively. She would feel something, like the urgency to have the "good bike," and then act on her feelings without thinking first. Children who meet their wants and needs of the moment without thinking a moment ahead can pose a challenge in the preschool room. At clean-up time, they may continue playing because they don't want to stop and don't feel like cleaning up. When it's time to go outside, they may refuse to stop for a moment to put on their jacket because putting on a jacket isn't as much fun as playing outside.

Punishing impulsive behavior does nothing to teach impulse control. Instead, this teacher might have tried to validate Grace's feelings and then guide her behavior. She might have said, "You really wanted that bike, huh?" When Grace agreed, the teacher might have said, "You want the bike real bad and Campbell is already using it. Let's see what we can do now to keep everybody safe." Maybe the teacher could have started a waiting list for the bike. Or the teacher could have helped Grace find the words to ask Campbell for a turn. The teacher might decide to add various strategies to the daily program to help Grace learn to think before acting. By working on the missing strength instead of on the behavior, the teacher could have helped Grace learn what she needed to know to manage her own impulsive behavior.

Transitions

As the children finished cleaning up and got in line to go outside, Freddy jumped on top of Emilio and tackled him to the floor. "He just attacked Emilio for no reason," Mr. Karo reported to the director as he brought Freddy to the office. "This is the third time this week that Freddy has hurt a child. I have no idea what to do." "Why did you jump on Emilio, Freddy?" the director asked him. Freddy shrugged.

The director decided to spend the next morning observing the classroom. Sure enough, Freddy pushed and hit others several times—while gathering for morning meeting, during cleanup, and when getting in line to go outside. All three times were transitions. Was this merely a coincidence?

Young children thrive with organized time, space, routines, and rituals. Transition times often lack this organization and for children like Freddy, transitions can feel unpredictable, frightening, and chaotic. Freddy became very anxious at transition time and he expressed that anxiety by striking out at other children. Punishing Freddy for his aggression did nothing to stop the problems. For Freddy, the solution turned out to be a simple matter, giving him structure at transition times. When he was given the task of pushing in chairs at every transition and then reporting directly to one of the teachers, he immediately calmed down and stopped hurting others.

Organization

Organization is important for children all day long, not only for transition time. The importance of organization and the impact it has on behavior cannot be emphasized enough. When children feel organized inside, they are more purposeful and directed. An internally organized child has a stable idea about her place in the world and what to expect. Without a sense of organization, young children struggle to make sense of how the world works. Their behavior may be chaotic, random, and unfocused.

For children to become internally organized, they must experience external organization in their daily lives. *External organization* refers to the efforts we make to organize the child's environment with routines and rituals, organized space, and clear expectations—all of which lead children to internal organization.

"Louis never seems to relax and have a good time here," his teacher said. "He doesn't get involved in play. His eyes are always darting around the room. At snack time, he hoards food instead of just taking one portion at a time. During group activities, if a child even bumps against him lightly, he makes a big deal of it and complains that he was hurt on purpose."

Louis's actions might tell us that he looks at the world as a scary and unpredictable place. As he goes through his day, he stays constantly on guard for potential changes and surprises. He has no idea about what might happen next, who's in charge, or the rules of the game. Most of Louis's day is spent feeling anxious, apprehensive, confused, and fearful. To Louis, the world is a random and unstructured place where one never knows what might happen next.

Here are three keys to providing external organization:

- Make the physical environment orderly and predictable.
- Structure time so children can begin to predict what will happen next.
- Set clear and consistent expectations.

As children experience this external organization, they are able to relax into work and play. Children begin to predict what will happen next in their day and where to find the materials and supplies they need. They find it easy to comply with expectations and guidelines because those limits are consistent from moment to moment and day to day.

Guiding Principles of Behavior

The core element of limits and expectations are the classroom's guiding principles of behavior. Children use these guidelines and expectations to help them organize themselves and make positive choices. As you think of what kinds of rules might be most useful in the classroom, keep the following questions in mind:

1. Does the rule teach an important life skill? And if it doesn't, can it be reworded so that it does? For example, "No running" isn't a very good life skill, since there are many times in life when running is not only appropriate, but also essential. If the no-running rule was created to prevent accidents, perhaps the rule might be better worded "Keep yourself and others safe."

2. Is the rule or guideline stated in the positive? Developmentally, children are not able to flip a negative to a positive until they are in first or second grade. For young children, "Bite" and "No biting" can sound like the same thing. Also, children have a much easier time "doing something" than "not doing something." If the true meaning of "don't bite" is to treat each other gently, the rule might be worded "Treat each other gently."

3. Is the rule a guiding principle of behavior? A guiding principle is a general statement that can be applied in many circumstances over a long period.

Try this exercise to better understand the concept of guiding principles of behavior. Think of someone who you greatly admire. This can be someone you know personally such as your grandmother or it can be a famous person, such as Abraham Lincoln. Now imagine that the person you admire has one rule that they use to guide their decisions, large and small. Write that rule in the box below.

Did you write something like "Always be your best," or "Do unto others," or "Be kind and work hard," or "Follow your beliefs"? These are all examples of guiding principles of behavior. They are all general guidelines that can be applied in many circumstances over a long period.

Establish the same kinds of broad guidelines for members of your classroom community.

Here is a sample of guiding principles of behavior:

1. We take care of ourselves.

2. We take care of others.

3. We take care of things.

Notice how broad these guiding principles are. Instead of five or six detailed rules like "No running" and "Keep your hands to yourself," the guidelines help children develop an internal compass or measuring stick to evaluate thousands of different possible behaviors. The guidelines are timeless life skills, which will be useful beyond preschool.

Maybe you are thinking that these rules are too vague for very young children who are still such concrete thinkers. You may be wondering how a child can get from "treat each other gently" to "don't hit Ralph just because you want his digger." Abstract concepts become understood over time with many hands-on, immediate, concrete examples. Teach these global concepts with the same kinds of strategies you use to introduce children to any new concept. When you teach the concept of *red,* you talk about red paint during painting, tell kids who are wearing red that they may wash for lunch, or gather a basket of all the red things they can find in the room.

Many of the strategies in this chapter and elsewhere in this book will give you some ideas on successful ways that teachers have introduced and reinforced their guiding principles of behavior.

Time Out

Traditionally, time out has been used in classrooms as a punishment for poor behavior choices. Should a child be separated from the group when they are angry and out of control? How does time out fit with our goal that children become intrinsically motivated and learn to manage their own behavior? Is time out being used as an extrinsic control to make a child feel bad in the hopes that they will then act good? Or is time out a self-regulation skill that children can take with them through life?

Just as a match is a tool that can be used to light the stove or burn down the house, time out is a tool that can be used to build up or to tear down. It's not the tool itself that is good or bad, it's how the tool is used and the intent behind the use that determines whether it is helpful or hurtful.

Let's look at time out as a possible life skill for a moment. When adults are out of control, when adults are angry and acting impulsively, what would we hope that they do? We would hope that they can begin to identify feelings in themselves when they're going to be dangerous to themselves or others or property and pull themselves away to a place where they can cool off. Waiting until the police officer comes to send you to time out in jail is not the answer. We want children and adults to be able to identify in themselves when it's time to pull out of a situation to avoid acting impulsively, foolishly, carelessly, or dangerously.

We teach what we model. One way to teach the skill of pulling out before things get dangerous is to model this for kids. We might say to children early on in the year, "Sometimes I start to feel anxious. When I feel like that, I'm afraid I might make some poor choices. So this is what I do: I go to the window, look outside at the trees, and take a few deep breaths. And then I come back and join the class. So if you ever see me say excuse me and walk to the window, it's probably because I need to center myself."

Take a moment to model this behavior for the kids. Say, "Excuse me," walk to the window, take some deep breaths, and return so that kids can see what it looks like. Have a group discussion to share with each other that everyone feels the need to pull out sometimes. Brainstorm different places in the room where people might go to cool off.

Should we be sending children to their cool-off area? Certainly—if you model it as caring behavior for our community of learners. Tell the children that sometimes you get anxious and irritated, and you don't even notice what's happening to yourself. Tell them that if they see that happening, to say, "Do you need to go to your centering place?" Model and role-play how that looks and what tone of voice would be appropriate as a reminder to somebody that they might need to go to their cool-off place. Make it a group practice that when you see someone—adult or child—losing control, anyone can take it upon herself to suggest to that person that perhaps they might want to go to their cool-off area.

But what if you suggest that a child uses her cool-off place and she doesn't want to go? Do you drag her there, kicking and screaming? If you force a child to go to her cool-off place, does it become a punishment?

When strategies don't work the way we envisioned, it's important to step back and regroup before acting. Somehow, dragging someone to a place that we are trying to define as a comforting area doesn't make much sense to me. At the same time, adults often sense that a child is overstimulated and needs to take a break from the action. What then might be some options that respect the peace and calm of a child's chosen place while at the same time helping an overstimulated child to calm down?

- You might take the child with you to your own calm-down spot and attempt to help the child calm down there.
- You might make it a point to spend some warm and comforting one-on-one time with a child in her chosen spot during center time when she is calm. During that time you might comment on how nice and comfortable the spot feels.
- You might find that if the child is too overwrought, he is hard to redirect, and you might try to spend a few days observing him more closely so you can catch him as soon as he starts to get anxious. Inviting him to join you in his calm-down spot to spend some one-on-one time together for a few moments may be inviting enough to get him to try it out.
- And you will do well to remember that not every strategy works for every child. Going to a calm-down area is just one of many centering strategies you will accumulate. If this particular strategy doesn't work for this particular child, introduce other strategies until you find a good fit.

What about children who, in the middle of group time or story time, stop and go to their cool-off area? Isn't that disruptive to the rest of the group? Shouldn't they have to wait until the activity is over? In fact, getting up and leaving immediately is exactly what we want children to do. We want them to become aware of when it's time to remove themselves from a situation and regroup. If we insist the child stay in the activity even when they know they need to remove themselves, their anxiety and their behavior will probably only escalate further. Quickly, we'll reach a point where we intervene and send them to time out, to the hallway, to the office, or home for the day. It's far better for everyone in the room if children are permitted and encouraged to leave and cool off when they need to do so.

Help children learn to appreciate taking some time out. Instead of using it as a tool to punish children who have disappointed, hurt, or frustrated you, present time out as an essential life strategy, a gift for children who need to "take a moment."

Remember that regaining control of emotions is an important step, but is often only the first step when dealing with problems and conflicts. Problems and conflicts cannot be addressed until all the people involved have managed their emotions and reestablished internal organization. Once everyone has moved from their emotional selves back to their thinking selves, the hard work of problem solving and conflict resolution can begin. Because this is such a broad and complex area, an entire chapter is devoted to these additional skills.

As you work with out-of-control children, don't lose sight of the real goals. You don't want to be tethered to that child all day, trying to control and manage his behavior. The goal is that children learn to manage their own feelings and take responsibility for their own behavior. When children have made good choices, we want them to feel satisfaction and pride in themselves. When children have chosen behavior that has damaging consequences, we want the child to attempt to fix things the best they can. Think twice about interventions and strategies that shift responsibility away from the child and put it on you, the adult. Be the child's ally in celebrating his success and profiting from his mistakes as he learns how to manage himself.

Supportive Interactions

Help children take ownership for the consequences of their actions on themselves, others, and their environment.

"Marcus hit me," Hernando cried to Mr. M. "I saw," said Mr. M, giving Hernando a hug. "You tried to push him off the bike, so he hit you, huh?" Hernando had a confused look on his face. "Marcus hit me," he said again. Hernando made no connection between his pushing Marcus and Marcus hitting him. To him, they were totally random and separate acts.

Once children make the connection between action and consequence, they can start to control their impulses and make more deliberate choices based on their predictions of the results.

Cause and Effect

Sometimes, we mistakenly assume children understand that there is a connection between their behavior and what results from that behavior. However, most preschool children are just beginning to connect their actions with the consequences.

Use reflective language that focuses children's attention on cause and effect. One simple way is to use the sentence template "You (action) and (result)."

- "You turned the crank and the clown popped up."
- "You mixed red and yellow and look what you got."
- "You wiped up that spill and now the table is all clean again."

Behavior Affects Others

Sometimes we give children a false sense of their power over the feelings of others. While children's behavior may have an impact on somebody's feelings, it is important not to encourage children to think they can control the feelings or behavior of others. Some hurting and troubled children will try to use this mistaken view of their power over others to be hurtful in an attempt to help themselves feel better. Be crystal clear that while feelings are a reaction to events, nobody can make others feel or do anything.

INSTEAD OF USING THE WORD *MAKE* . . .	TRY "WHEN YOU___, I FEEL____."
"Tell Raymond how he made you feel."	"Tell Raymond that you don't like it when he calls you names."
"Don't make me call your mother."	"When I call and you don't come in, I feel very frustrated."
"Look at his face. How did you make him feel?"	"When you told Benjamin he couldn't play, he felt bad."

Help Children Learn School Limits and Expectations

"At School We . . ."

It is helpful to remember that rules and expectations at school are specific only to your classroom. Even though we may assume that guidelines such as "Wash your hands before you eat," or "We don't use that kind of language," or "No hitting," are universal, not all families or cultures might agree. Children do best when we are able to support home expectations while at the same time enforcing school expectations. How then can you avoid statements that start with "But my mommy said . . ." (I should hit him, I don't need to wash my hands, I can go outside with no shoes, and so on).

Start your enforcement of school rules with the consistent use of the phrase "At school we . . ." When you preface with "At school we . . ." you help children identify immediately that what will follow is an expectation of behavior at school.

- At school we walk to the outside door.
- At school we use words not hands.
- At school we throw away our own snack trash.

If a child responds with, "But my mommy said I don't need to throw away my own trash," simply respond, "It's okay that your mommy told you that rule for your house. At school we throw away our own snack trash." The "at school we" phrase is even more important when guiding about sensitive issues such as nudity, touching, hitting, profanity, and inclusion.

You will find this phrase useful, too, when talking with parents. If a parent is worried because you won't let a child defend herself with physical aggression, avoid moral debates on violence as a means to resolve conflict. Instead, you can say something such as, "I understand you don't want Nathanial to be bullied. I don't want him to be bullied either. At school we will find other ways to deal with bullying besides hitting back." Notice that this response also follows the template of "validate feelings before guiding behavior."

Where Are You?

"At school we" is one way to introduce the concept of behavior changing based on the context. However, children can easily forget to monitor where they are so they can successfully adjust their behavior to match the environment. Are they are home? At school? At grandma's?

Many children are visual learners instead of auditory learners. Help children use their vision as a guideline for appropriate behavior. Use a phrase such as, "Look around you. Where are you right now?" This prompt often works to help the child switch back over to their "school persona."

- When Shea gets up during circle time and starts twirling around, bumping into others, say, "Shea, stop a minute. Look around. Where are you right now?"

- When Santo is on the loft tossing baby dolls over the railing, say, "Santo. Look around. Where are you right now?"

Guiding Principles of Behavior

Guiding principles are the two or three timeless, umbrella guidelines you have established for your classroom. Help the children in your class internalize these principles as a way they can evaluate their own behavior. Do this by referring to the principles when you state a school rule. Use the template "At school we (rule) because (principle)." In the example below, the guiding principles of the classroom include

1. We take care of ourselves.
2. We take care of each other.
3. We take care of our stuff.

AT SCHOOL WE . . . (RULE)	BECAUSE . . . (GUIDING PRINCIPLE OF BEHAVIOR)
At school we walk on the step	because we take care of ourselves.
At school we use words not hands	because we take care of each other.
At school we throw away our snack trash	because we take care of our stuff.

Reflective Feedback

One of the most powerful tools we have to help children learn the guiding principles of behavior is to give them descriptive feedback when you see them behaving. First, when you use this feedback instead of saying, "Good job," or "I like the way you . . . ," you are helping the child build intrinsic motivation. The child begins to internalize the guiding principles and starts to construct an internal compass that they can use to manage their own behavior. Second, recognition invites repetition—the behavior that gets our response is more likely to be repeated again in the future if it is acknowledged.

One sentence template that is useful is "You (action) because (principle)."

- "You washed your hands before you ate because we take care of ourselves."
- "You waited for a turn at the slide because we take care of each other."
- "You put all the blocks back on the shelf because we take care of our stuff."

First/Then

Working and playing in the school community sometimes requires doing things kids don't feel like doing. Maybe they are involved with clay work when it is time to clean up for lunch, or they're feeling full of energy and ready to go when it is time to sit quietly and listen to a story. Threats, punishments, or bribes might get the child to comply, but this keeps the burden of responsibility with us. Our ultimate goal is that children learn to do undesirable but necessary tasks without this external motivation.

Help children develop the understanding that sometimes we need to do a less desirable action before we do actions that are more desirable by using the first/then technique.

INSTEAD OF SAYING . . .	TRY . . .
"If you don't pick up the blocks, you won't go outside."	"First pick up the blocks, then you can go outside."
"You're not going to get snack if you don't come inside right now."	"First come inside, then you can have snack."
"If you finish your job, I'll let you have a turn at the cooking table."	"First finish your job, then you can cook."
"If you lie quietly at rest for ten minutes, I'll give you a sticker."	"First rest quietly for ten minutes, then you can get up and play."

Help Children Learn to Manage Their Emotions

Children need time to explore feelings as an important step to building self-regulation. They need to be able to identify feelings in themselves and others, they need to understand that feelings change over time and are not permanent, and they need to be able to separate their feelings from their actions. As children gain a deeper understanding of their feelings, they can begin to learn how to manage their feelings by self-soothing and other strategies. Finally, they are ready to learn how to express their feelings to others and use assertive language instead of impulsively striking out when they are upset.

Feelings Are Responses

Many young children have no idea where their feelings come from. Before they can manage feelings, children need to have an understanding of what triggers their feelings. Help children understand that feelings are responses to outside events. Not only do events and other people affect them, but they themselves have an impact on the feelings of others as well. Weave sentence templates such as the following into your daily language with children to guide them to make these connections.

WHEN . . .	TEMPLATE . . .	EXAMPLE . . .
Outside events have an impact on their feelings	You feel (emotion) because (event).	"You feel excited because March is coming for supper," or "You feel tired because you worked so hard on the climber."
Other people's actions have an impact on their feelings	When (person)(action), you felt (emotion).	"When Margaret said you couldn't go to her birthday, you felt sad," or "David shared his blocks and you felt good."
Their actions have an impact on other people's feelings	When you (action), (other person) felt (feeling).	"When you pushed Denise, she felt angry," or "Jose liked it when you asked him to sit by you at circle."

Label and Validate Feelings

We might fall into this trap with children: we not only want to control their behavior but we also want to control their feelings. Is feeling happy superior to feeling sad? Many of us were raised to believe that some of our feelings were okay, and some were not. "Happy" might feel whole lots better than "sad" but the feeling itself is not superior. Making value judgments on children's feelings blocks their ability to monitor their behavior effectively. It takes the full range of feelings for children to develop their moral compass. Children learn as much from the feeling of disappointment as they do from the feeling of joy. When something they do triggers feelings of disappointment, it serves as a message to them to reexamine their behavior.

Strive to validate all the feelings that children express in your classroom. A good way to validate feelings is to reflect back to children your best guess about what they are feeling while withholding any judgment.

INSTEAD OF SAYING ...	TRY ...
"What's that face supposed to be all about?"	"I wonder if you are feeling frustrated (hurt, scared, disappointed)."
"Pouting isn't going to get you anywhere."	"It looks like you want to use the soccer ball first."
"There's no reason to be angry."	"You're angry and that's okay."
"There's nothing to be upset about."	"I can see you're upset and I understand."
"Don't feel that way."	"I'm sorry you feel that way."
"Go sit on the beanbag chair until you're ready to stop crying."	"What do you need? What do you want?"

What's Underneath "Angry"?

Anger is sometimes called a "secondary emotion," which means that it is used to cover up a more vulnerable emotion such as frustration, disappointment, hurt, or fear. Whenever possible, guide children to identify their primary emotions instead of using the more aggressive word *angry*.

Frustrated: You want something and are having trouble getting it.

Disappointed: You thought something was going to happen and it didn't.

Hurt: You feel physical, emotional, or social pain.

Fear: You have anxiety about the unknown.

INSTEAD OF SAYING ...	TRY ...
"You seem angry that you have to wait for a turn."	"You seem frustrated that you have to wait for a turn."
"I bet you're angry that it isn't your 'Show and Tell' day."	"I bet you're disappointed that it isn't your 'Show and Tell' day."
"When Emmaline said your shoes are ugly, you felt angry."	"When Emmaline said your shoes are ugly, you felt hurt."
"You're angry that we have a new teacher-helper today."	"You're scared about the new teacher-helper today."

Here's a final suggestion about anger management: Discourage destructive or violent outlets for anger such as tearing up an old phone book or using a punching bag, which produce chemical changes in our bodies. These chemicals might relieve difficult feelings and lead to feelings of excitement and euphoria. Children might find these feelings very pleasurable and make a dangerous connection between violence and destruction and feeling good. This misconception can escalate later to vandalism and violence toward others.

Validate Feelings, Then Guide Behavior

Help children distinguish between feelings and actions. Children are not in control of their emotional responses to things that happen, but they do need to learn to take responsibility for their behavior choices. If someone grabs their toy, they may feel angry. Feeling angry is fine. However, they're the ones to make the decision to either grab the toy back, use assertive words to get the toy back, find adult help, or walk away. Their reaction to their feeling is their responsibility. Our role is to guide children to handle that anger with control and make a purposeful decision.

To validate a child's feelings, make your best guess of what the child is feeling. One way to start out is to use the words "you wish" or "you want." Other words that might work are "You look frustrated," "Are you disappointed," "I wonder if you are afraid," or "Are you hurt?"

Only after you have helped the child identify the feeling do you limit and guide behavior. By doing this, you validate for the child that the feeling is acceptable and that the action needs some thought and channeling.

Practice validating feelings then guiding behavior until it becomes second nature. Try to use it on a regular basis whenever you approach a child to redirect their behavior. It's one of the most important techniques to use with young children to help them understand and manage their powerful feelings.

INSTEAD OF SAYING . . .	VALIDATE FEELING BY SAYING . . .	GUIDE BEHAVIOR BY SAYING . . .
"Stop grabbing that doll. Arsenio is using it."	"Do you want to use that doll?"	"You can ask Arsenio for a turn or I will help you find another one."
"Quit kicking Jarvis's block tower."	"Do you want to play with Jarvis?"	"At school we don't kick blocks. You can ask Jarvis if you can play with him."
"Move away from the sink. Sophia has been waiting a long time."	"It looks like you are having fun in the water."	"This sink is for washing. Let's find a different place to play in water."
"No throwing shoes."	"Are you frustrated with those shoes?"	"We need to keep kids safe, so no throwing. I can help you tie if you like."

Self-talk

Some children talk in negative terms about themselves when they're upset. The words a child says to himself are part of what builds that child's view of reality. When you hear a child using destructive self-talk, encourage the child to replace that talk with more empowering language. Here are some examples of how you might approach this:

INSTEAD OF ...	SUGGEST ...
I can't stop.	I am the boss of me.
I hate her.	I'm angry.
I'm gonna punch you.	I need to walk away.
I can't do this. I'm dumb.	I can do this. I'm a smart kid.

Feelings Change

Young children don't realize that feelings ebb and flow over time. When children are upset, they expect to feel that way for the rest of time. To be able to self-regulate, children need to know that they can manage their emotions and that feelings change over time. Help children notice that happy isn't permanent, and neither is sad. Make it a habit to recognize and reflect to children when their personal feelings have changed. Use a sentence pattern such as "You felt (feeling) and now you feel (feeling). Feelings change."

- "This morning you were angry with Jhon, and now you two are having fun with the police cars. Feelings change."
- "You used to not like to eat salad and now you do! Feelings change."
- "You were so sad this morning when your nana left. Then you played with your friends and you felt better! Feelings change."

I Hear You

Ms. Garcia: "Who knows which animal gives us the eggs we're using in the cooking project today?"

As hands wave wildly in the air, Topanga yells out, "Chickens, chickens."

Ms. Garcia: Topanga, I'm calling on kids who are raising their hands right now. Hunter, do you know which animal gives us eggs?"

Topanga crosses her arms over her chest, juts out her chin, and her eyes fill with tears. She wonders what she did wrong. Ms. Garcia wanted to know which animal gives eggs, she was able to help, and instead Ms. Garcia asked Hunter, who doesn't know anything about farm animals. If Ms. Garcia wanted to know something and Topanga knew it, why couldn't she tell the teacher. "This is a dumb school!" she cries out.

If there are some children in the group who need to be the ones to answer, it can be helpful to develop a signal to use with them. Teach them that if you look at them and touch your nose with your index finger it means, "I hear you," which lets them know that you know that they know the answer. It gives other children the space they need to think and respond as well.

What's Your Plan?

Impulsive children act before they think. They chatter during story time, they run instead of walk to the door, or they serve themselves seven scoops of pudding at lunch. These children move through the world reacting to what's around them without stopping a moment to think first. The objective of "What's Your Plan?" is to help the child put a moment of thoughtful behavior into their impulsive activity.

Use this technique when you see a child who appears to bounce around the room without getting involved anywhere. Over time, this practice in impulse control will pay off in less random and more thoughtful behavior overall.

1. Approach the child, get down on his level, gently hold his hands in yours, look into his eyes, and ask, "What's your plan?"
2. A child's plan can be as simple as pointing to the water table or as complex as "I'm gonna give the dinosaurs a bath in the water table."
3. Say, "Okay, go," and release the child.

Support Self-Regulation through the Classroom Culture

Many of the challenges that preschool children pose can be traced back to a lack of self-regulation. When you infuse your daily schedule, rituals, and routines with opportunities for children to develop and practice self-regulation skills, you will find your days magically smoothing out and becoming more peaceful.

Help Children Understand Consequences

Children need opportunities daily to explore cause and effect in many different contexts before they can take ownership of the consequences of their own actions. Look for opportunities to point out the action-consequence connection in the classroom routine and in children's literature.

Cause-and-Effect Activities and Toys

Children need an understanding that their behavior has consequences, both positive and negative, before they can develop self-regulation. For children to learn that their actions have an impact on things and people, they need to experiment and explore every day. Through this exploration, children form an understanding of how actions and behavior affect the outside world. Be patient as children test their understandings by repeating the same thing many times. Provide children with materials and activities that reinforce cause-and-effect understanding.

- Include materials such as a jack-in-the-box, surprise boxes, marble mazes, balls and ramps, and magnets.
- Place cups, funnels, and bottles in the water table for children to explore. Set out red, yellow, and blue water and eyedroppers so children can experiment with mixing colors. Provide cooking projects and open-ended exploration with a variety of art materials.
- Point out cause and effect as you read storybooks to children. Ask the children questions such as "Why do you think the Little Red Hen kept all the bread to herself?" "Why do you think the wolf couldn't blow down the brick house?" "Why do you think the hungry caterpillar's belly is getting bigger and bigger?" Children find these questions interesting because they are just beginning to realize that events are related in cause-and-effect chains. Dirty Harry rolled in the mud and got dirty, so his family didn't recognize him, so he got the scrub brush, so they washed him, so he turned white with black spots again, so they recognized him. These are not random events. They logically follow one another in a cause-and-effect manner.

Beginning-Middle-End Stories

Guide children's understanding of the flow from feelings to actions to consequences by helping them break down stories into three steps: the feelings that started it all, the action the character decided to take, and the consequences or results of that action. You can do this with many of the picture books you already read to the children. You can also use stories you make up about incidents in the classroom.

For example, in *The Kissing Hand*, the little raccoon feels scared to go to school and be away from his mother. His mother gives him a kiss on his palm to take with him to school. The result was that the raccoon child felt better. Guide children to see this by asking the questions:

- How did the little raccoon feel at the beginning of the story? (focus on the trigger feeling)
- What did he and his mom finally decide to do that worked? (focus on the action)
- How did everyone feel at the end of the story? (focus on the main character and the other characters that got involved)

When there have been problems in the classroom, make up a story with pretend names. One approach is to tell the whole story with a solution already in place. For example:

"Once upon a time, in a school far, far away, a bunch of children came to circle to listen to a story. They all sat down, and then Logan came from the cubbies and he couldn't find a place to sit. He looked and looked and there was no place. Logan felt very sad and lonely. He looked at Peter and he looked at Casey. 'Casey, can I sit by you?' he asked. 'Sure,' said Casey. Casey moved over and Logan sat down. He had a big smile. 'You're my friend, Casey,' he said."

- How did Logan feel at the beginning of the story? (sad, lonely)
- What did he decide to do? (ask Casey to move)
- How did Logan and Casey feel at the end of the story? (happy)

As the children learn problem solving, let them help you finish the story. For example:

"Once upon a time, in a school far, far away, a bunch of children came to circle to listen to a story. They all sat down, and then Logan came from the cubbies and he couldn't find a place to sit. He looked and looked and there was no place."

- How do you think Logan felt?
- What do you think he might try to do?
- How would everyone feel if he did that?

If you're interested in storytelling as a way to help children, you may find Trisha Whitney's book, *Kids Like Us*, helpful.

Tell and Retell the Story

Help children analyze their personal stories with the three-step story process. Help them find the trigger feeling, their response, and what resulted.

To use the stories when a child has made an unsuccessful action choice, use the "tell and retell" method. This process helps children revisit a situation and discover alternative responses that they might have made. By using this process regularly, you will help children learn to think through their own personal situations before they choose a response—something that few children are able to do by themselves when they are sitting in a time out.

1. First, tell the story in the same three steps, the way it happened. Use the third person point of view to tell the story. Focus on the three major points:

- What was the trigger feeling?
- What did the child decide to do?
- How did it turn out for everyone?

"Once there was a girl who wanted to ride a bike. She looked and looked for the bike, and then she saw that somebody else was riding it. She was very disappointed. (Trigger feeling) The kid went over and pushed the bike over. (Action) The bike fell and the kids cried. (Result) That's how that story went."

2. Continue by working with the child to come up with another response that might have a happier ending. Say something such as, "Let's do the story again and figure out what that kid could do to have a happy ending." Start by retelling the story as closely as you can to the original, but pause before the character decides on an action.

"Once there was a girl who wanted to ride a bike. She looked and looked for the bike, and then she saw that somebody else was riding it. She was very disappointed. (Trigger feeling) Last time she pushed the bike over. That didn't work. I wonder what else she could try?"

Allow the child to come up with another solution and continue the story from that point.

"Okay. So, she decided to get the teacher. The teacher came and helped the children decide how to take turns. The girl and the other child took turns on the bike and they had fun. That's how that story would have ended."

Or,

"Okay. So, she decided to call the kid StinkyButt. The kid got mad and told the teacher. The teacher came over and told her, "We don't name-call at this school. Go away from the bikes now." The girl had to walk away. She was still sad because she wanted the bike. Uh-oh, that didn't work. Let's think of another ending."

When telling and retelling, it is usually more effective to tell the story in the third person. Instead of saying, "You wanted the shovel," try saying, "The boy wanted the shovel." Many children have an easier time talking about a theoretical child than they do talking about themselves. Also, when the story is told specifically about the child, children will focus on the details and will do a lot of correcting and sidetracking such as, "I didn't say that," or "He said I could have it."

Equipment and Supplies

As children learn to take responsibility for the results of their actions, it is important that they have the supplies they need to maintain their environments. Provide child-sized brooms, mops, and spray bottles filled with water to help children clean up after themselves.

Establish and Uphold Limits and Expectations

Kids have trouble organizing their space, time, and actions when they are confused about the expectations set for them. The clearer adults are about the community expectations, the more organized and calm children become. When children don't have to expend a lot of energy figuring out the system, they can relax and use that energy to learn, explore, and make positive connections with others.

Story Time and Puppetry

Children need to see guiding principles in many different contexts if they are to internalize them as their own standards. Use your normal story time to reinforce these principles as one way to weave the guiding principles of behavior into your daily curriculum.

As you read books to children, take notice of examples of characters who demonstrate your guiding principles of behavior. For example, if the children in the story wash the dog, it could be used as an example of "we take care of each other."

Point out the activity in the book. "Look, the children are washing the dog. He was all dirty and they gave him a bath. The kids were following our guideline . . . they were taking care of each other."

Use puppets to act out other examples of your guiding principles and have children figure out which principle you are demonstrating.

HAVE THE PUPPET(S)	ASK
Wash his hands before snack.	"Is he taking care of himself, taking care of others, or taking care of his things? What do you think?"
Put a bandage on his friend's nose.	
Put the puzzle pieces back in the box.	

Who Can I Match?

Matching others is a life skill. I don't go to the opera very often. But when I do, I make sure to match others in the audience so I know when to applaud and when not to applaud. When I attended religious services in an unfamiliar church, I needed to match others to know when to sit, stand, or shake hands.

Don't be afraid to use "child experts" in the classroom as visual models for children who are still learning limits and guidelines. When a child is struggling to figure out what to do in certain social situations, invite them to "match" somebody who does know.

1. Chat with the challenged child and brainstorm with that child to decide who in the class might know the expected behavior for the problem situation. For example, say to the child, "Who in our class seems to know how to do 'Music Special' really well?" "Who seems to know how to do lining up?" "Who in our class seems to know circle time?" Help the child find somebody who demonstrates the expected behavior in a skilled way.

2. Talk a bit about what it is that the skilled child does that lets us know they are doing it well.

3. Help the child who is still learning the skill to use the more skilled child as a cuing system. Say, "Remember, you can take a look at Adam or Bethany if you forget what to do at circle. Usually they know what they are doing and then you can match them and get back on track."

Avoid saying, "Do like the other children," because often the child will choose someone who is equally challenged and off task. You want them to pick somebody who is competent at the skill.

Self-serve Snack

Use self-serve snack as a tool to help children practice compliance with community standards. Teach children how to use a portion sign on the serving table as a guideline for what to serve themselves.

For example: Take two crackers and one string cheese. Illustrate the portion sign with picture cues. Tell children that they can come back for more food if they need it, but each time they are limited to the portions on the sign. Some teachers bring the sign to morning meeting to review with children before they transition into center time.

Mandatory and Optional

Young children have a fascination with new and unusual words. Make the most of this natural interest to introduce the concepts of *mandatory* and *optional* to the children in your group. When you label certain activities as mandatory or optional, children can make more sense of your requests and demands. What once appeared to be merely whim on your part now falls into cleaner categories.

Consistency is key to help children form useful definitions of these words. The meaning of the word *mandatory* is "nonnegotiable." It must happen. For children to clearly understand this meaning, make sure to follow up when an activity is labeled "mandatory." If an activity is mandatory and the child does not do it and slips through the cracks, she will have trouble forming the correct definition of the word.

Make the word familiar to children by announcing one activity each morning that will be mandatory. Then make clear some other choices that are optional.

- "There is new smelly fingerpaint out on the red table. That is an optional activity today. Remember, though, that doing your job from the job board is mandatory."
- "I want everyone to do some work on the fish mural today. That is mandatory. All the other center activities are optional."

After the word has been in use in the classroom for a while, begin to use it for things like cleaning up, hand washing before snack, or coming in from outside. Help children begin to internally organize the concept that sometimes there are mandatory and nonnegotiable tasks that must get done whether they want to do them or not. Use the label "mandatory" for these activities to remove it from debate. When a child whines "But I don't want to wash my hands," instead of rationalizing and debating you can simply reply, "I understand. Washing hands is mandatory, though. Sorry." By setting yourself up as an empathic support for the child but one who reminds the child of mandatory events, you can pull yourself out of personal power struggles. Children quickly learn these terms and use them to make sense of the world. One teacher who implemented these words in her classroom reported on how fluent the children became with the terms.

"Is the gingerbread house project mandatory or optional," asked four-year-old Ahbre. "Optional," Samantha answered. "But remember that choosing a book to take home this weekend is mandatory, so you might want to get that done now so you don't forget." A parent of another child in the same class reported that when she told her child to get into the bathtub as part of the bedtime routine, her daughter looked up from her game and said, "Is that mandatory or optional?"

"I Don't Want to and I'll Do It Anyway"

Young children love predictable books, rhymes, and rhythm. Use this natural attraction to help children do things they would rather not do. Teach children the singsong mantra "I don't want to and I'll do it anyway."

1. Begin by modeling the sentence yourself when you do something you'd rather not do. For example, when you need to clean up spilled flour, say, "I don't want to and I'll do it anyway."
2. Use puppets and dramatic play with the children to rehearse and practice the skill.
3. After children have learned the chant, help them put it into practice in real life situations. When a child is resistant, try saying "I don't want to and . . ." and

hesitate to allow the child to finish the sentence. For most children, once they have said the words "I'll do it anyway," they find it easier to comply.

Help Children Learn to Manage Their Emotions

Earlier in this chapter we talked about children using a calm-down area as a tool to help them manage their emotions. Calm-down areas are only one of many strategies that children find useful to help them regain control when they become anxious or agitated. Introduce children to a variety of calming strategies that they can begin to make a part of their own self-soothing techniques.

Self-soothing

Self-soothing is an important tool for managing emotions, yet we often make the mistake of trying to break children from self-soothing habits! Respect and honor children's self-soothing techniques unless they present a danger to self, others, or property. Some children already have coping techniques such as rocking, thumb-sucking, hair stroking, or cuddling a baby blanket. Expose children to wide ranges of soothing strategies to help broaden their available repertoire.

- Some kids do well with a familiar comfort item to help themselves calm down when they are agitated. Some ideas for items that a child might use are family photos, a Koosh ball, a small cloth, a teether, or a small stuffed animal.
- If a child ends up tossing these things around, see if you can attach the item to their belt loop with a short string. Some things like picture frames or Koosh balls can be found attached to keychains, which can then be easily attached to clothing.
- While many kids do well storing their comfort items in backpacks or cubbies, some children need their items closer at hand. Have them use a fanny pack and encourage children to take out the items when they need help regulating their emotions. If they can keep items close without holding them in their hands the whole time, they will be freer to participate in activities.

Exploratory Materials

Children find it easier to express themselves with actions rather than with words. Many children discover that working with sensory materials helps them to calm down and relax. Other children find that they are able to express a full range of emotions through manipulating these materials.

Provide kids with daily opportunities to work with open-ended materials such as water, wood, clay, and sand.

Water as a Soother

Many people are able to describe anger as red or hot. These people can find relief by using water as a soother.

If you have a child in your group who has frequent angry outbursts, you might want to explore this idea with them.

1. Very soon after the child has calmed down, ask, "Is your anger a color? What color do you think it might be?"
2. Another time you might ask, "How does your head feel when you are angry? How do your hands feel?"
3. If a child describes the feeling of anger as the colors red or orange or describes it as a hot feeling in their head or hands, suggest that next time you will show them a way to chase the red or the hot away.
4. The next time you see them begin to escalate, invite them to get a drink of water, wash their hands or face, use a spray bottle of water to clean a table, or play at the water table.
5. If this strategy works, make sure that the child has access to water as a soother whenever he feels the need. Let the child know that many people use water as a way to calm themselves down.

Plan-Ahead Charts

Children start out with very few strategies to manage their emotions. Some children, in fact, think that they are the only ones who ever feel anger or sadness! Help the children in your class understand these truths:

- Everyone feels strong emotions.
- Different kids use different ways to manage their emotions.

1. At large or small group meetings, introduce the subject by talking about your own experience. Say something such as, "Last night I was so scared. I was sleeping and then the storm came and the thunder woke me up! I was real scared. Does anybody else here ever get scared?" This introduces the ideas that everyone, kids and grown-ups alike, might get scared sometimes. Let children share their own experiences of times when they were scared. Many will copy you and talk about being scared of the storm. That's fine. Others will want to share how brave they are and that the storm didn't bother them at all. That's fine too.

2. Validate each child's experience with reflective feedback. For example, say, "So, Brandon, you aren't scared of thunder," and "Emilia, big dogs can be scary, can't they?"

3. Next, begin sharing techniques to manage fear. Again, start with your own experience. "You know what I did when I got scared last night? I turned on the light. When I was a kid, I used to go to my mom's bed. Then I felt better. I wonder what you guys do to help yourselves feel better when you get scared." Invite each child to share techniques they use to successfully manage fear.

4. You might want to record children's ideas on a chart. You can later have children illustrate their emotion and technique for a page in a class Big Book.

5. Repeat this activity at another time with another emotion, such as excitement or frustration.

6. Review the compiled lists of ideas or Big Books often, and add to them over time. Refer to the lists when a child is struggling to manage a difficult emotion.

Don't forget to look for examples of people managing their emotions in storybooks. Help children identify how the character managed that emotion.

Relaxation Techniques

Different people have different temperaments and use different types of strategies to cool off. At home, I clean the refrigerator. Some people like to run, some people like to listen to music, some people like to chat with a friend, some people just want to be in a quiet corner and read a book. Give children the space and opportunity to explore different avenues and different strategies for soothing and relaxing when they are feeling anxious or stressed, or are beginning to feel out of control.

- Some children find they can calm themselves by taking deep breaths.
- Becky Bailey, author of *Conscious Discipline,* describes a variation on this method that she calls STAR strategy: Stop, Take a deep breath, And Relax. Cut a star out of cardboard or buy a stuffed star to give children a physical and visual cue to remember the strategy.
- Children can sit alone in a beanbag chair or a rocking chair.
- Some children find that working with art materials helps them manage emotions.
- Music helps some children relax. Keep a tape player and headset available for those children who need it.

- Many boys and some girls find that large motor activities help them calm down. Either take the child outside for a few minutes to burn off the energy or provide a large motor area in the classroom for the child to use when they need it. This might be a two-foot square area with a hop ball or a platform on which to climb and jump down.
- Some teachers conduct large group breathing and stretching exercises for relaxation during morning meeting. Other teachers find that vigorous dancing or calisthenics helps their group to relax and get ready for more quiet work. Many teachers play soothing music at rest time to help children unwind from their active mornings.

Places and Spaces

Learning how to regroup when we are losing control is an important life skill. Many people find that leaving the situation for a short period of time helps them regain control and perspective. Help children explore this strategy by including places within the classroom where they can go to center themselves when they begin to spin out of control.

- One-person areas—Some people like solitude while they calm down. Have one or more one-person areas in the room where children can retreat without being bothered by others. You can make an "office" area with a small desk, drawing tools, and maybe a lava lamp. You can make a "cave" on the bottom shelf of a built-in wall unit and use carpeting for the floor and pillows. A table fountain or aquarium helps to soothe other children.
- Squiggly square—Some adults choose to go for a run or shoot baskets to cool off when they are angry. Provide something similar for the children in your classroom who need physical activity to pull themselves back together. One teacher makes a "Squiggly Square" in a corner of her classroom. She marks off a three-foot square on the floor with masking tape. When children want to jump up and down or let their bodies go loose and silly, they are invited to use that small, safe area. This is a great technique to give children the physical release they need without waiting for outside time.

Symbolic Organizers

When children do break down and have a tantrum or lose control, envision that as a temporary disruption in their internal organization. Our task is to help them move from that disorganized state back to internal organization.

Just because a child has stopped the tantrum or the swearing and shouting does not necessarily mean the child is back into an organized state. Be careful about sending these children back into the mainstream while they are still a bit internally disorganized. In this state, they are more vulnerable to having another breakdown. How can we make sure they are truly ready to rejoin the group?

Most children find that working a very simple puzzle helps them to regain their internal organization and control. Children use this symbolic activity of moving the puzzle from disorganization to order as a way of moving themselves from disorganization to order at the same time.

1. Sit the child at a small table on the floor with a small simple wooden puzzle.
2. Remove the pieces, and ask the child to put the puzzle back together.
3. Sit with the child while they do this small task. While they put the puzzle back together say, "You are putting everything back where it belongs," or "The pieces are all getting put together again," or similar type statements. Emphasize that they are making order and putting things right.

You can use other materials in the same way.

- Give the child a handful of Unifix cubes and have them attach them all together. Some older children do well if you make a pattern with about six cubes and ask them to continue the pattern with more cubes. Use a very simple A-B pattern such as red-blue, red-blue.
- Give children a handful of math sorters and have them sort the objects into meaningful piles. Some examples are a handful of mixed coins, buttons, seashells, or jewels.

Sand Tray

Children can work through many emotional issues in their play when they are given the right props and opportunities. Many children find sand trays ideal for this purpose. Although sand trays are traditionally used for play therapy, you can adapt them for the classroom too.

1. Fill a bus tub or similar-size container with a few inches of clean sand.
2. Provide some containers with a variety of small props. Include the following items, and add other tiny toy and representational figures:
   - People figures of all ages, abilities, and colors
   - Animal figures including some wild animals, dinosaurs, snakes, and bugs
   - Plastic trees and fences

- Fantasy figures including queens and kings, fairies, witches, wizards, jewels, and crystals
- Helper props such as police and firefighters, doctors, and ambulances
- A variety of small vehicles

3. Set the sand tray in a one-person area out of the traffic paths of the room. Invite children to use the sand tray to make a world. If you wish, when a child appears to be almost done, invite them to tell you about their world.

Recently, a teacher reminded me of Bentley. His mother was recently remarried and they had just moved to a new house. Bentley had been more disruptive than usual and nothing seemed to help very much. One afternoon we pulled out the sand tray and all the props and invited Bentley to play. He immediately took the three boxes of props and dumped them into the tub. We thought the activity was a failure until we asked him, "Tell us about your world." His answer? "My world is a total mess." How revealing! No wonder this child was having such a hard time at school. We used this information in the classroom to make sure that Bentley's school day was simple, orderly, and predictable, and very soon his school behavior improved.

Keep in mind that teachers are not therapists. If children reveal disturbing information while using the sand tray, refer the child to the appropriate support personnel or agencies.

Support Children's Management of Time, Space, and Change

Children can't look at a clock to figure out what happens next. The way they tell time best is with predictable rituals and routines. If they are outside playing, lunch must be next. If lunch is over, it must be rest time. And if afternoon snack is done, it must be time to go home.

"Who will I sit next to? Will I be line leader? Will there be a space for me?" Provide additional support to these children by giving them a predictable place to be at transition time and a clearly defined space to work and to play.

As useful and reassuring as rituals and routines are, however, life is full of change as well. Help children cope with change and transition by weaving supportive strategies throughout your program.

Picture Schedules

An important component of self-regulation is the ability to understand the passage of time. A regular daily schedule is one way to build this sense of time into the daily program.

Reinforce your daily schedule with a picture schedule posted at the children's eye level to help them visualize their day.

1. Take pictures of all major program portions of the day. For example, morning meeting, center time, outside time, afternoon meeting, lunch, rest, quiet play, outside time, go home.
2. Label each picture with its title, such as "Morning Meeting." For young children, it is not necessary to add the actual clock time, although you can if you wish.
3. As you move from activity to activity, refer to the posted schedule to help children learn how to use the tool. For example, point to morning meeting on the schedule and say, "We're done with this activity. Let's look now and see what comes next. Who knows what this is a picture of? You are right, next is center time . . ."
4. When an individual child asks you if it's outside time or go-home time yet, instead of just answering the question, bring them over to the picture schedule and help them find the information they need.

Some teachers put their picture schedule in a pocket chart and have children move the pictures from the left to right column as the activity is completed. Others bind the pictures in book form with a plastic spiral binder and have the children flip the pages as each activity is finished to see what comes next. It wouldn't be overkill to use all of these methods in one classroom if you had a number of children who needed help getting oriented.

Timers

Timers can empower children and help them to organize their understanding of how the world flows. Young children have little concept of how long "five more minutes" or "in a minute" are. Timers are an interesting, visual, and concrete way to introduce children to the concept how time is measured. Try using timers along with your five-minute warning for cleaning up or to structure a child's turn at "Show and Tell." There are many inexpensive timers available at local stores and discount outlets. Try the kitchen department for egg timers and kitchen timers.

Timers have many advantages over the teacher keeping time:

- First, you don't have to add "timekeeper" to your already full job description.
- Children can learn how to use common timers and build an understanding of how time keeping and turn taking works.
- Children are much less likely to argue with a timer than they are to argue with a person keeping track of time.

Use timers sparingly, however, to limit children's access to an activity. Allowing children to use a center or piece of equipment for as long as they want encourages children to get deep into their play. It's a better strategy to have the eyedroppers out for a week without limiting "turns" than to have them out for a day or two giving each child a three-minute turn. For sharing and taking turns with materials or areas, consider using wait lists instead. Each child then can use the activity for as long as they like during that session. When they are done, or when the next session begins, the next person on the list has the opportunity to use the activity.

Talking Stick

Use a talking stick or a small stuffed toy to help children learn to predict when it will be their turn to talk at group time. The predictability of when the stick will arrive helps some children with the waiting process.

1. Make a talking stick by having children decorate a small branch with paint, glitter, beads, and other decorations.
2. Explain that the stick will be passed around the circle and that everyone will get a chance to talk.
3. The child who is holding the stick or the toy is the speaker. Those children without the prop are the listeners.

Waiting Lists

When teachers take on the role of Timer Police, moving children in and out of activities in an attempt to let everyone have a turn, they cheat children of the opportunity to learn how to manage scarce resources on their own. Use waiting lists for popular areas such as computers or the art easel or when new and interesting toys are added to the classroom. Waiting lists have a number of valuable advantages over teachers keeping track of turns.

- Waiting lists are concrete, visual representations of taking turns. Many children find it easier to learn visually than by just listening to the teacher.
- Children can consult each other to figure out whose turn is next.
- Waiting lists are objective and children are less likely to dispute something in writing than they are to debate endlessly with the teacher.
- Children can eventually learn to manage waiting lists with minimal adult help. This gives them a life skill and the teacher extra time for more essential roles.
- Waiting lists help children develop an internal organizational vision of how turn taking works.

Here are different ways to use waiting lists, based on your teaching objectives and the children's skill levels:

- Put up a clipboard and marker. Teach children to "write" their names, one under the other when they want a turn. It doesn't matter that some children can't make any letters. Teachers might want to keep an eye on the sheet and lightly print the child's initials next to their "signature" until they can recognize each child's typical mark. When it is the next child's turn, the teacher can cue the next child by saying, "Is this your name here? That means it's your turn."
- You can use charts with pockets or Velcro boards as waiting lists. Children put their name cards in the slot. When the child completes his turn, he puts his name card back where it belongs.
- Make photo cards for each child using a digital camera and printer. These cards are used in the same way as the name cards above.
- Put names or attach small photos to spring-clip clothespins. Have children attach their clothespin to a piece of posterboard to show that they want a turn next.
- As the children become accustomed to waiting lists, you can establish that when each child is done, she looks at the list, crosses off her name (or removes her name card), and lets the next child know it's his turn. Completely teacher-free turn taking!

Concrete Cues and Props

Props and visual cues help children begin to define their personal space and the space of others. As they mature, they'll be able to define space without these cues. Children will be at different developmental levels in your classroom. It is perfectly acceptable to use these props and cues with those children who still need them and to allow more mature children to negotiate their own personal space.

- Use carpet squares, masking tape, or hoops on floors to define a child's personal workspace.
- Have children decorate colored construction paper. Cover the paper with Con-Tact paper to make durable sit-upons.
- Set a large appliance box on its side in the block area to make personal space for one child.
- Help children define personal space at the water table by using individual dish-pans.

- At an art table, try cookie sheets to define workspace for individual children.
- Make sure children have individual, labeled cubbies to keep a few personal belongings.

Body Bubbles

When children are ready to move on from concrete and visual props to define personal space, use "Body Bubbles" to help them visualize an imaginary bubble that surrounds their bodies.

1. Use your arms to make a circle around your own body to demonstrate and have the children do the same.
2. Have children try to dance or walk around the room without "popping" each other's bubbles.
3. When gathering for a meeting or beginning a movement activity, review the "body bubble" concept to help children negotiate space.

Preview Changes

Help children prepare for new events, new people, and other unusual activities. Even small changes can throw off some young children and cause them to become anxious. Anxious children will either externalize their anxiety by hitting, running around, acting the fool, or being defiant, or they will internalize by withdrawing from activities, weeping, whining, or acting helpless and pathetic.

Prepare children for a field trip to the state fair, for a grandmother who will come in to read a story, or for moving the classroom furniture around. Help children focus on what will be the same and what will be different.

When talking about rearranging furniture, one class made the following discoveries.

WHAT WILL BE THE SAME?	WHAT WILL BE DIFFERENT?
We will have the same toys.	The blocks will be in a different place.
We will have the same kids.	We will read books in the other corner.
We will have the same teachers.	The water table will be on the other side.
We will still have snack.	I don't know where dress up will be.
We will still have a window.	
My friends will be here.	
We still go home to sleep at night.	

Transitional Objects

Young children are still learning the concept of *object permanence,* that things exist even when they are out of sight. Before children fully understand this concept, they can be very anxious when transitioning from home to school. These children are not sure that home and family exist when they aren't visible.

Concrete transitional objects help them know that home and family exist although they are far away. Suggest to families that they allow their child to bring a significant transitional object with them to school such as a family photo, a set of old keys, or a piece of a parent's clothing.

In the same way, some children fear that school will disappear when they go home. You might find these children with their pockets stuffed with small school items at the end of the day. To support these children, find a school token they can take home at the end of each day. You might want to send home their name card from the attendance pocket chart or from the job board. Children know that this item is important to the classroom and will feel comfort in bringing it back and forth from school to home. Some children may have trouble bringing objects back to school for various reasons. Rather than continuing to send items home, you might want to explore a different strategy. One teacher gave the child the essential job to turn on the lights in the classroom in the morning. This important job helped the child look forward to coming to school in the morning in the same way that returning a school book might help another child.

"1, 2, 3, It's Me"

Transitions can be difficult for children who need predictability in their environments. Transition most often means that the child will be moving physically from one space to another. If this transition will require a negotiation of space, such as when children are told as a group to line up to go outside, some children will become so anxious that they strike out at others for no apparent reason.

Assign the child a special numbered place to be on line every time the class has to line up to minimize this child's anxiety and acting out behavior. Whether the child gets there first, last, or sometime in between, that child knows she is always in the same spot. Number three is a useful position since many children can count to three and the singsong "1, 2, 3, it's me" is catchy and fun to say. Third in line is also a "neutral" place, unlike "line leader" and "last kid."

Make sure all the children know that Freddy's place in line is number three so that they move to make space for him when he gets there. Most children will be very helpful and supportive with a 1-2-3 child in their group. Children typically will support strategies that lead to more peace and safety.

Red Dot

This strategy is similar to 1-2-3, except it is used for group time when children do not have assigned seats or sit-upons.

Put a red sticky dot on the floor to indicate the child's predetermined place at group time. Make sure everyone knows that the red dot is Freddy's space. Having a clear vision of where to go helps some children calm down and reduces inappropriate behavior.

Sit-Upons

If many children get anxious when gathering for group time, consider using a system to assign predetermined places for each child. One method do this without assigning permanent seats is to use individual sit-upons.

1. Have each child make their own sit-upon with colored paper and art materials.
2. Cover the sit-upons with Con-Tact paper to make them durable.
3. Assign a rotating job to arrange the sit-upons in the group area before children gather.
4. When children transition to large group time, each child finds their sit-upon and sits in the designated spot.
5. Make sure that there is a firm rule that children must sit where they find their sit-upon. If children are permitted to move their sit-upons, the predictability is lost.

Clean-Up Job Board

Cleaning up after center time can be one of the most challenging transitions of the day. "I didn't take that out"; "I already put some blocks away. Anthony needs to do the other blocks"; "I never played there." Time and attention that you need to spend helping anxious children transition gets siphoned off by the constant distraction of monitoring the clean-up activity.

Make life easier for the children and for yourself with a "Clean-up Job Board."

1. Put photos of each center in the left-hand pockets of a pocket chart.
2. Assign pairs of children to be in charge of each center and put their names in the right-hand pockets next to each job.
3. If there are too many children, add additional transition jobs such as pushing in all the chairs, using the carpet sweeper in the carpet area, or washing the tables.
4. Have the assigned children clean up their assigned area regardless of whether they used the materials that day.

5. Scan the room to see if the area is clean. Send the assigned children back to finish an area if it isn't done.

6. Try not to rotate jobs more often than once a week. Predictability and routine are key for children to feel calm and in control.

When you use a clean-up board like this, make sure to also require children to pick up after themselves as they move from one area to another during the work period.

Self-Regulation Activities

Provide activities to help children take ownership for the consequences of their actions on themselves, others, and the environment.

Cause and Effect

These activities help children make the connection between their actions and the effects they have on the world around them.

"What If"

For children to make good behavior choices, they need to be able to visualize the effect of each choice. Give children practice in visualizing the future with "What If" games. Ask children questions like these:

- What if cars could fly?
- What if we went to school at night and slept in the day?
- What if it snowed in the summer?
- What if kids could drive cars?

Have children share their ideas. You might also have them make "What If" Big Books to help them visualize possible futures.

Limits and Expectations

These activities help children explore the guiding principles, experience limits on their behavior in a nonthreatening way, and come to term with school expectations.

Class-Made Books

Children need concrete visual reminders and much repetition in order to learn guiding principles of behavior. Help the children in your class to make a Big Book that uses practical examples of the guiding principles.

1. Use one guiding principle for each Big Book. For example, "We take care of each other."
2. Give each child one blank page.

- Help each child come up with an example of how they can help to take care of others. Some children have an easier time with this task if you have them complete the sentence "I help other people when I ______." Print their words on the bottom of the page.
- Have each child draw an illustration for their example.

3. Add a page where parents can write responses.
4. Bind pages and cover.
5. Read the book to the children and allow them to take the book home overnight to share with their families.

Looks Like/Sounds Like

This is a variation of making guiding principle Big Books. Instead of putting together books, work together with the children to make a chart for each guiding principle. Hang these charts on the wall at children's eye level so that they can see the pictures often during the day.

For example, make a "Looks Like/Sounds Like" chart for "We take care of our stuff."

1. Divide the chart down the middle. Label the left-hand column "Looks Like" and the right-hand column "Sounds Like."
2. Work with the children to fill in the chart. For example, title a chart "We take care of our stuff" and brainstorm with the children what "taking care of our stuff" might look and sound like.
3. Have the children describe it, act it out, and see what it looks like and sounds like.
4. Take pictures of the children "taking care of stuff" and post these pictures on the chart. Since visual cues work much better for many young children than verbal cues, these pictures are invaluable.

5. As children act out what taking care "looks like" you may hear them say things like, "Use the markers on the table," or "I'm gonna wipe the water up." Take dictation of these words for the "sounds like" side of the chart.

Who should be the models for the "looks like" pictures? Choose the child who is least proficient at the skill. Ask the child if they would like pose "taking care of stuff." Now you have a picture of appropriate behavior that includes a picture of your struggling child doing the activity successfully. Each time that child sees that picture, they see themselves as successful at that task. Seeing this message over and over starts to reprogram their self-concept: "Yes, I'm a kid who can take care of stuff. There's the proof right up there on the wall. That's me taking care of things."

Picture Cues

Use the same idea for a child who might have trouble with a more specific expectation such as standing in line. Post a picture of this child doing the skill. There it is! A "standing in line at school" posterboard with a picture of the struggling child modeling the skill! This visual proof begins to change the child's self-talk and self-image. When they see themselves as successful, they begin to believe themselves successful and in turn they become successful.

Managing Emotions

Help children learn to recognize their emotions by having them notice how they feel physically. Teach children how to recognize feelings in others based on what they see and hear. Whenever there is talk of feelings, remember to emphasize that people can manage their feelings and that feelings will change over time.

Emotion Necklace

Prepare children to be able to read the emotions of others by using emotion necklaces. Children find it much simpler to identify an emotion by looking at a simple happy or sad face card than they do by attempting to read individual faces.

1. Prepare ten small cards about two inches square with simple happy and unhappy faces.

2. Punch a hole at the top of each card and lace a long piece of yarn through the card. Tie the ends together to make a "necklace."

3. Keep these emotion necklaces in a small basket easily available to the children.

4. Teach the children how to select and put on an emotion necklace that expresses how they are feeling. Make sure that you wear these cards yourself.

5. Model for the children how you can tell how somebody else is feeling by looking at their face card. Say something such as, "I see Maddy has a sad face necklace on. I wonder why she's sad today. I think I'll go ask her." Or, "Luci, you have a happy face necklace on today. I wonder why you're feeling so good. Did something special happen?"

Simon Says

"Simon Says" is a wonderful game for children to practice impulse control. The trick of "Simon Says" is to stop and think before you act. The problem with the game in its traditional version is that the kids who have the most problems with impulse control are eliminated early in the game; in other words, the child who most needs to practice impulse control is the child who ends up getting the least practice! In this version of "Simon Says," nobody is out and everyone gets the practice they need.

1. Gather the children into either a small or large group. Have them stand a couple of feet away from each other.
2. Tell the children that you are going to play "Simon Says." Tell them that you are going to do things with your body, and sometimes they should copy you. If you tell them "Simon says," then they should copy you. If you don't say "Simon says," then they should not copy you. Remind them that it is a very tricky game and that they need to listen carefully before they copy you.
3. Modify the original game so that when children make a mistake, they are not eliminated from the game. They are merely prompted to listen carefully and try again. The goal is to keep all the children in the activity for the entire game so that everyone gets to practice impulse control.

Here's an example of Randi playing a round of "Simon Says" with her kids.

"Remember, stop and think," Randi reminded the children as they began the game. "Before you move, what do you need to think about?" she asked the group.

"Do the same thing," suggested Marisella.

"Uh huh," agreed Randi. "You are exactly right. You do the same thing if I say the words 'Simon says.' Remember? And Mari, if I don't say 'Simon says,' you stay . . ." Randi paused here for Marisella to finish the sentence.

"Stay still," said Marisella.

"Ok, ready? Here we go. Listen hard. Simon says put your hands on the floor," she modeled the motion as she talked. Randi waited until all the children had their hands on the floor. "You waited to hear me say 'Simon says.' Yes."

"Ok. Here's a tricky one. Listen hard. Put your hands way high in the air." Randi kept her hands on the floor. Two children put their hands up. A few children called out "Simon didn't say," and Randi waited for the two to put their hands down again. "That was so tricky. Let me trick you again. Listen hard. Simon says put your hands up in the air." She said "Simon says" louder than the rest of the words, and put her hands up. Again, she waited until all the children had their hands up before moving on.

Randi included one "stop and think" song or game in her lesson plan three times a week. After a few weeks, she was able to play "Simon Says" a little faster and with fewer prompts. The children were beginning to learn how to "stop and think" before they acted.

Obstacle Course

Many children are challenged by shifting gears from active play to more quiet play. These children need more practice with modulation activities. These activities are specifically designed to help children move from loud to quiet, from using large muscles to using small muscles, from moving quickly to moving slowly. When children practice modulation in play activities, they can begin to transfer that learning to other times when you need the children to settle down, such as for rest time. "Obstacle Course" is one of these modulation activities that you might want to organize from time to time.

1. Set up an obstacle course with large motor activities, such as climbing through a tunnel and jumping over a log.
2. In the middle of the course, set up a small table with a small motor activity on it. This can be something like stringing a few beads or putting together a three-piece puzzle.

When children go through this course, they need to be able to shift themselves from one mode to another. This shifting helps develop internal controls needed to "stop and think."

Call-and-Response Songs

Call-and-response songs are another way to help children process information before they act. These are game-type songs where a leader sings a line first while the children are quiet, and then it's the children's turn to sing a response. When children become familiar with a song, it's challenging for a kid to hold back and not sing until it is time for a response. Two popular children's call-and-response songs are "Did You Feed My Cow?" by Ella Jenkins and "Candy Man" sung by Greg and Steve.

As a bonus, "Candy Man" helps teach the concept of whispering and thinking the words—both useful life skills. After children have learned the skill of thinking the words, teach them to use the strategy when they have the urge to say something hurtful or to call out of turn. "That is a time to just think the words." Some teachers like to use the singsong "Should it be said or kept in your head?" as a prompt to just think the words.

High-Low ABCs

Another song for modulation practice requires children to sing with energy, then immediately shift to a whisper and back to singing forcefully again. Songs like these help children learn to quiet down from energetic play.

1. Sing the "Alphabet Song" while sitting and patting your legs with your hands.
2. Sing and pat one line loud, quietly on the next, loudly on the next line, and so on. For example: "A, B, C, D," (loud) "E, F, G," (quietly) "H, I, J, K," (loud) "L, M, N, O, P," (quietly) "Q, R, S," (loud) "T, U, V," (quietly) "W, X," (loud) "Y, Z" (quietly).
3. Like the obstacle course, this game requires children to be conscious of their energy and activity levels, and gives them a fun way to practice modulation control.

Freeze Dancing

Like "High-Low ABCs" and "Obstacle Course," "Freeze Dancing" gives children an enjoyable and nonthreatening way to practice controlling their impulsive urges.

1. Play music while the children dance freestyle.
2. Turn the sound off. Tell the children when the music stops they have to freeze in position.
3. If you call out, "Stop and freeze," when you turn off the music, the same words can be taught for emergency situations such as on field trips or in the play yard.

You can also use the Ella Jenkins song "Stop and Go" (this song is on two of her recordings, *Play Your Instruments* and *Did You Feed My Cow?*) to practice a similar dancing game. Another variation is to play "Freeze Tag" outdoors. The rules for "Freeze Tag" is that one person is "it." The rest of the children run about and must freeze in position when touched by "it." There are no winners or losers in this game. The fun is in the freezing. Some people use the rule that children who are free can tag children who are frozen to "unfreeze" them, which can make the game last longer!

If You're Happy and You Know It

By modifying this song, you can help children not only label emotions but also come up with strategies to manage those emotions.

1. Make up new verses for the song, using the emotions that the children are learning. Some common ones for children are happy, scared, angry, and hurt.

2. The second line of each verse should be a strategy that children can use in the classroom. Some ideas:

- If you're happy and you know it, give a smile.
- If you're scared and you know it, find a friend.
- If you're angry and you know it, count to five.
- If you're hurt and you know it, get a hug.

Here's an example of how one teacher sang this song with her group. Notice how she handled the child who came up with an inappropriate strategy for handling anger.

The children gathered around Holly for a song before lunch. Holly started clapping and had a big smile on her face. "Happy, happy, happy," chanted Teddy, jumping up and down.

"If you're happy and you know it," she started singing. Most of the kids joined in with big smiles. "Clap your hands!" they finished. "If you're happy and you know it, clap your hands," they all continued together. "If you're happy and you know it, then your self will surely show it" (they all smiled and squirmed around), "If you're happy and you know it, clap your hands."

"What should we do next?" asked Holly.

"Scared. Do scared," called John. "Okay. Let's do scared. What does scared look like? Show me how you look when you get scared," she said to the group, as she modeled herself what her own scared looked like.

"What can you do if you get scared in school? Who has an idea?" continued Holly.

"I want a hug. I get scared," said Brandy.

"Okay. Let's sing that we get a hug. Ready? If you're scared and you know it, get a hug. If you're scared and you know it, get a hug. If you're scared and you know it, then your self will surely show it—let me see your scared self! If you're scared and you know it, get a hug. Okay, go find somebody to get a hug with."

The children sang and acted out the scared verse and then gave hugs to each other.

"Let's do one more feeling. We did happy and we did scared. I wonder what we can do now. Who has an idea?"

"I wanna do mad," said Francisco. "I punch his face when I get mad."

"Okay. Let's do mad. How can we do mad at school so we can all be safe, Franny?"

"I punch his face," Francisco answered.

"You get mad and you feel like you want to punch. At school, we keep everyone safe. Do you have an idea how to do mad with no hurting at school?" Holly gave Francisco time to think of an answer.

"I don't know," said Francisco.

"Hmmm," Holly said to him. "I wonder who you can ask in our class who might know. Who would you like to ask?"

"I ask Mitchell. How you be mad, Mitchell?" he asked.

"Count to five," answered Mitchell. Holly had taught the children to count to five if they felt they were getting out of control.

"Ok, count to five is safe. Let's use that," said Holly. She led the children in the last verse of the song.

Class-Made Books

Help reinforce the concept that children can manage their feelings and that feelings can change. When you make a class-made book with the children's ideas and artwork, they will be drawn to the book over and over again, giving them the practice and review they need to learn the difficult concepts.

1. Make a Big Book with the class, called "Feelings Change," on managing feelings. Have children fill in sentence models such as "I get afraid when__________. I help my feelings change by ____________." Print the words on the bottom of the page and have the children illustrate their idea.
2. Bind the book together with a cover and back page. Label the front with the title and the back page as a parent response page.
3. Read the book to the children and allow children to take turns bringing it home to share with families. Invite families to comment on the back cover.

Managing Time, Space, and Change

Temper tantrums often are the only recourse children have when they have not yet learned delay of gratification or socially acceptable ways to achieve their goals. Use some of the following ideas to teach children to wait for a short time.

Dramatic Play Themes

You already know that children learn best through play. Use your dramatic play centers to help children practice waiting and taking turns in real-life settings. Some ideas are setting up a doctor's office with a waiting room and sign-in sheet, a bakery with number tickets, or a post office with a line where you wait for a turn at the counter. Because many children come to these activities with little experience, be sure to join in the play at first to model how the system works.

1. Sign in, take a number, or get in line.
2. Say something like, "I see there are some people ahead of me. I'm gonna have to wait 'til it's my turn."

3. Each time somebody's turn is done, say something like, "It's getting closer to my turn, but not yet. I still have to wait."

4. When your turn comes, show the children how you know. Say something like, "My turn. My name is next on the list," or "My turn, I'm next in line."

While I Am at School

Some children are distressed at school because they have trouble understanding that people still exist even though you can't see them. For some children, the distress can be so great that they try to act out enough to get sent home from school! Help children learn to visually imagine what home or family looks like while they are away at school. Children who learn to visualize often show much less anxiety when they are away from home.

Children can practice this skill in large or small groups.

1. Model the skill yourself first. Say something like, "I am thinking of my mom. I bet right now she is cooking supper at her house."

2. Ask the children if they can guess what their grown-up from home is doing right then. For children who have trouble with this skill, encourage families to share something of their daily plan with their child during the good-bye ritual.

3. Children can draw or paste pictures of their images to make a class Big Book called "While I Am at School."

Homemade Picture Books or To-Do Lists

Classroom schedules highlighting major activities of the day—such as meals, outdoor times, and rest times—are enough support to help most children navigate their days. Some children do well with even more personal supports.

1. Work together with children to make little photo-illustrated picture books or to-do lists to help them visualize their days.

2. These pictures should feature the child doing the activity. Include activities as well as transitions, and make sure to include their arrival to and departure from school. Be especially careful to include pictures of the more difficult transitions of the child's day.

3. Read the book often to the child, send the book home for families to share, and use the book to "preview" the next event. For example, as lunch ends, bring the book or list to the child. Help them find the lunch picture and then guide them to identify the next event.

Discussion/Reflection Questions

1. What guiding principles of behavior might you design for your classroom and why?
2. Describe how an adult who has never established the four building blocks for self-regulation might behave.
3. How might you "validate feeling, then guide behavior" for each of these situations:

- Matt is climbing up the slide ladder after you called the children to the gate to return to the classroom.
- Dee-Dee is weeping because Ebony is washing tables, but it was supposed to be her turn.
- Giuliana's birthday is tomorrow and she's bouncing around today interfering with other children's play.

Exercises

1. Think of a child in your class who has demonstrated a low level of self-regulation. Briefly talk about two or three incidents that have happened recently and identify one or more of the four building blocks that you think this child might be lacking. What one or two strategies will you implement to help the child build those strengths?
2. Look at your schedule, the physical environment, and your classroom rules and limits with an eye toward "organization." What are some of the strengths of your current program? What changes might you make to improve external organization?

Reflection/Journal Assignment

Design a bumper sticker for your car with a slogan that captures your personal guiding principle of behavior. How did you come about settling on this guiding principle for yourself? How have you used this principle to make major life decisions?

Resources

Bailey, Becky. 1997. *There's gotta be a better way: Discipline that works.* Oviedo, FL: Loving Guidance.

———. 2000. *Conscious discipline: Seven basic skills for brain smart classroom management.* Oviedo, FL: Loving Guidance.

Brooks, Robert, and Sam Goldstein. 2001. *Raising resilient children.* Chicago: Contemporary Books.

Committee for Children. 1997. *Second step: A violence prevention curriculum.* Seattle: Committee for Children.

Covey, Stephen R. 1997. *The seven habits of highly effective families: Building a beautiful family culture in a turbulent world.* New York: Golden Books.

Devereux Foundation. 1999. *Classroom strategies to promote children's social and emotional development.* Lewisville, NC: Kaplan Press.

Dinkmeyer, Don, and Gary D. McKay. 1973. *Raising a responsible child: Practical steps to successful family relationships.* New York: Simon and Schuster.

Gestwicki, Carol. 1999. *Developmentally appropriate practice: Curriculum and development in early education.* Albany, NY: Delmar Publishers.

Gordon, Thomas. 1970. *P.E.T.: Parent Effectiveness Training: The tested new way to raise responsible children.* New York: Peter H. Wyden, Inc.

Gould, Patti, and Joyce Sullivan. 1999. *The inclusive early childhood classroom: Easy ways to adapt learning centers for all children.* Beltsville, MD: Gryphon House.

Hewitt, Deborah, and Sandra Heidemann. 1998. *The optimistic classroom: Creative ways to give children hope.* St. Paul: Redleaf Press.

Shore, Rima. 1997. *Rethinking the brain.* New York: Families and Work Institute

Taylor, John F. 1997. *Helping your hyperactive/ADD child.* 2nd ed. Roseville, CA: Prima Publishing.

Wheat, Rebecca. 1995. Helping children work through emotional difficulties—Sand trays are great! *Young Children* 51:82–83.

Whelan, Mary Steiner. 2000. *But they spit, scratch, and swear! The do's and don'ts of behavior guidance with school-age children.* Minneapolis: A-ha! Communications.

Ziegler, Robert G. 1992. *Homemade books to help kids cope: An easy-to-learn technique for parents and professionals.* Washington, DC: Magination Press.

6

Initiative

"I can grow and change and learn new things."

Ms. Ruiz sat down by Misael in the home living area. "Do you need help?" she offered. Misael was trying to put a tiny sweater on a tiny baby doll and seemed to be having trouble. "No," she answered. "I can do it." Ms. Ruiz's fingers itched to give a helping hand, but Misael persisted and finally got the sweater on the baby. "Look," she proudly announced. "I did it!" "You sure did," answered Ms. Ruiz. "You're a kid who keeps trying until you get the job done." "I'm gonna make the baby a hat from the art area," said Misael as she bounded down the loft stairs. She gathered papers, tape, and glitter and began to work. Before she was done, Ms. Ruiz gave the signal for clean up. Misael gathered her materials and asked her teacher if she could put them in her cubby to finish tomorrow.

What Does Initiative Look Like?

Misael, like many typical four-year-olds, had the basic building blocks for initiative.

Children with initiative:

- Can persist, focus, and complete a task, even when frustrated
- Are competent and confident about growing and learning new things
- Look forward to the future

When Things Go Wrong

"I'm done," said Du'A. His job was to pick up the chalk pieces from the sidewalk. The bucket was half full but there were five more pieces clearly in sight. "No, you're not," said his teacher. "Go back and finish up." "I did it already," Du'A answered. "I worked a long long long long time already." "There's still chalk out there. I see it from here. Go on back and get them." Du'A wandered back to the chalk area and found another piece to put in the bucket. "Here," he said as he handed the bucket back to the teacher. "Still more chalk out there. Go back and find the rest," his teacher said. "I'm too tired," Du'A whined. "My leg hurts. See my owie?" He pulled up the leg of his pants. "I'll look at your owie later. Go back and get the chalk." The teacher put the bucket back in Du'A's hands, he took two steps and dropped the bucket. Chalk flew everywhere and Du'A began to cry. "I can't do it," he cried.

Children are often oblivious to what is so obvious to us. In fact, Du'A usually had trouble finishing a task and would often find excuses not to finish if pushed. He really had no idea how to check to see if a task was done so it seemed to him that there was never an end to a job. He would get easily distracted or discouraged. Du'A needed some support and guidance to help him figure out ways to tell if a job was done. His teachers could have started him with self-correcting toys like puzzles. They could have given him descriptive feedback when he did complete a job so that he could begin to understand what "done" looked like. They might have tried to use checklists during the day so that he would be able to see that any task was finite and that there was a way to tell when you were done. Given these tools and experiences, Du'A would have soon developed the understanding and skills he needed to finish a job.

"I can't draw my family. You do it for me," insisted Monte. "You can too draw your family. Just do your best," encouraged Mr. T. Monte put a few lines on his paper, tore it up, and threw it in the trash. He went back to the table and threw the markers on the floor. "Pick up the markers, Monte," Mr. T said gently. "I hate school. This work is stupid," answered Monte. He got up, dumped his chair over and hid behind the wastebasket.

Mr. T followed him and crouched down beside the wastebasket. "You have until the count of three to get back to the table and pick up the markers, Monte," he said firmly. "Go away! I hate you! Get away from me!" screamed Monte. He kicked the wastebasket and it shot across the room. "Enough," said Mr. T. "Go to the color chart and pull a card now." "I hate you. I hate you," Monte screamed as he melted into a tantrum kicking everything within reach. Mr. T. picked up the struggling child and called over to his co-teacher that he was taking the child down to the office—again. Monte's mother was called and told to pick him up.

One of the pleasures of working with very young children is their endless enthusiasm, excitement, and can-do attitude. Most children in this age range are full of initiative and are a delight to work with.

Some children, however, have already been written off as failures in life before they even turn six. These are the little guys who pose incredible challenges to parents and teachers with behavior that are rude, aggressive, weepy, manipulative, hurtful, or generally unlikable. Every day they are given feedback that they are somehow deficient, failures, or hopeless. Days full of sad-face cards, time-out chairs, notes home, and more subtle "failure" messages become so much of a way of life for the child that they begin to make that outside message their inside self-talk.

Monte's life was full of snowballing problems. His low level of self-regulation had led to many years of negative and discouraging messages. His mother referred to him as her "problem child," and he was well known among peers as the "bad one" and the "troublemaker." He had already been kicked out of two other preschools for being bad and was about to be asked to leave this one as well. As the negative messages increased, Monte's initiative decreased. He felt increasingly more inadequate and incompetent, which made each day harder and harder to handle with his already low level of self-regulation.

Monte's problems weren't going to be solved in a day. However, Monte's teachers made a commitment to consciously begin to change the way they reacted and interacted with him. They used more encouraging language and descriptive feedback for those times he was doing well. They worked on changing Monte's vision of himself by helping him keep a journal of his successes. They eliminated the use of the color chart that only served as a visual cue for Monte that he was a failure. And they began to help Monte's mother appreciate her child's strengths by frequently sending home notes about the delightful things he had done during the day. Gradually, Monte's behavior both in the classroom and at home improved.

"When something bad happens to Ciara, it's as if her whole world is over. I'm not talking about just big things here. I mean if somebody won't play with her right then, or if she has trouble printing her name, or if she was hoping to be the one to turn off the lights but it's somebody else's job that day. She totally falls apart and starts that "I never get to . . ." or "Nobody ever plays with me," kind of stuff. I try to explain to her that "Feelings change," or that I will help her, or her turn will come, but she just can't move on. Her whiny ways begin to really get on my nerves. I just want to scream, "Get over it, will you?" The teacher laughed self-consciously at this point. "Of course, I don't," she continued. "But I'm so tired of hearing her complaining all day. Now I just hope that ignoring her will make it stop."

Some kids like Ciara have trouble visualizing that time passes, feelings change, and events move on. This can lead them to feel hopeless, stuck, and powerless over their fates. Before children can learn effective problem solving and decision making, they need to understand that time passes and that they have a hand in designing their futures. Ignoring Ciara might just make things worse by confirming to her that indeed, nobody cares and life is hopeless. Instead, the teacher might try some activities and language that help Ciara begin to understand that later is another opportunity and tomorrow is another day.

Our goal for children is that they never lose hope and that they always look forward to a better and stronger tomorrow.

Supportive Interactions

Use language in your daily interactions with children to help children develop positive attitudes about themselves and their potentials. By fine-tuning the words you use with children, you can help them achieve the following:

- Persist at tasks even when things become challenging
- Learn to carry out a task to completion
- Feel confident and competent
- Feel hopeful about themselves, their potential, and the future

Recognize Persistence

Our talk to children becomes their self-talk. And children's self-talk becomes their reality. Use language that lets children know that we notice their efforts and trust in their abilities. Instead of extrinsic motivators such as saying, "Good job" or handing out stickers, use descriptive feedback when children exhibit persistence, focus, and task completion. Descriptive feedback allows children to take ownership of their own strengths. When children receive praise or rewards for their efforts, their focus shifts from valuing their strengths to working to please others. Remember, too, that what gets recognized gets repeated. Children who are consistently recognized for persisting in a task, are more likely to persist again in the future. Use descriptive phrases like these:

- You've been working a long time.
- Look how hard you've been working. I bet you're proud of yourself.
- You can do this.
- You're trying and trying.

Recognize Accomplishment

Some children naturally find pleasure in completing tasks and others will even get uncomfortable if you don't allow them to finish their work. Some children, however, find it easy to abandon work that they find boring or challenging. Prepare children for the demands of school and adulthood by helping these children learn to find internal satisfaction in getting a job done. When you observe children completing a task, use reflective language to recognize their accomplishment.

- You're a kid who tries over and over again until you figure it out.
- Look at that! You got all the puzzle pieces put back.
- Let's look at how great the block area looks. Every block is back in its spot. That was hard work to finish all that.

Are We Done?

Help children recognize when a task is complete by demonstrating how to check over their work one last time.

- Make it a practice to say to the children, "Are we done?" You can do this after you set the table for snack, after you put all the sand toys back in the baskets, or at the end of reading a picture book.
- For individual children, try saying such things as, "Let's check one more time. Are there any blocks (puzzle pieces, chairs, trash, and so on) out of place? Okay, that means we're done."

One More Thing

When you are working with a child who flits quickly from one activity to another, try to keep him engaged for one more moment by saying, "One more thing." Often, this strategy will even extend a child's focus past that "one more thing."

WHEN YOU ARE PLAYING WITH A CHILD . . .	TRY SAYING . . .
in blocks	"One more thing. Can we add three more blocks to the tower?"
in home living	"One more thing. Would you get me some pretend supper before you go?"
at the water table	"One more thing. Would you hold this funnel a minute so I can pour this big pitcher?"
at the writing table	"One more thing. Would you find me Orson's name card?"
in the book center	"One more thing. Before you go, would you find me a fun book that I can read from our bookshelf?"

Beware of "Doing For"

"Draw me a horse," "Zip my coat," "I can't pour without spilling," "Can you write my name?" We can do it better, faster, and easier than they can. After all, adults have had many years of practice. However tempting it is to "do for," children need opportunities to practice skills for themselves in order to perfect them.

Be particularly aware of "doing for" when it comes to social and emotional skills. When one child hits another, instead of jumping in to defend the child who was hit, teach and coach that child to use assertive language to defend himself. Teach, show how, coach, guide, but don't "do for."

INSTEAD OF SOLVING . . .	TRY TEACHING AND COACHING . . .
"Nakita, don't hit Faith. Hitting hurts. She doesn't like that."	"Faith, you can tell Nakita you want her to stop hitting you. Say, 'Stop hitting me.' I'll stand by you to help."
"Oops. You spilled some milk. Move over and let me wipe it up before it gets all over the place."	"Oops. You spilled some milk. Do you need help to get some towels to wipe it up?"
"The red marker is broken? Here, let me get you another one."	"The red marker is broken? I wonder where you can find another one."

Use Encouraging Language

Praise and criticism are two sides of the same coin. Both praise and criticism are external rather than internal evaluations. Children who are often praised don't develop the skills they need to self-evaluate. Rather than trusting their own perceptions, they depend on others to do the evaluating for them. Work and learning lose their intrinsic value and instead become ways to get attention and verbal reward from others.

Some children who get frequent praise become "praise junkies." They sound like this:

- Do you like this?
- Is this pretty?
- Did I do this right?
- Is mine better?
- Whose is best?
- Are you going to put a sticker on my paper?
- Mine is better than José's, right?
- Is this good?

Praise and criticism can cause other children to become "discouraged." In fact, the more they are praised, the more discouraged they may become. Compliments such as, "That is the most beautiful painting I ever saw," become words for worry. If that's the most beautiful picture (which I suspect it's not, thinks the child), then what do I do for an encore? If mine is the most beautiful, why did I hear her tell Jon the same thing about his? I feel like just experimenting with mixing the paint, but I better not cause it may turn out ugly and then the teacher will tell me it's ugly and she only likes beautiful pictures. Discouraged children sound like this:

- This is ugly.
- I can't do this.
- Mine is the stupidest one.
- I'm gonna tear mine up and throw it away.
- José's is nicer than mine is.
- Do it for me.

Instead of praising children's work, try giving them descriptive feedback, focusing on the process instead of the product, or making a comment to encourage the child to reflect on their own work. Encouraging and descriptive feedback is especially important when working with children who seek adult attention and praise, and for children who appear discouraged.

Try these responses when a child asks, "Is this good?"

DESCRIPTIVE FEEDBACK	FOCUS ON PROCESS	ENCOURAGE SELF-REFLECTION
"I see you made it all swirly up here on top."	"Tell me how you made this swirly part up here."	"What's your favorite part of this painting?"
"Look how many different colors you used."	"How did you decide what colors to use in this?"	"Do you like the colors you used for this painting?"
"That tower is almost as high as you are."	"That must have been tricky to build a tower so high."	"What do you think of that tower?"
"You got all the way across the monkey bars."	"You worked hard to learn how to get across those monkey bars."	"How do you feel about getting all the way across the monkey bars?"

Strive Up instead of Belly Up

Most young children love to challenge themselves and "be big." They love the fact that every day they gain more skills. For a preschooler, *tomorrow* is an opportunity to be even better than he was today! Because they are asserting their independence, it is very difficult for them to "belly up" and do something "just because I said so."

Use this knowledge of typical child development when you are faced with a child who chronically or stubbornly won't comply because they need to be big. Learn strive-up language instead of belly-up strategies to motivate children to do what needs doing. Reframe a task for them as something tricky or challenging and most children will put their energies toward achieving the goal.

Turn compliance into a sign of strength rather than a sign of weakness.

INSTEAD OF SAYING . . .	TRY . . .
"Get out from under that table right now."	"I wonder if you're a kid who knows how to get out from under the table all by herself."
"I'm counting to three and you had better get yourself inside this door."	"I wonder if you can get all the way into the classroom by the time I reach blast off. Here I go . . . five-four-three-two-one-blast off."
"You took all those puzzles out, so you need to put them all back on the shelf."	"Do you think you're a kid who can put all seven puzzles back on the shelf with no help?"
"Why do I have to keep reminding you to put your shoes in your cubby?"	"Pretty soon you'll be a kid who can put his shoes in his cubby all by himself."

Approach Problems as Opportunities

Problems, challenges, and mistakes are a part of life. Kids who do well accept this fact and focus their energies on fixing or solving issues instead of looking for excuses or the opportunity to place blame. The language we use with children when there are problems sets them up to look back or to look forward. Approach problems and misbehavior as opportunities for future growth and development. Help children look forward to solutions rather than dwelling on the problem.

INSTEAD OF FOCUSING ON THE PROBLEM	TRY TO FOCUS ON WHAT HAPPENS NEXT
"Do you want to stay in from recess?"	"How can we solve the problem?"
"I warned you about that, didn't I?"	"Let's figure out a way to fix this."
"You should know not to do that. Go pull a color card."	"Everyone makes mistakes. Let's figure out a way to fix this."
"Why did you do that?"	"What can you do differently next time?"

Acknowledge the Child's Positive Intent

Everyone's days are a mix of successful and not so successful experiences. One of the tricks of life is to figure out how to work through the hard stuff and continue to move forward. Help children develop this forward-looking attitude with words that convey your trust and belief that at her core, the child has a positive intent.

WHEN A CHILD . . .	SAY . . .
has been working on being quiet at story but had a hard time today	"I know you are working hard to stay quiet during story time."
has been working to come inside at the signal but continued to play today instead	"Pretty soon, you'll be a kid who can come inside when the chime rings."
is learning to share supplies and refuses to share the markers today	"Pretty soon, your brain will be strong enough to tell your body to share the markers."
is learning to stop using profanity and slips	"It takes a long time to learn how to use new strong words."

Here are some more encouraging things to say when children have disappointed themselves.

- I'll teach you whatever you need to know to do school.
- You can do it.
- Don't worry, it takes practice.
- Don't give up, I have faith in you.
- It's okay to make a mistake.
- Let's think about what happened. I wonder what else a kid might try?
- Well, this choice didn't work so well. There must be some other way to do it. What could that be?
- You sure have a big pile of work to do. What kind of help do you need?
- You tried real hard. Soon you'll get it.
- I know you'll find a way to do this.
- I know you can fix it.
- I'll bet you make it next time.
- You are a smart person. You can figure this out.

Classroom Culture

Most preschool children see themselves through rose-colored glasses. Because they grow, change, and learn so rapidly in the early years, they have confidence that if they are lacking a skill today, they are sure to have it tomorrow. Help children keep this enthusiasm to learn by making sure that the daily program is accessible to all styles of learners. Establish a classroom that supports persistence, focus, and task completion. Provide a supportive environment where children can feel confident and competent as learners.

Help Children Concentrate

Sitting still and focusing on a task can be more challenging for some children than for others. These kids may be interested and excited about the work, but they find the physical environment so distracting (or uncomfortable) that they can't focus or complete the task.

Try a number of different strategies to help children concentrate on a task.

- Help distractible children focus by giving them a toy to hold quietly during work.
- Some children concentrate best when they can sit on a large ball or stand when working at a table.
- Make sure that chairs allow children to sit with their feet flat on the floor.
- Kids who get distracted by noises sometimes do well with earmuffs or headphones that are disconnected.

Going to the Office

Another strategy for children who get distracted is to set up a small area of the room as an "office" where children can go to work without being disturbed by others. This is not a punishment area or a time-out area. It's a quiet place in a room full of activity to which a child or adult can withdraw to concentrate on work.

Some teachers set up a small desk in an attractive corner of the room. Face the desk toward the wall and decorate it with a lamp, calendar, pencil cup, discarded telephone, and other items to help make it look like an attractive office space.

Invite children who get distracted easily to take "their work" to the office. Make sure children understand that when someone is using the office, they are not to be interrupted or disturbed.

When you first set up an area like this, expect that all the children will want to explore it and have a turn to work in it. You might want to post a sign up sheet on a clipboard and hang it on the wall next to the desk. Once the novelty wears off, you will probably find that those who don't need the area quickly lose interest, while those who do keep returning for more.

Self-Correcting Tasks

Young children often have trouble figuring out what "done" means when they are doing a task. For example, a child who has wiped the paint off the floor for a minute or two might assume the job is finished, even though there is still paint on the floor. Help children learn how to reflect upon their work and evaluate for themselves whether or not it is done.

Puzzles are a convenient, self-correcting tool for task completion. When children have put a puzzle together, help them determine if the task is finished. If all the pieces are in all the spaces, the task is done. If there are extra pieces or extra spaces, the task is not done.

Label shelves so that everything has a place. For example, take a photo of each musical instrument and attach the photos to the shelf. Store each instrument on top of its corresponding photo. After music time, have a child check the shelf to make sure each instrument has been put back in its place.

Assign the rotating job of "Clean-up Inspector" to check all the areas at clean-up time to make sure everything has been put away.

Checklists

Checklists are a useful life skill for people who need external organizers in their daily lives. Children can begin to use picture checklists to help their focus and complete tasks. Checklists are particularly useful for children who have been diagnosed with ADD or ADHD. One way to integrate checklists into your daily program is by using one at your morning meeting.

- Make a picture posterboard of your morning meeting routine.

Take a photo of each of the activities and paste them on the board. Make sure they are posted in order, either from top to bottom, or on a long strip from left to right, which also reinforces early concepts of reading.

- Laminate the board so that you can write on it and erase every day.
- Check off each activity with a dry-erase marker as it is completed.
- At the end of the meeting, have the children evaluate the list with you to make sure everything got done.

Long-Term Projects

Part of developing the concept of hope is the ability to look forward to tomorrow. One way to help children grasp the concept of hope is to include some project work that takes two or more days to complete.

When you do long-term projects with children, make sure to help the children review the progress that was made each day and to anticipate what will be done the next day.

Some ideas include the following:

- Have children make items from materials that harden and dry over time, such as plaster of paris, papier-mâché, or playdough. When the items dry, allow the children to paint and decorate them.
- Build and decorate a gingerbread or graham cracker village.
- Make simple puppets one day, and put on a puppet show the next day.
- Bake muffins one day, and serve them for snack the next day.
- Plan a celebration with the children. Brainstorm with them what they need and how to do it. Help them execute the plan.

- Conduct one or more long-term studies, which can take place over a number of days, weeks, or even months. Some classes have done studies on different kinds of shoes. Others have studied how a house gets built or that geese come from eggs. For more information on how to conduct long-term studies, check the bibliography at the end of this section for books by Sylvia Chard, Margie Carter and Deb Curtis, and Lilian Katz.

Study Planning Form

Bring the learning to the children, not the children to the learning. When you design lessons and activities, make sure that they are accessible to all the children in your class. Each child will have his own two or three preferred ways that they learn. Some learn best by seeing, others by doing. Some kids have to touch things or use their hands in some way in order to learn. You might see these children fiddling with things while you read them a story. Some children need to be able to move their whole bodies; they might rock or bounce about during story time. Some children don't process new information unless they can chat aloud about it. Some kids learn best with others, some best by themselves. In addition, you may have a child who is allergic to feathers, a child who can't touch anything sticky, a child who only understands Russian, and a child who lives in a homeless shelter. Regardless of what knowledge you are presenting to kids, whether it is learning to read or learning about animals or behavior, help children explore the concept by providing a broad range of activities for all learning styles and individual needs.

One teacher uses the study planning form below to make sure she has addressed the many learning styles of children in her group.

Seeing	(include photos, pictures, posters, books, watching puppets shows and dramatic plays)
Doing	(include hands-on activities, play acting, opportunities to practice, journal writing, experience charts, field trips, play sequences)
Using their hands	(include artifacts, books, American Sign Language)
Moving	(include dramatic play, puppets, dance, learning centers)
Chatting	(include discussions, buddy work, group work, scripts)

Working with others	(include dyad, small group, large group opportunities)
Exploring alone	(include opportunities for children to explore by themselves or with adult guidance)
Accommodating cultures, interests, and challenges	(be aware of family, culture, language, differing abilities and challenges)

Use Learning Styles for Teaching Social Skills

Keep children's learning styles in mind when you are teaching children social and emotional skills as well. "I tell her repeatedly, and she still grabs toys from the other kids. She can even say the rules back to me. She'll tell me, 'Use your words.' I can't tell you how many times I've gone over the same thing with her. 'Don't grab toys. Use your words.' Is she just being defiant or what?" We may tell and tell, but the problem is that most young children don't learn from hearing words.

The teacher in the above example took another look at her technique for teaching children to use words instead of grabbing a toy. Using the study planning form on the previous page, she made the following lesson plan to help children learn the concept.

Seeing	Take photos of children who are sharing. Use the puppets to illustrate asking for a turn. Read picture books that highlight children sharing and taking turns.
Doing	Have children act out asking for a turn at circle time. When children grab, use guidance and coaching to redo the situation, and have them ask for a turn.
Using their hands	Teach all the children ASL for turn and have them use the sign at the same time they use the words.
Moving	Have children act out situations of asking to use something. Have children roll a ball back and forth to each other at circle.

Chatting	Teach a "use your words" script to the kids. "Can I use that?" with a response of "Okay," or "Not now, maybe later." Have kids practice the script at circle time. Have kids do an experience chart on what they can do if they want something that somebody else is using. Have kids notice when others have asked for a turn, and take dictation for leaves on the "I Can Do It" tree.
Working with others	Buddy children up to ask each other for a turn with a toy. Do a transition game from group to center time where each child in turn asks another child for a turn with the "Talking Bunny." (The child who gives up the bunny transitions to the next activity—the child left holding bunny is asked next for a turn by another child. Be aware that an adult must ask the last child for a turn!)
Exploring alone	Picture books of children sharing and taking turns. Practice sessions with teachers on asking to use something.
Accommodating cultures, interests, and challenges	Maya's family feels it is too forward to ask for something that others are using. They want her to stand by quietly and wait a turn. Teach the children to be aware of others who stand by watching. Have them say, "Did you want a turn?" or "I'll give you a turn when I am done."

Backward Chaining

When a child is overwhelmed by a complex task, they may decide that they can't do it at all. Instead of working to master the task, they will avoid it or constantly ask others to do it for them.

Backward chaining is a way to help children master a complicated task bit by bit. When backward chaining, the teacher does everything but the very last step. Then the teacher teaches, coaches, and guides the child to finish the task. The sense of completion and success encourage children to keep working on mastering the entire task.

For example, after rest time, the teacher might put both socks and one shoe on the child. Then the teacher might loosen the laces, put the child's toe in the other shoe, and have the child pull the shoe the rest of the way on. When the child masters pulling the shoe on, the teacher might stop the next time after loosening the laces. Each time the child masters another skill, the teacher does less and less of the task. By using backward chaining, the child enjoys the satisfaction and pride of completing the task.

You might find it useful when using backward chaining, to first make an ordered list of the steps needed to accomplish the big task. The steps to get a turn for something that someone else is using might look like this:

1. Approach the child who has the thing you want to use.
2. Say, "I want a turn to use the (thing)."
3. Find something to do while you are waiting for your turn.
4. Take your turn.

To help a kid learn this skill:

1. The first step is to walk the child through the whole process. When the child says to you, "I want a turn on the computer," say, "Okay. Let me show you how to do this." Walk with the child over to the computer. Say to the child who is using the computer, "Ebony says, 'I want a turn to use the computer.'" The child will probably respond, "She can have it when I'm done." Help Ebony find something to do while she waits. When the child on the computer is finished, find Ebony and bring her to the computer for her turn.
2. After a few times, do everything except for the last step. When you see it is Ebony's turn, if she hasn't gone over herself, just remind her.
3. When Ebony has demonstrated success in taking her turn, back off some more and have her do the last two steps. Have her find something to do by herself and take her turn independently.
4. Again, after a few days, when you bring Ebony over to ask for a turn, have her be the one to say the words. You might need to prompt her with "Ebony, say 'Can I have a turn?'"
5. Once she's mastered "using her words," you can send her over to ask for turns by herself.

Activities to Support Initiative

Many children learn best when they can see and experience the concepts they are trying to learn. Help children visualize their growth and development by recording their reflections and by having them use their new skills on a regular basis.

Each One Teach One

Nothing reinforces learning more than teaching. Help children gain confidence in their skills and knowledge by using them as teachers for other children in the classroom or for children in younger rooms.

- A child who has learned to recognize the names of classmates can teach a child who is still learning to set out nametags for an activity.
- A child who can count can teach other children at the snack table when the snack portion card says to take three crackers.
- A child who can tie shoes can teach another child how to tie.
- A child who can pump on the swing can teach a friend how to pump.

"How I Am Growing" Journals

Young children are so focused on the here and now that they have trouble recognizing their growth and change over time. When they are struggling to learn a new skill such as tying shoes or managing hurt feelings, children need to be able to envision future success—to have hope. Help children remember how they overcame obstacles in the past to help them develop a sense that they will be able to continue to grow in the future.

1. Staple together a book of blank pages for each child.
2. Have children decorate their book covers.
3. Establish a weekly ritual of helping each child record a stepping-stone. Look for such stepping-stones as tasted a new food, played with a new playmate, worked with a new art medium, put on their own shoes, or put together a new puzzle. Major milestones are built from such tiny accomplishments.
4. Encourage children to illustrate their page, or give children photos of themselves engaged in their achievements to mount on their pages.
5. Have children bring their journal home to share with families. Leave room on the pages for families to comment. Add more pages as necessary to keep a running record for the entire year.

6. Some discouraged children benefit from having an adult regularly reading through their journal with them to reinforce the self-talk that they are kids who have proven they can learn new things in the past and that they will continue to do so in the future.

Daily Reflection Notes Home

"Hey, Erik. Tell me why you aren't sitting at story with the other kids," said Julie.

"'Cuz I be's bad," Erik answered.

"Oh, sometimes you do stuff the teacher doesn't like, huh?" Julie probed.

"No, I be's bad all the time. All the days my teacher give me a sad face to take home to my momma."

"I bet sometimes you get a happy face."

"Nuh uh. Only good kids get happy faces."

Many parents and teachers feel a need to send home daily reports from school, especially when a child is struggling with behavior issues. Notes such as "Veronica hit three times again today," or "Elliot refused to come inside again when he was called," are not useful tools to help children develop the skills they need to be more successful the next day. While notes such as these can act as a report card of behavior, they neither serve as plans for improving the future nor do they help children see themselves as people who have potential for doing better tomorrow. Instead, use daily reports that help everyone maintain a healthy vision of the child as a complex individual with strengths, challenges, and plans for future improvement.

For example, one report might say, "Today I was proud that I helped set the table for lunch. Tomorrow I will try to ask for a turn with words instead of hands."

1. Help children reflect upon their own behavior by involving them in completing the daily report. Say something like, "Powell, let's do your note to take home to your Auntie Nicole."

2. Plan a meeting time each day when you and the child can reflect on the successes and challenges of the day and select one of each to report on.

3. Begin first with a success. Say, "Okay, first we need to write down a wonderful thing you did today." If the child can't think of something, gently remind him of two or three things from which to choose. "Let me think. Oh, I remember seeing you set the table for lunch. And I saw you reading a book quietly on your rest mat today. And what else? Didn't you and Saffron play Mr. Potato Head together at center time?" Record the child's success for them.

4. Next address one challenge of the day. Ask the child to recall one and then prompt them to switch from the problem itself to how they will address the problem tomorrow. For example, if a child says the biggest challenge was that he

and Luke threw sand in the play yard, ask the child what they will try to do tomorrow instead of throwing sand.

This step is very important. Help the child envision what a better choice might have been. Often at this point, the child will say, "I'll play nice." That isn't going to help the child tomorrow. Coach the child to be more specific. For example, say, "What will you do tomorrow with the sand that will keep everyone safe? Will you build tunnels with the sand? Will you keep the sand on the ground? Will you put water in the sand to make a river? How will you be safe with the sand?" Record the child's choice on the note.

5. If the child can't remember a challenge, prompt them in a similar way as you did for the success. Tactfully suggest, "Hmmm. Let me think. Wasn't there some kind of problem out in the sandbox today? Something with Luke? And sand?" Keep slowly, tactfully, and respectfully adding bits of detail until the child can "remember" the incident.

6. It's at least as important to recognize success each day as it is to report on problems. Initially, you will have to do a lot of coaching and asking guided questions to help the child remember successes and to reword challenges as plans for tomorrow. After a few weeks, however, most children can begin to construct these answers with less help from adults.

Hope Books

Help children anticipate a positive future by making "Hope Books," either individually or as a class Big Book project. Some possible themes include these:

- When I Turn Five I Will Know How to . . .
- When I Go to Kindergarten I Will Learn . . .
- When I Grow Up I Will . . .
- Someday . . .

1. Select a theme for the book.

2. Help children to complete a sentence template for their page of the book. Take down their dictation and have the child illustrate their page. For example, ask the child to complete the sentence "When I get big, I'm going to get a job as a . . ."

3. Put the pages together with a front cover and family response page on the back. Read the finished book to the children either individually, at small group, or during large group time.

4. Allow children turns to take the book home to share with their families. Invite families to comment on the family response page, and then keep the book in the classroom library.

My Life Books

Young children are just beginning to learn the concept of the passage of time—that there is a past, a present, and a future. Understanding the concept that time and events move along is a prerequisite to feeling hope and anticipation for the future. Making past, present, future style books helps children visualize and internalize this understanding.

1. Give each child a blank page for the class Big Book called "My Life."
2. Take dictation from each child to complete three sentences: When I was a baby, I used to ______________. Now I am (age), and I can ________________________. When I am a grown-up, I will be able to ______________________.
3. Have the children illustrate their pages with photos or drawings.
4. Bind pages together into a Big Book with a cover and a family response page in the back. Read the book to the class and let children bring the book home to share with families.
5. Keep the finished book in the class library.

Discussion/Reflection Questions

1. How might you respond to boost initiative?

- When a child asks if you like the way they cleaned up the table toy area
- When a child says they can't put on their shoes
- When a child asks you to draw a tree for them because they don't know how to do it

2. Were you a child who got stickers, prizes, and praise, or a child who rarely got these kind of external reinforcements? For what kinds of accomplishments did you get them? Describe a specific memory of something you tried very hard at and either were or weren't rewarded for. How did the experience feel? How do you think it affected your ability to take initiative?
3. How do you feel about a child who will only play in the block area day after day and who won't try any other activities? Would you allow them to keep doing that? Would you restrict their time in blocks? Would you try to lure them into trying other activities? How would you approach this situation and why?

Exercises

1. Design a lesson using the study form plan for any concept you wish. Plan to have all the activities completed in one week and implement the plan. How did it work for the children?

2. Make one of the hope books or a "My Life" book with the children in your classroom. How did that work for the children?

Reflection/Journal Assignment

Begin a "How I Am Growing" journal for yourself. Start it by recording ways you have grown and changed personally and professionally since beginning this study. Add to your journal weekly.

Resources

Bailey, Becky. 2000. *Conscious discipline: Seven basic skills for brain smart classroom management.* Oviedo, FL: Loving Guidance.

Brooks, Robert, and Sam Goldstein. 2001. *Raising resilient children.* Chicago: Contemporary Books.

Chard, S. C. 1998. *The Project Approach: Making curriculum come alive.* New York: Scholastic.

———. 1998. *The Project Approach: Managing successful projects.* New York: Scholastic.

Devereux Foundation. 1999. *Classroom strategies to promote children's social and emotional development.* Lewisville, NC: Kaplan Press.

Dinkmeyer, Don, and Gary D. McKay. 1973. *Raising a responsible child: Practical steps to successful family relationships.* New York: Simon and Schuster.

Hewitt, Deborah, and Sandra Heidemann. 1998. *The optimistic classroom: Creative ways to give children hope.* St. Paul: Redleaf Press.

Katz, L. G., and S. C. Chard. 2000. *Engaging children's minds: The Project Approach.* 2nd ed. Norwood, NJ: Ablex

Kohn, Alfie. 1999. *Punished by rewards: The trouble with gold stars, incentive plans, As, praise, and other bribes.* Boston: Houghton Mifflin Company.

7

Problem Solving and Conflict Resolution

"I can solve problems and resolve conflicts."

Problems and conflicts are part of everyday life. The question isn't how to avoid problems and conflicts, but how to manage them when they happen. We will be using the word problem *here for one-person problems (for example, Ben can't find his shoes or Joni threw her snack trash on the floor) and the word* conflict *for problems that are between two people (for example, LaVita and Doug both want to use the pink marker).*

What Do Problem Solving and Conflict Resolution Look Like?

Children need two basic building blocks for problem solving and conflict resolution:

1. They need to develop a problem-solving attitude.
    - They have to believe that problems can be solved.
    - They must trust that they can come to agreement when resolving conflicts.
    - They need to have the intent to solve the problem, not to place blame, make excuses, or retaliate.
2. They must learn problem-solving and conflict-resolution skills. With adult support they can do the following:
    - They can manage their emotions and be assertive about their needs.
    - They can start to define problems and brainstorm potential solutions.
    - They can begin to make purposeful choices about which solution to try.
    - When a solution doesn't work, they have the initiative to go back and try the process again.

In this chapter, we're going to look at solution-based strategies for the four kinds of problems that come up most frequently when working with young children.

- When a child comes to you with a problem. For example, "I can't find my shoes."
- When you go to a child because you have a problem with them. For example, you see a child spill some water on the floor and walk away.
- When two kids are having a conflict with each other. We all know this one! Two children both want to use the same kickball or both want to be first in line at the drinking fountain.
- When you and a child's family are in conflict over a childrearing practice. For example, the parent dresses their daughter for school in her best clothing and wants you to keep her clean all day.

Regardless of the type of problem or conflict, the basic four steps will always be the same.

1. Find out what is wanted or needed.
2. Define the problem.

3. Brainstorm and choose a solution to try.
4. Check in to see if the solution worked.

Developing Problem Solving

"All day long I feel like I'm solving problems for the kids! This kid wants a red marker, that kid can't find his jacket, the other kid wants to know if there's room to play at the sticker project table," Alisha grumbled. "When are they going to learn to solve some of these little problems by themselves?"

"Little children, little problems. Big children, big problems." Today it's a problem about finding a red marker. In ten years, it will be a problem of what to do when someone offers her drugs. Just as a new skier starts learning on the bunny hill, where there is a minimum of risk, a new problem solver must start on the problem-solving bunny hill. It's only by practicing on low-risk problems like red markers and missing jackets that children develop the problem-solving skills they will need to tackle the major problems just around the corner. Children learn to solve problems the same way they learn everything else. They watch others, they practice and experiment, and eventually they master the skill. Some children master the skill very easily, while others require more direct instruction, scaffolding, or support to become proficient.

Teachers are especially fast and efficient problem solvers. As they multitask throughout their days, they solve dozens of children's problems, large and small. "Let me tie those for you," "There's an extra pencil on my desk; go get it," "Scoot over and make room for DeAndre."

The irony is that the skilled adult who least needs practice gets all the practice. Less skilled children, who most need practice, get fewer opportunities to practice solving daily problems. Give children opportunities to learn and practice problem solving on a three-year-old's problems to build the skills they'll need later for a five-year-old's problems, twelve-year-old's problems, teen's problems, and eventually, an adult's problems. How do we do this? Start by acknowledging that the child has a problem and turning it back on them to solve. When a child says she can't find a red marker, reply, "You want a red marker and can't find one. That's a problem."

"Clean up, clean up, everybody everywhere. Clean up, clean up, everybody do your share," the teacher chanted. Celina ignored the signal and continued to work with the blocks. "Time to cleanup," the teacher reminded her as she walked by. When the teacher looked a few moments later, Celina still hadn't begun to pick up. "Celina, did you hear me? Clean-up time," the teacher said as she walked over to the child. Now what?

It's not always easy to think of solutions for problems. Many of us are in the habit of thinking that if a child does something inappropriate, we should give consequences or punishments instead of using a problem-solving approach. Sometimes we think of offering rewards, but they're not solutions either. They are just the flip side of punishments.

Figuring out the difference between punishment and solution is not always easy when we are thinking of working with children's problems. It may help you to clarify your thoughts if we shift for a moment to the adult world.

Imagine that the gas gauge is broken in your car. You have already been late for work twice because you have run out of gas. Come up with three ways you could solve this problem.

1. ______________________________

2. ______________________________

3. ______________________________

Did you put yourself in time out or take away TV for a week? Probably not. Neither of those strategies would have solved the problem of running out of gas and being late for work.

The things you listed were probably genuine solutions to the problem. Maybe you thought to get the gas gauge fixed, take a bus to work, fill the tank up every night on the way home, or leave for work an hour earlier each day just in case. These solutions are ways to get done what needs to get done.

When we work toward solutions, we work toward ways to solve the problem and reach the intended goal. We don't look for ways to retaliate, punish, or blame someone for having a problem.

Look again at the exercise you did in chapter 1 when we compared strategies to teach children rhyming words and typical consequences for challenging behavior. We will be using that activity again now, so if you haven't done this exercise yet, you might want to do it before you read on any further.

Look at the interventions on the left side. Many of these are probably strategies to punish or "teach a lesson." Those interventions on the left are probably focused on an adult doing something to the child. Now look at the right side of the chart. Most of these are probably solutions to the problem. They are strategies intended to help the child overcome obstacles and learn the task at hand. These strategies are an attempt to work together in a supportive way to fix things.

"How can we solve this problem?" This sentence is one of the most magical things we can do for children to help them take responsibility for their own behavior. We don't need to write their name on the board, give check marks, or take away recess. What we need to do is help the child find a way to do what needs doing. We need to look for solutions rather than fall back on punishments.

Some of these approaches are summarized on the following chart.

PUNISHMENT	SOLUTION
Place blame	Take responsibility
Look back	Look forward
Pay for wrong	Fix things
Me against you	Support and mentor
Power and control	Cooperation

Na'Quan bit Manuel on the arm, hard enough to leave marks. "He got paint on my paper on purpose," he said through his sobs as he tried to explain his biting to the teacher.

"You can't come to my birthday," Arial spat out to Shastina after she refused to share the stickers. "And you're not my friend anymore. Daija's my best friend now and you can't play with us."

"Tae'Hun knocked down my blocks so I knocked down his blocks back," Celine said to the teacher. "He did it first."

"My daddy tell me if somebody hit me or call me names, I supposed to punch them back," said James to Mrs. Lewis.

You hurt me so I'll hurt you is common playground logic. Retaliation works on the belief that if a child can make the offender feel bad enough, they themselves will feel better and the offender might shape up. Most young children work on the theory that in order to get others to behave and cooperate, they need to use force, threat, exclusion, and other methods of coercion. Moving children from blame and retaliation to peaceful conflict resolution is one of the most challenging tasks facing caregivers of young children. "Go back and use your words," may work from time to time, but the skills required to resolve conflicts are very complex for young children. During the preschool years, children depend on adults to teach and facilitate the process.

"Triviana's mother doesn't want her to play in the sand anymore. She says it gets in her hair! For goodness sake, can't she just wash the child's hair in the tub at night?"

"Matthew is barely a year old and his grandma is insisting we sit him in the potty chair every hour! I gave her a flyer on appropriate potty training but she still insists on starting now."

"Shawna is dead tired after lunch and her momma refuses to let her nap here. The child keeps falling asleep, even when I sit her at the puzzles to keep her up. What am I supposed to do, wake her? That's crazy."

We've all been there. Families want us to do something with their child that just doesn't fit into our program or philosophy. Often, these conflicts can erode our relationships with families to the point that they withdraw from the program.

When we focus on the "practice" instead of on the underlying need or want, we can easily lose sight that we and the parents most often have compatible goals for children.

- When Triviana's teacher asked her mother to share why the sand was such a problem, she discovered that for some children, sand gets so embedded in braids or hair oil that it can be a day-long process to clean the child. Her teacher shared that Triviana loved playing in sand and that she learned science and math concepts in that area.
- Matthew's grandma said that in her culture, children were expected to be toilet trained by a year old and that everyone in her family for generations had done it that way. His teacher said that the center didn't usually begin training children until two years old, and she didn't want to make him sit on the potty if he cried and struggled to get off.
- Shawna's mom said that Shawna had trouble sleeping at night if she took a long nap during the day. The teacher let the mom know that Shawna was falling asleep whether or not she was put down for a nap.

Discovering needs and wants is the first step toward resolving the problem. As the teachers and families worked together to share their goals, beliefs, and problems, they were able to come to mutually acceptable solutions that worked for everyone.

Triviana's mother allowed her to play in the sand if the teachers made sure her head was covered with a scarf or cap. Matthew's teacher agreed to sit him on the potty as long as she could let Matthew up if he fussed or cried. Shawna's teacher and mother decided the child could sleep for up to half an hour and must be awake by three o'clock.

There may be times that families ask you to do something that is considered abuse or neglect by your state laws. Help the families understand the state laws and work to find another way to help families reach their goals for their children. If you suspect neglect or abuse in the home, follow your center guidelines and state laws for reporting the incident.

Let's use the four-step process now to revisit Celina and the blocks.

1. Find out what is wanted or needed.

   Before we can start thinking of solutions, we need more information about Celina. We know the problem from our point of view. It's clean-up time and she won't clean up. What we don't know yet is what Celina needs or wants. Seek first to understand.

   "Celina, you're still playing with the blocks. What is it that you want?" asked her teacher. "I didn't finish making the Barbie castle," Celina answered. "I still have to finish the top part here where she waves to the people."

2. Define the problem.

   Now that you know what Celina wants and why she is frustrated, can you begin to more clearly define the problem?

   At first, it might have appeared that Celina was being defiant or oppositional. Now we have more information and can understand that the problem is that Celina wasn't done with her work and work time was over. Clarifying the problem opens the door to finding solutions.

3. Brainstorm and choose a solution to try.

   Look again at Celina's problem about the blocks. She wasn't done with her project, and it was time to clean up to go outside. Think about the right side of the rhyming chart. What might you suggest as solutions to the block problem? Did you think of things like leaving her structure out to work on after the class comes back inside? Or putting a sign on the structure so nobody else uses those blocks? Maybe letting her stay inside while one teacher does lunch setup so Celina can finish her work. Giving her five more minutes to finish up. Or letting her get a couple of friends to help her finish building before going outside. These would all be possible solutions to the problem.

4. Check back to see if the solution worked.

Problem-Solving Roadblocks

The four steps of problem solving were easy to apply in Celina's case. Often, though, we might encounter roadblocks to the problem-solving process. These are some common roadblocks:

- Children (or adults) are so emotionally charged that they can't engage in problem solving.
- Even when they are calmed down, some children can't tell you what they need or want.
- Children often don't have the skills to define the problem or the conflict.
- Children have very little experience at solving problems and might need help to learn how to think of and choose solutions.
- Sometimes, solutions don't work!

Help Children Calm Down

Kids might be so emotionally charged that they can't even begin to engage in the problem-solving process. Before they can start, they need to move from their emotional state to a thinking state.

When faced with a problem or a conflict, the first natural reaction is an emotional one such as fear, anxiety, frustration, disappointment, hurt, denial, or justification. Problem solving is a "thinking" process involving the cerebral cortex portion of the brain. When children are in a highly charged emotional state, the thinking part of the brain goes on vacation while the "emotional brain" takes charge. The first step, then, is to use self-regulation skills to move from an emotionally charged state of mind to a thinking state of mind. Until children are proficient at these skills, they will need a lot of support from adults to calm themselves down enough to begin to think about problems and solutions.

Help children regain control by listening, acknowledging, and reflecting back their feelings. Refer back to the chapters on attachment (p. 37) and on self-regulation (p. 105) for specific language and approaches for validating children's emotions and helping them move into an internally organized state of mind.

Teach Assertive Language

Even when they are calmed down, some children can't tell you what they need or want.

As children move into their thinking mode, the next step is to begin to clarify the problem. A problem or conflict exists when the child has a want or need that isn't getting met. To be able to express that need effectively, the child must develop assertive language.

Many classroom problems can be traced to children's lack of assertion skills. Assertion is somewhere in the middle of a continuum that runs from passive on one end to aggressive on the other. When there are problems or conflicts, children may respond from anywhere along that spectrum. Typically, a child will use one of these three communication strategies regardless of the problem at hand.

Children who use a passive approach can be exploited or bullied by others. They allow more aggressive children to get their own way and may be reluctant to express opinions or preferences. Children who use an aggressive approach frequently get into physical confrontations with others. They may be described as all-about-me or selfish and self-centered people.

Children at both ends of the spectrum need help to develop assertion skills. Assertive children neither bully nor are the victims of bullying behavior. When children use assertion, they are neither afraid to state their preferences and limits, nor do they run over the rights of others. Assertion balances needs of self with needs of others.

APPROACH	LOOKS LIKE/SOUNDS LIKE
Passive	"Whatever you want." Just gives up and retreats.
Assertive	"This is how I feel and what I want." Open to hearing what the other party to the conflict feels and wants.
Aggressive	"My way or the highway." "Give it to me or else." Might refuse to negotiate or use physical means to get what they want.

It's as important to teach limit-setting language to children who use a passive approach as it is to do social-skills training for children who are more physically or psychologically aggressive. It can be difficult to avoid the trap of "rescuing" passive children. Because they don't stand up for themselves, adults often jump in to enforce their rights and set boundaries for them. If Kianna grabs a doll from Geoff and Geoff allows it, a teacher who witnesses the scuffle might step in and tell Kianna to return the doll. Without support to develop assertion, a child who is victimized in this classroom is likely to become a child who is victimized in many different settings. Passive female children are at particular risk of becoming victims of abuse later in life. Help passive children learn assertion to set boundaries now by teaching all children how to use assertive language to state their needs, assert their rights and set boundaries for others. Later in this chapter, you'll find language and strategies to support passive children.

Help Define the Problem

Even when children can state what they want and need, young kids have trouble defining problems. Defining a problem requires seeing two sides to the story, and young children are developmentally at an egocentric stage. They can only see a problem from their point of view. It's often up to the adult to look at the clues and to make their best guess as to what the problem is really about.

THE CLUES	THE PROBLEM IS . . .
Gabriel is arguing with Kyrha over who will use the wagon.	Two kids want to use the same wagon.
Shay is crying when his mother leaves for work.	Shay wants to stay with his mom and can't because she has to go to work.
Jeana tears up her paper and dumps the markers on the floor when her picture of her dog isn't turning out the way she wants it to.	Jeana wants to draw her dog and is not able to make it look the way she wants it to.

Notice that in each case the problem is defined in neutral language that doesn't make assumptions about who is at fault or invalidate children's strong feelings.

Help Children Choose Solutions

Help children begin to brainstorm possible solutions. First graders and older usually like to generate a long list of possible solutions before moving on to the next step of choosing the solution. Younger kids do much better when we combine the two steps. Each time a solution is proposed, move on to evaluate the solution and decide whether to try it. If the solution is discarded for some reason, think up another solution.

Some common solutions to young children's problems include sharing, trading, waiting, getting a duplicate item, leaving, finding something else to do, getting adult help, making amends, and fixing what went wrong. While these are common solutions, children are amazingly inventive and often think of solutions far out of the ordinary that work out just fine. For example, two children may decide that they will both wash the baby doll at the same time, one washing the head end while the other washes the feet end. If both children agree, be willing to try it out.

Be wary of deciding that a proposed solution isn't "fair" until you hear what the children think of it. For example, suppose that Ella took the red truck from Ivan, who was playing with it. In the problem-solving session, Ella might propose that she gets to play with the truck as a solution. This might not seem fair to an adult, since Ella took the truck from Ivan to start with. But we don't know what Ivan's truth is. He might have been done with the truck, or not care very much about playing with it. He might be willing to let Ella have it once he feels that justice has been served through the problem-solving process. If Ivan says he doesn't want to let go of the truck, then the adult can support him and Ella in finding another solution. But if Ivan is happy with Ella's solution, it's not up to the adult to decide that it isn't "fair."

What if you are concerned that Ivan is afraid of speaking up to Ella, that he really wants the truck but will concede just to keep the peace? Of course you can coach Ivan to use assertive language with Ella (see above). But in the end, Ivan is the only one who can decide when it's worth asserting himself. If adults decide for him, he may never come to the point of saying, "No," or asking for what he wants. If the class models assertion and problem solving over and over, eventually children like Ivan find their own voices.

Nonetheless, not every solution a child suggests will be acceptable or feasible. Help children evaluate whether a solution is a good choice or a poor choice.

- The solution must fit in with the community's guiding principles of behavior.
- The solution must be doable.
- The solution must be helpful and not hurtful.
- The solution must solve the problem, not make anyone pay for having a problem.

When a problem is a conflict of the needs of two kids, have the children check out their suggestion with the other child. Keep the children checking with each other until they find a solution that works for both of them. There is an example on page 203 that shows what conflict resolution might look like between two children with a teacher facilitating.

Evaluate the Solution

Some solutions work and some don't. When they do, give children descriptive feedback to focus their attention on how the process worked. For example, say, "You wiped up that water and took care of us and our stuff! You figured out a good solution."

When a solution doesn't work, simply guide the child through the process again. For example, perhaps a child has been noisy at rest time and has suggested moving her nap mat to the other side of the room. After the move, you find the child has found a new audience and is still chatting. Say, "Oops. Moving your nap mat didn't work. Let's find another solution to try."

Punishment

Maybe you are thinking now that if we don't punish children then we are allowing them to get away with things. Recall, for a moment, the building blocks for the strength of problem solving. We want children to believe that problems can be solved without blame or retaliation, and we want them to learn the skills they need to solve problems.

Punishment is an attempt to get a child to pay for undesirable behavior. Our practice of punishment and retaliation shows children that these are viable solutions when there are problems.

Let's look at another unintended message we send when we use threats of punishment with children. What we are really saying to the child is, "You have a choice not to comply if you are willing to pay the consequence." Seen in this light, perhaps it's when we do punish children that we let them get away with things. It's when we say, "How are you going to solve this problem?" that they take ownership of their behavior.

This willingness to pay the price of punishment differentiates our difficult kids from our "easy" kids. Typical children will understand the threat to mean, "Don't do that." Challenging kids hear us giving them a choice. They can either comply or they can pay a price. They weigh whether the price we have put on hitting is a price they are willing to pay and often purposefully choose the consequence over being socially appropriate. Is that the message we intend to send with our threat?

Someone told me recently of a friend who loves to drive fast. Every year or so he gets a speeding ticket, which he refers to as his "license to speed." He's more than willing to pay this price to drive the way he wants to drive. Many corporations use the same reasoning, preferring to pay fines as the price for violating expensive environmental or labor laws. When they look at the bottom line, it's more cost effective to ignore guidelines and pay the fine than it is to comply.

The problem-solving approach comes from a different perspective. Instead of asking if the child is willing to pay the price for making poor choices, problem solving says, "This needs doing. Let's figure out how to get it done." The problem-solving approach doesn't even entertain the notion that something mandatory might not be done, because once we do that, we have told the child it is optional.

Using a problem-solving approach, we might say to a child, "It looks like you're having trouble staying quiet at rest time. How do you think you can get that job done?"

The problem-solving method passes along an important life skill. We don't want to raise a generation of adults who are willing to be antisocial and pay the price for it. We want a generation of adults who can figure out how to take care of business even when it's not a convenient or pleasurable choice. Examine your own life for a moment. Is there a dry-erase board in the break room at work where you write your name when you mess up? Probably not. Do you have someone following you around to reward you with stickers when you hang the towel back on the rack? I doubt it.

Successful adults have figured out the process of "it's a challenge but how am I gonna get it done?" We have alarm clocks to wake us up. We close the office door when we have a report due. We get an exercise buddy to encourage us to work out regularly. These are all "how are you gonna get it done" strategies—life skills. Begin now to build that same attitude in the kids that you teach. Instill in children the belief that all problems can be resolved, and teach them the skills they need to make that belief a reality.

Supportive Interactions

Many young children quickly learn how to solve their own problems such as wiping up spills or finding materials and supplies. Resolving conflicts with others, however, is much more complex. Most young children need a lot of support and guidance from adults to solve those kinds of problems peacefully. Convey your belief that problems can be resolved. Help children stay mindful of expectations and limits of acceptable behavior. As you interact with children, make sure to model and use all the skills needed for problem solving and conflict resolution often.

Model Cooperative Language

When children are uncooperative, perhaps it's because parents and teachers have failed to create an environment in which children are truly involved in creating plans, making choices, and brainstorming solutions. Many children have more practice protecting their sense of self through resistance and rebellion than through self-control and cooperation. Model cooperation rather than aggression, bribery, threats, or control in your own interactions with children throughout the day.

INSTEAD OF SAYING . . .	TRY SAYING . . .
"Do it because I said so."	"Let's figure this out together."
"Whoever cleans up fastest gets to be line leader."	"Let's see how fast we can work together to get the room cleaned up."
"You took them out so you put them back or you don't get to use them again."	"Let's help Bianca put the blocks away. She needed to use so many for the airport she made, and she needs some help."

"That's a Problem"

Get out of the habit of solving children's little problems. Instead, turn those problems back to them with the phrase "That's a problem." Avoid giving children suggestions on how to solve their problem unless they are truly stuck.

WHEN A CHILD SAYS . . .	TRY SAYING . . .
"I can't find my shoe."	"Wow. That's a real problem."
"The paintbrush fell on the floor and there's paint all over the place."	"Uh, oh. You have a real problem."
"Is it my job to be snack helper?"	"Hmmm. You don't remember your job. That's a problem. I wonder how you might find out what your job is?"

Lying

Tooth fairies, Easter bunnies, cartoon characters, and wishes on birthday candles—the lines of reality and fantasy are still blurred for preschool-age children. "If I say it is so, and I wish it were so, then it becomes so," is truth for children at this age. Yes, Deanna hit Brady on the head with a shovel. But when she is asked, she can say, "No, I didn't hit him," and mean it. She believes that if she said she didn't hit him, then she can rewrite the past.

When you know a child was responsible for a particular event, instead of asking whether they were responsible, begin with the mutual assumption that they were.

INSTEAD OF SAYING . . .	TRY SAYING . . .
"Did you grab that toy from Connie?"	"Tell me what happened about the toy."
"Did you spill that water?"	"Uh, oh. I see the water spilled. Let's find the paper towels to clean it up."
"Did you finish cleaning the home living area?"	"Let's go to the home living area to check it out."
"Did you knock over the bookshelf?"	"I see you knocked over the bookshelf. You must have been pretty angry."

Coach Assertive Language

Both passive and aggressive children need to learn language of assertion. Whether a child uses aggressive or passive behavior, you can use these teachable moments to help children learn assertive responses.

WHEN . . .	CHILDREN CAN SAY . . .
A child is being controlled by another child	"I don't want you to help. I'll do it myself."
A child is the object of name-calling or profanity	"I don't like those words. Stop it."
A child is being bullied	"I don't like that. I'm going to play with somebody else."
Someone is grabbing a toy from them	"Stop it. Ask for a turn."

Scaffold Assertive Language

When you give children assertive language, you may have to tailor your response depending on how passive the child is. For example:

- You might say, "Did you like when Kianna took the doll?" If John says no, say, "Go tell Kianna, 'Stop, I don't like it when you grab.'"
- You might say, "John, it's okay to tell Kianna you were still using the doll," or "John, do you need help to get the doll back?"
- If John tends to talk softly and avoid eye contact, have him rehearse his "strong voice" with you. Model and practice a firm yet respectful tone of voice and assertive body language.
- Provide your own physical support if the child needs it. Get down to John's level, put your arm around him, call Kianna, and say, "Kianna, John has something to tell you." Then say to John, "Tell her 'I was still using the doll. Give it back please.'"

Break down assertive language into baby steps. Some children need to start with very simple assertive language while others are ready for more sophisticated language.

	TEACH	INCLUDES . . .	FOR EXAMPLE
FIRST	"Stop" or "No."	A single word to set a boundary	"Stop."
SECOND	"I don't like that."	Expression of a feeling	"I don't like that."
THIRD	"I don't like it when you (behavior)."	Expression of feeling as a result of the action of another	"I don't like when you call me names."
FOURTH	"I don't like it when you (behavior). I want you to (suggestion for change)," or "I don't like it when you (behavior). I'm going to (action)."	Expression of feelings, the action of another, and a suggestion for change or action	"I don't like when you call me names. I'm going to play with somebody else."

Walking away can be an assertive skill. Model it for children, and coach them on how to leave a bad situation with a feeling of strength and control. Emphasize leaving as a sign of strength and wisdom instead of a feeling of intimidation, defeat, weakness, or shame.

Model Assertive Language

Of course, one of the most powerful tools you have to teach assertive language and behavior is to model it yourself in your daily interactions with children.

WHEN A CHILD . . .	INSTEAD OF . . .	TRY SAYING . . .
Calls you a name	Sending the child to time out	"I don't like those words. I'm going to walk away right now."
Talks while you are trying to read a story	Saying, "That's so rude to talk while I'm reading."	"When you talk I have trouble reading. I wish you could be more quiet."
Calls another child a rude name	Saying, "Be nice."	"When you call Passion names, I wonder what you are trying to say. Let's see what's wrong and find another way to say that."
Grabs a toy from another child	Grabbing the toy back and returning it to the child	"I don't like it when you grab toys. We take care of people in our classroom. I want you to give the squirter back to Dana."

Reword Profanity

Some children use profanity to express their strong feelings. Children are much more likely to cooperate when they are feeling heard and understood. By listening and reflecting a child's feelings, and supporting the child's right to have those feelings, children can see us as allies rather than opponents. Listening skills and compassion says to children, "Yes, you are very distressed and that is understandable. Let's work together to help you move forward."

Help children find descriptive feeling words to use instead of profanity to express strong emotions. For example:

INSTEAD OF USING . . .	TEACH THEM TO SAY . . .
Profanity for frustration	"This is too hard for me."
Profanity for disappointment	"I wanted to do that."
Profanity for hurt feelings	"I didn't like when he said that."

When you say, "You look so angry," or "I see your tears. I bet you're very sad about something," you acknowledge that the child's message has been heard and understood. This can be one of the most effective ways to help children pass through the "acting out" part of their emotions.

Bad Timing

Problems can come up at inconvenient times. Sometimes you will be in the midst of other pressing issues and won't be able to help a child immediately.

That happens often in our adult life. You may be at work and a friend calls in distress. Your break starts in fifteen minutes. What might you say? Perhaps, "I hear you're really upset. I can't get away right now, but I can spend some time with you in about fifteen minutes. I'm so sorry. Can you wait?" The language you would use to convey caring and respect for a friend while still setting limits is the same language you would use with a child. "I can see you are frustrated about something. It'll take about ten more minutes to finish this lesson, and then I'll come and help you. You can go over to the book corner or the aquarium if that would help you hang on until I can get to you."

Parameters of Solutions

Not every solution can work. Often certain "givens" must be taken into account when thinking of a solution. For example, if children are fussing over who gets to use the wagon, they might suggest that the school buy another wagon. While that may be a potential long-term solution, it doesn't address the fact that right now there is only one wagon.

If children are coming up with many unworkable solutions, clarify the problem by defining some of the parameters.

ACCEPT THE FEELING . . .	SET THE PARAMETERS . . .
"You wish you could take that bike from Kyrha."	"Kyrha is going to use that bike for now. Let's find another way to solve the problem."
"I know you want to be with your Mommy."	"It's Mommy's time to go to work and your time to go to school. Let's figure out something for you to do while you are here."
"Drawing a dog is hard for you right now."	"Markers need to stay on the table. Is there something I can do to help you with your drawing?"

School Behavior vs. Home Expectations

Sometimes, the way problems are solved at home might be different than the way problems are solved in the classroom. Perhaps at home siblings are encouraged to "fight it out" when they have conflicts. In some homes, family members might find it hard to tolerate children's sadness, and they may bend their rules in an effort to get children to stop crying. Some family members may throw or break things when they are angry or frustrated. Remind children of the way things are done at school with the phrase "At school . . ." to help children think of appropriate solutions.

WHEN . . .	"AT SCHOOL . . ."
Children physically fight over a bike.	"At school we use words, not hands, to solve problems."
Children cry to intimidate adults into meeting their demands.	"At school, the rules stay the same, even when children cry."
Children act helpless to get adults to do tasks for them.	"At school, (zipping, flushing, drawing, pouring, and so on) is a kid job."

Model Guiding Principles

"Do what I say, not what I do" does not work with young children. Children learn best by watching others and using others as models. They observe carefully as the adults in their lives deal with children's frustration, disappointment, and conflict. They also pay careful attention to how their adult caregivers respond to their own feelings and conflicts. Be the kind of person you want your children to be. Demonstrate your own personal commitment to upholding your class's guiding principles of behavior in everything you say and do.

There is a discussion about the role of guiding principles of behavior for self-regulation in chapter 4. These guiding principles can also be woven into the problem-solving process to help set the parameters for acceptable solutions.

WHEN THE CHILD . . .	WEAVE IN THE GUIDING PRINCIPLE . . .
Wants to grab a bike from another child	"You wish you had that bike. At school, we can't just grab things because we take care of others. Let's find another way to solve this."
Cries for his mama	"You miss your mama so much. Let's see how we can help you because at school we take care of ourselves."
"Borrows" things from school without asking	"You would love to take this toy to your house. We take care of our stuff at school, so we'll leave it here to play with tomorrow. Let's find something that you can take home with you."
Hits a child to get she wants	"We take care of others at school. If the kids won't listen to your words, come get me and I'll help you."
Throws markers on the floor because he's frustrated by not being able to draw a dog	"You can't draw that dog the way you want. At school, we keep markers on the table because we take care of our stuff. Let's see if there is some way to help you."

Brainstorm Solutions

It's important that we guide children to begin to think of their own solutions to problems. Use coaching and encouraging language to help children think of potential solutions.

- What are you going to do?
- Tell me some ideas.
- How could you solve this problem?
- What could you do now that is helpful?
- What could you do to solve your problem?

Sometimes children might not come up with possible solutions. For some children, it's because they are new at the skill. Others are used to having adults solve things and they are just waiting for the ax to fall. And still others have learned to avoid taking responsibility by letting adults take on the entire burden. As tempting as it is to jump in, save time, and solve the problem yourself, control your impulses. Children will only learn the process by stretching and practicing.

IF . . .	TRY . . .	SOUNDS LIKE . . .
The child is very new at brainstorming solutions	Give a choice between two acceptable solutions.	"You have a choice. You can get another book or find another area to play in right now. What will you choose?" "Would you rather do (this) or (that)?" "What would be better for you? (This) or (that)?"
	If the dispute is over space or stuff, common preschool solutions are to share or take turns. When children are first practicing solutions, propose one or both of these strategies whenever you can.	"Some kids decide to take turns with the shovel. Other kids like to find a way to play with shovels together."
When a child has had ample experience brainstorming solutions	Encourage the child to find a peer to help.	"Would you like to find another friend to help you think?" "Who might know?" "Who can you ask?"
	Help the child break through their block.	"Pretend you're a kid who has an idea. What would you say?"

Use a Solution-Based Redirection Script

Use this very simple, three-step script when redirecting children. The goal is solution, not punishment.

1. Identify child's needs or wants.
2. Define the problem.
3. Help the child find a solution.

Let's look at this script in closer detail.

1. Identify child's needs or wants. Reflect your understanding of the child's point of view. When the child hears that you understand their perspective, you have put yourself in the role of an understanding mentor instead of an arbitrary dictator. An easy way to word this step is to begin with "You wish" or "You want." For example:

   - "You want to use the magnifier."
   - "You were in a hurry."
   - "You wish we didn't have rest time at school."

2. Define the problem. Clarify the conflict between the child's behavior, want, or need and the existing situation. Keep the message short, sweet, and clear. Use the word *and* to connect the two parts of the sentence. For example:

   - "You want to use the magnifier *and* Blossom is using it."
   - "You were in a hurry *and* you knocked the chair over."
   - "You wish we didn't have rest time at school *and* that's what's next on our picture schedule."

Notice how the examples used the word *and* instead of *but.* For instance, "You wanted to choose our story book *and* I let Harold choose one today" instead of "You wanted to choose our story book *but* I let Harold choose one today." The use of *and* is intentional. When we use the word *but,* we are trivializing the first part of the sentence. In this case, that would be the child's feelings. The use of the word *and* conveys the message that the child's feelings are as important as the limit or expectation.

3. Help the child find a solution by saying something such as these:

   - What can you do now?
   - What's your plan to solve this?

Some children will need prompts to help them find solutions. Over time, they will need less help.

- Give a choice: "Would you like to ask Blossom for a turn or do you want to get another magnifier from the science shelf?"
- Guide the child to undo the harm: "Uh oh. Do you think you can pick that chair up all by yourself?"
- Redirect: "Come, I'll help you find a book, and we'll bring it to your rest mat," or "Let's go to the water table now, and I'll get you when there is a magnifier to use."

Fortunately, the three steps are much simpler to use in practice than to read on a page. Here are some examples of how it might look in your classroom. Each of the three steps are marked:

- "Bruce, (1) you're so hungry you rushed to snack *and* (2) you forgot to wash your hands. (3) How can you fix that?"
- "(1) You wanted to get a swing *and* (2) you pushed Barbie down while you were running. (3) Come help me see if she's okay.
- "(1) You're having fun throwing the foam blocks *and* (2) those blocks are just for building. (3) Would you like to toss beanbags into the clown mouth with Diana, or do you want to wait to throw balls when we go outside?"

Classroom Culture

Give children props, prompts, space, and your guidance so that they can practice and develop problem solving. The more often you guide children through the problem solving steps, the sooner they will begin to use the steps on their own.

Problem-Solving Center

A problem-solving center in the classroom is visual and concrete evidence that problem solving is valued.

The requirements for a problem-solving center are few. It might be a small table with two chairs or a corner with a beanbag chair. The wall might have photos or drawings of children talking out their differences. Most problem-solving centers also have pictures and words to help guide the process. One example is the chart below:

PROBLEM-SOLVING STEPS
1. What do I want? What do you want?
2. What can we do?
3. What did we decide?
4. How did it work?

Peer Mediators

Once the group has learned the conflict-resolution method, children can learn to be peer mediators. Even children as young as four years old can guide their classroom peers through the process. It is helpful to have a problem-solving center or table set up when using peer mediators, since the environmental cues help keep the children on track.

- If a child wants the job as a peer mediator, let him join you for a few conflict resolutions with other children, and coach them through the mediator process.
- When a simple conflict comes up between two children and you are too busy to handle the problem, ask the children involved if they would like a peer mediator to help.
- Have the three children go to the problem-solving center to work on the problem. Most four-year-old peer mediators use a rather free-flowing facilitation style, which is fine.
- If the children still can't resolve the conflict, make an appointment with them to help out as soon as you have a moment. If they do resolve the conflict, congratulate the three children for their productive work.

Tattling

Tattling is a tricky topic. On the one hand, we encourage children to solve their problems with words instead of hands. On the other, when children feel unable to resolve conflict peacefully, we call their attempts to get adult support "tattling." We work hard to form a classroom community where everyone looks out for the welfare of each other. And yet we call it "tattling" when they warn us that another child is not following community guidelines. To get a better grip on tattling, shift for a moment to the adult world.

- You're at a stoplight and somebody rams into your car from behind. What do you do?
- You're at work and someone persists in making suggestive comments to you even after you have told them to stop. What do you do?
- A child in your room is still biting other children, even after you have done everything you know how to do to help her stop. What do you do?
- You witness a mother beating her child with a belt in the parking lot. What do you do?

An important life skill we develop is to know when we can handle a situation alone and when to seek help and support from others. When you call a police officer, talk to a supervisor about harassment, refer a child to the school counselor, or call child protective services, you are demonstrating wisdom in seeking support. Allow children to develop the same trust and interdependence by supporting their efforts to seek help when they feel unable to handle a situation themselves.

Young children lack the wisdom and life experience to distinguish dangerous from nondangerous behavior. Children who are victims of adult abuse are often threatened by their abusers to keep it a secret. Instead of asking children to make judgment calls they lack the maturity to make, encourage children to report incidents that trouble them, whether they are participants, victims, or witnesses.

While we want children to feel free to come to us with their concerns, we don't want to encourage "getting others in trouble" as a way to get attention. A simple way to handle all incidents of tattling is to have an automatic and scripted response such as the following.

IF A CHILD REPORTS . . .	TRY SAYING . . .
An incident in which they are involved—e.g., "He won't let me get on the slide."	"Do you need help solving this?" If the child says yes, you can move into problem solving or conflict resolution.
An incident involving other children—e.g., "Kim won't let Dallas get on the slide."	"Thank you." If the child pushes for a greater response, you might say, "I'm taking it under consideration."

If you decide to intervene with Kim and Dallas, avoid referring to the child who reported the incident.

INSTEAD OF SAYING . . .	TRY SAYING . . .
"Kim, Dow said you won't let Dallas use the slide."	"Dallas, it looks like you're trying to use the slide. Is there a problem?"

Conflict Resolution in Action

1. Regain emotional control—Allow each child to briefly talk and be heard about the issues so they can move from their emotional state to their thinking state.

   • Listen, but don't get involved in the backstory.

   • End this exchange by saying, "What is it that you want?"

Here is a sample script:

Mr. R: Okay, you guys. It looks like we have a problem here. Shanae, you talk first and then Tre'vone it will be your turn.

Shanae: I was doing the computer game and I was winning, and Tre'vone came over and he pulled me and made me lose.

2. Assert needs and wants.

Mr. R: Uh huh. So what do you want? *(During conflict resolution, Mr. R focused not on what happened but on what happens next.)*

Shanae: Tre'vone needs to go away and leave me alone.

Mr. R: Okay. Tre'vone, tell me what's going on.

Tre'vone: Yesterday you told me I could do computer after circle and I was supposed to do it, and she sat down fast and started to play and it's my turn so I made her stop.

Mr. R: Okay. So what is that that you want now?

Tre'vone: I want to do my turn.

3. Define the problem or the conflict.

   • Make a neutral statement such as this: "It looks like two children both want____________."

- Clarify any "At school . . ." rules or guiding principles that might apply to the situation.

MR. R: *(Trying to put together what both kids want and form a neutral problem statement)* So, it looks like two kids both want to be the one to have a turn at the computer now. Is that right?

TRE'VONE: It's my turn.

SHANAE: I was using it first.

MR. R: So two kids both think it's their turn. Is that right?

(The children agree.)

MR. R: So let's work together to solve this so that everyone is okay. Remember, at school we take care of each other and we take care of ourselves *(two of their classroom guiding principles of behavior)*, so we need to make sure that this works out for both kids.

4. Brainstorm solutions and predict the consequences of the solution on self, others, and the environment. Then select a solution to try.

- Have the children suggest solutions.
- Guide children to talk to each other at this stage.
- If kids are stuck, try saying something like, "I once knew some kids who decided to___________." *(When giving children suggestions, it most often works best to just have a memory of a past time and relate the story without directly suggesting to the children. Often, after another moment or two, one of the children will repeat the suggestion as their own.)*

MR. R: I wonder what you guys can think of that we can do now.

SHANAE: He needs to let me finish first.

MR. R: Ask Tre'vone if that would be all right.

SHANAE: Let me finish, okay?

TRE'VONE: No. You'll use all the time and I won't get a turn, and Mr. R said I could do it today.

MR. R: Nope, that idea won't work for Tre'vone. Let's think of another idea.

TRE'VONE: *(To Shanae)* Let me go first then you can have it back tomorrow.

Shanae: No. I was going first. You use it too long and I never get a turn.

Mr. R: Nope, that's not okay with Shanae. Let's keep thinking.

Shanae: *(Folding her arms)* Tre'vone won't let me do my turn. He never lets anybody do computer except him.

Mr. R: We'll keep thinking until we find something that works for everybody. You know, a few years ago some kids had a problem like this. And they decided to use the timer from the cooking center so both kids had time that day.

Shanae: We could use the timer.

Mr. R: Ask Tre'vone if that would be okay.

Shanae: Tre'vone, we could use the timer and then we both could have a turn.

Tre'vone: Okay. But I need to go first.

(Shanae did not respond.)

Mr. R: Shanae, Tre'vone said the timer would work for him if he can go first. He's waiting to see if that is okay with you.

Shanae: Okay, but I need to get a turn too.

5. Select and implement one solution.

- Commit to finding a solution where both children agree.
- Congratulate the children for finding a solution.

Mr. R: So, you guys will get the timer and each take a turn this morning. Do you need my help to figure out how much time to set?

Shanae: Yeah. You make sure I get time too.

Mr. R: Okay with you, Tre'vone?

Tre'vone: Yeah. I wanna go now. She can do the timer.

Mr. R: You guys figured out how to solve the problem. You took care of yourselves, and you took care of each other. *(Mr. R and Shanae went off to take care of the timer while Tre'vone went to the computer to start his turn.)*

Not every classroom problem calls for conflict resolution. Perhaps you saw one child push another out of the way at the swings. There's nothing wrong with moving in and resolving the issue then and there.

The biggest reason for using conflict resolution is to help children learn how to do the process. Use conflict resolution during teachable moments of the day when you have the time and space to do. The easiest and best conflicts to practice on are conflicts over space and stuff. For example, two children both want to use the red bucket or two children both want to be the line leader at the door.

USE CONFLICT RESOLUTION WHEN . . .	DON'T USE CONFLICT RESOLUTION WHEN . . .
You don't care how it gets solved.	You want the situation resolved your way.
You have space and time to work through the process.	You are rushed or too busy with other things.
Children are using the "thinking part" of their brains.	Children are in an emotionally charged state.

Problem-Solving Activities

Solution Wheel

A solution wheel is a quick reminder of some generic solutions to problems.

1. Draw a large circle on a piece of paper, and cut it into eight pie sections.
2. In each section, write down one generic technique used to solve young children's problems. Some ideas are share, trade, get another one, wait for a turn, play something else, fix what you broke, say 'I'm sorry,' and go to the problem-solving table to solve it.
3. You might remind kids of this resource when they come to you with a conflict and have them choose a solution from it.
4. Some teachers make small copies of the circle and glue it on posterboard cards with a spinner. The kids are then invited to spin the spinner to find a possible solution to their problem.

Some teachers let children spin the wheel over and over until it lands on a choice the child wants. Others just let the child choose from the available choices.

Discussion/Reflection Questions

1. Make a neutral problem statement for each of these situations. Start your statement with "It looks like two kids both . . ."

- Johnisha and Neil are physically struggling over a book in the library center.
- Ian comes to group time and sits next to the teacher. Wilbur approaches and tells Ian he was sitting there first but he had to wash his hands and Pablo was saving his seat. Ian says that he's sitting there and he's not moving and that once you get up you lose your seat.
- Maritza is absent today. Her job was to clean the guinea pig cage. Adrian decides to do her job at job time and begins to get the supplies. Meanwhile, Mychael has decided the same and tells Adrian he thought of it first. Mychael begins to open the cage to move the guinea pig to the carrier. Adrian yells for Mychael to go away because he was there first.

2. For each of the scenarios above, select one of the children and give examples of one line of dialogue for that child if the child were (a) passive, (b) assertive, or (c) aggressive.
3. For each of the scenarios above, what might be an example of a punishment that a teacher might impose? What is one way that the children might resolve the conflict without punishment?

Exercises

1. Try to use the conflict-resolution process with children four or five times. Did you find it hard not to get involved in the backstory? What did you find challenging? What went well? How did the children respond?
2. Try the "That's a problem" technique consistently for a week. Did you notice any changes in the children?

Reflection/Journal Assignment

Where are you on the passive-assertive-aggressive continuum? Do you have a consistent style, or does it vary depending on whom you are with? What impact has your style had on your professional life? Your personal life?

Resources

Bailey, Becky. 2000. *Conscious discipline: Seven basic skills for brain smart classroom management.* Oviedo, FL: Loving Guidance.

Brooks, Robert, and Sam Goldstein. 2001. *Raising resilient children.* Chicago: Contemporary Books.

Committee for Children. 1997. *Second step: A violence prevention curriculum.* Seattle: Committee for Children.

Covey, Stephen. 1997. *The seven habits of highly effective families: Building a beautiful family culture in a turbulent world.* New York: Golden Books.

Dinkmeyer, Don, and Gary D. McKay. 1973. *Raising a responsible child: Practical steps to successful family relationships.* New York: Simon and Schuster.

Fisher, Robert, Bruce Patton, and Robert Ury. 1991. *Getting to yes: Negotiating agreement without giving in.* New York: Penguin Books.

Gestwicki, Carol. 1999. *Developmentally appropriate practice: Curriculum and development in early education.* Albany, NY: Delmar Publishers.

Gordon, Thomas. 1970. *P.E.T.: Parent effectiveness training: The tested new way to raise responsible children.* New York: Peter H. Wyden, Inc.

Hewitt, Deborah. 1995. *So this is normal too?* St. Paul: Redleaf Press.

Koralek, Derry. 1999. *For now and forever: A guide for families on promoting social and emotional development.* Lewisville, NC: Kaplan Press.

Levin, Diane E. 1994. *Teaching young children in violent times: Building a peaceable classroom: A preschool–grade three violence prevention and conflict resolution guide.* Cambridge, MA: Educators for Social Responsibility.

Mize, Jacquelyn, and Ellen Abell. 1996. Encouraging social skills in young children: Tips teachers can share with parents. *Dimensions of Early Childhood* 24 (3). http:/www.humsci.auburn.edu/parent/socialskills.html.

National Association for the Education of Young Children. 1988. Ideas that work with young children. Avoiding "Me against you" discipline. *Young Children* 44:24–29.

Nelson, Jane, Lynn Lott, and H. Stephen Glenn. 2000. *Positive discipline in the classroom: Developing mutual respect, cooperation, and responsibility in your classroom.* 3rd ed. Roseville, CA: Prima Publishing.

Saifer, Steffan. 2003. *Practical solutions to practically every problem: The early childhood teacher's manual.* Rev. ed. St. Paul: Redleaf Press

Whelan, Mary Steiner. 2000. *But they spit, scratch, and swear! The do's and don'ts of behavior guidance with school-age children.* Minneapolis: A-ha! Communications.

8

Respect

"I have unique gifts and challenges, and so do others."

At the end of each day, Ms. C helped the children reflect upon their day at school. "Jackie," Ms. C said. "Tell me what you are proud of today." "I proud of that I share the paint and I listen to the story," Jackie answered quickly. Jackie is a child who can easily reflect upon her day and identify times she has demonstrated positive behaviors. She believes herself to be a good person generally, and each day she adds evidence to support this belief.

"I'm an expert at riding the red bike," volunteered AJ when the teacher led the children in making an "Expert Chart." "How about you, Lexi?" the teacher asked. "What are you an expert at? What can you help other children with in our class?" "I don't know," Lexi answered. "Well, I know you like to draw pictures of your dog Max. Do you think you might be our class expert at drawing dogs?" Lexi broke into a big smile. "I can draw the goodest dogs."

Children like AJ and Lexi are able to identify strengths and talents, sometimes independently and other times with adult support and guidance. They learn to recognize and take pride in their skills and accomplishments.

"What you wearin' that hat for, Hanif?" Ryker asked. "Boys 'posed to wear it.

My daddy say so," Hanif answered. "My daddy don't say so," Ryker replied. Their teacher, Samantha, heard the exchange and came over. "In Hanif's family, boys wear those kinds of hats. In Ryker's family, boys don't wear those kinds of hats. Each family decides what the boys will wear and it's all right." "Okay, I'm gonna wear the cowboy hat, and Hanif can wear his family hat," Ryker said, and the two boys ran off to play.

What Does Respect Look Like?

Children who respect themselves and others

- Recognize and appreciate their own gifts and challenges.
- Recognize and appreciate others' gifts.

Children first develop respect by carefully observing the qualities of the significant adults in their lives. Because they desire to be like the grown-ups around them, they begin to take on those qualities as their own. By being the person you wish children to be, you will be modeling the traits that they will build into their own definitions of respect. Developing self-respect is the first step for a child to develop respect for others.

Children with a sense of respect value themselves and other people. They recognize and appreciate their own unique qualities, their strengths, and their challenges, as well as those of others.

When Things Go Wrong

"So what are you real, real good at?" teacher Alicia asked Christian as they made his personal page in the Big Book.

"Nothin'," he said.

"Let's think together," his teacher coached. "I remember outside I saw you go all the way across the monkey bars."

"Uh-uh. I fall when I do monkey bars," Christian countered.

"Well, look here. Look how you write your name with all the letters. You are good at that, huh."

"That paper is stupid," Christian said, and he grabbed the paper and tore it into small pieces.

"I'm a bad boy," Sebastian told the visitor to his classroom. "I don't do nothing right and I always get in trouble and I need to take a sad face home 'cause I am bad every day."

"Oh, I'm sure sometimes you do things right," said the guest.

"Nuh-uh. I hit kids and break stuff, and I don't listen to nobody," Sebastian answered.

So often as we try to help children grow and learn new things, we focus on their areas of challenge and weakness. After all, those areas need work. For children with many areas of challenge, their reflected reality may seem to be that they are a big mess of problems with no arenas of strength or talent.

Before children are three years old, everything they believe about themselves comes directly from what others tell them. Gradually over the next two years, however, the talk that children hear about themselves becomes their self-talk. Their minds become like tape recorders, playing and replaying those messages again and again. Many times a week, Sebastian is told that he is taking a sad face home because he had a "bad day" at school. His mother, seeing yet another note with a sad face, says to him in the evening, "I see you were a bad boy again for Ms. F today." With these repeated messages from the important adults in his life, it's no wonder that Sebastian has begun to define himself as a bad kid. What children believe about themselves becomes their reality. Children who tell themselves they are failures fail. Children who tell themselves they are stupid have trouble learning. Children who are told that nobody likes them behave in unlikable ways. One of the first steps in helping children to change their unsuccessful behaviors is to change their self-defeating self-talk.

Help children develop self-talk that honors their abilities to grow and change in positive ways. Give them tools and language to visualize and celebrate their successes.

"Lola can't play with us, huh," Dewey said to the others at the sand table. "She don't got no teeth in the front. She too ugly to play with us."

"Go 'way, Nicholas. Only girls can play with the dress-up," Ramona said.

"Who is that kid over there with the red shirt?" the visitor asked.

"She's Svetlana," Sadie said.

"Is she one of your friends here at school?" the visitor asked.

"Nobody her friend. She don't talk in English."

As children grow and mature, they begin to identify their own characteristics and the unique characteristics of those around them. They may develop fear or discomfort with differences and might avoid those who aren't like themselves. Acknowledge and model respect for diversity to reduce children's anxiety about differences and to guide them to appreciate the contributions of each member of the community.

Cooperation vs. Competition

When is cooperation a winning strategy, and when is competition a winning strategy? Our adult lives call for both skills. Developing a mission statement with a committee calls for cooperative skills. Playing chess calls for competitive skills. As children learn to both respect themselves and respect others, they need to develop both skills. Begin to prepare children by helping them learn when and how each is appropriate and productive and by giving them the life skills to do both.

Competitive children often choose ways to be different or stand out from the crowd. They have a need to be the fastest, the loudest, or the strongest, and they might not go along with the flow of the rest of the group. Children who must compete are sometimes very disruptive to school activities when we are expecting cooperation. For example, if we are singing the "Alphabet Song" as a group activity, this child might be at *z* while the rest of us are at *k*. And while we all attempt to finish the song, the competitive child is yelling, "I got done already. You guys are soooooo slow. You can't do it fast like me." For this child, being faster or louder means winning. Competitiveness permeates American society, so it is not surprising that some children pick this up at a very young age.

You may notice less competitive behavior and more cooperative behavior with children from cultures in which interdependence is more important than independence. In fact, these children will often shun activities that call for competition and may be very uncomfortable if they receive attention and glory as the winner.

Be very clear that some activities are competitive and some activities are cooperative, and include activities in your daily schedule to help children practice both skills.

Most children who have strong attachment and affiliation need little additional support to develop this strength. Some children, though, can benefit from additional interventions. Strategies from the attachment and affiliation chapters (chapters 3 and 4) can be used to supplement the suggestions in this chapter.

By accepting and honoring that we all come with our own set of talents and challenges, our hope is that children will approach life with an inclusive philosophy and the highest degree of respect for self and others.

Supportive Interactions

Since children form their ideas of respect by observing significant adults, it is important that you be aware of your interactions with and in front of children at all times. Verbalize your recognition and appreciation for the different personalities in your classroom. Finally, prepare to respond thoughtfully to children's frank observations of differences.

Recognize "Insides"

During the preschool years, children start to notice differences in people by external characteristics, such as gender, skin color, and material possessions. While this is a typical development stage, help children become aware that people are more than their outsides.

Emphasize character traits in your dialogue with children, especially when you first greet them in the morning.

INSTEAD OF SAYING . . .	TRY SAYING . . .
"Good morning. I like your new tennis shoes."	"Good morning. I feel happy when I see your big smile."
"What pretty hair ribbons."	"Tell me about your visit with your grandma."
"Aren't you a handsome boy today."	"I'm so happy to see you this morning."

We All Have Something in Common

Young children find the familiar comforting. They often don't want to try an unfamiliar food or a new babysitter, and they love to hear the same favorite book over and over. They may shy away from playing with kids who appear different from themselves.

Help children notice how they share similarities with other children, particularly with children of a different gender or with different physical characteristics. Focus your observations of commonalities on internal rather than surface qualities.

- You have a dog at home just like Iris has.
- I see two kids who both like to do linker cubes.
- Did you know that Leticia says that *The Hungry Caterpillar* is her favorite book too?

We Are Each Unique

Children can shock adults by the very frank observations they make about unusual features of others, such as "Look how fat that man is." Instinctively, we want to shush children and tell them, "That's not nice to say." However, young children aren't commenting on others to be rude; they are genuinely interested. Sometimes, these observations can also cause them to be a bit anxious, and their tone of voice might sound aggressive or defensive. Regardless, try to respond in a matter-of-fact way that validates the child's observation of the diversity of humanity.

To avoid being caught off-guard, take some time to practice supportive responses to children's observations of differences. Try a simple response that first validates the child's observation of a difference followed by generalization of commonality.

WHEN A CHILD SAYS . . .	ACKNOWLEDGE THE DIFFERENCE	GENERALIZE THE SAMENESS
"Dharma's lunch looks yucky."	"Dharma's lunch is different than yours."	"But everybody's lunch is yummy food."
"Karen's skin is all pasty white."	"Karen has light skin and you have dark skin."	"All people have skin on the outside of their bodies."
"Passion don't have no mama."	"Passion lives with her grandma and you live with your mama."	"All kids live with grown-ups who take care of them."

We're Different and We're Friends

Children have some things in common with others and some things that are unique, and they can be friends regardless. Focus children's attention on how two children can have differences and still be very good friends.

Be careful to use very benign surface differences when you do this activity. The safest one to use is a difference in preferences. Look for differences in what foods they like, what activities they like to do, what colors they are choosing for their paint project.

- You like to use the tire swing best, and Becka likes to use the rope swing best. You like different things and you can still be friends.
- You ate two servings of carrots, and Marcia doesn't even like to eat one carrot! You like different things and you can still be friends.

Support Respect through the Classroom Culture

There is tremendous power in bringing together groups of individuals with unique talents and gifts. The whole ends up being much more than the sum of its parts.

Teach children to celebrate diversity. Help them identify what unique qualities they bring to the community and how to respect the qualities that others bring with some of the following ongoing activities.

Reflecting Family Lives

Children do not enter the classroom as an empty slate. They bring with them their home language, traditions, preferences, and culture. Just as adults might keep mementos of home at their workplace, encourage children to bring similar items into the classroom.

Family pictures, familiar bedtime music, and special foods from home help the child to feel that school is their place and that their whole being is honored and respected.

- Display photos of children and their families on a family photo wall, in picture albums, or in individual or collage frames around the classroom. Have families bring in family pictures or take pictures at drop off, pick up, or home visits. Make sure that all children are represented with at least one family member. Some teachers have made a family photo album to keep in their home living areas. Others have framed photos and have hung or placed them in various areas around the room.

- Ask families to donate extra household items to the room. Some items you might request are small rugs, place mats, pitchers, rolling pins, curtains, tapestries, vases, picture frames, cookbooks, hats, and baskets. Use these items throughout the classroom to bring a homelike atmosphere that reflects children's lives and experiences.

- Ask families to donate old magazines, picture books, and cookbooks that reflect their cultures and traditions. Add these materials to the class library as well as to the dramatic play areas and other appropriate areas of the classroom.

- Lend families tape recorders and picture books and have them record their reading on tape. Use these books and tapes in the listening center to supplement other books on tape you might have. Include books and family recordings in all languages spoken by the children in the class.

- Encourage families to teach the class nursery rhymes, chants, and finger plays that the family use at home. Weave this rich variety of family cultural traditions into the classroom repertoire.

- Collect information from families about foods that are served both every day and for celebrations. Invite family members to make simple recipes with children as a cooking project or to share at snack time.

- Ask families to lend you CDs or tapes of lullaby music used at home, and use this music for rest times and quiet times in the classroom.

- Discover families' skills and talents. Ask these experts to enrich the curriculum and environment of the classroom. Look for talents such as playing musical instruments or singing, cooking, painting, woodworking, beading, sewing, working with clay, storytelling, and collecting (shells, rocks, dolls, bones, or snow globes).

Images of the Children

Another way to honor the children in your room is to use photos of the children from the classroom community in place of commercially produced posters. It is much more powerful for children to see images of themselves on the walls than it is to see images of total strangers.

- Take one or more pictures of children playing together, mount them on posterboard, and label it "We Play Together" to replace a commercial poster.
- Photograph children in the classroom who are washing their hands to replace the existing hand-washing procedure poster.
- Mount pictures of classroom children engaged in learning center activities in each center.
- Make a poster of parents and children reading books together to decorate your library center.
- Make sure there are one or more mirrors around the classroom so children can see themselves frequently.

Post Children's Work

Help children take pride in themselves and their work products by providing space for each child to display their own work.

Some teachers post small pictures of each child around the classroom to indicate to children where they can post one sample of their work. When a child chooses to post another sample, they take down the first one and replace it with the new one. Children can take care of this task themselves without adult assistance. Just give them the tape and let them go.

Class Experts

Everyone has a talent or skill they can contribute to benefit the classroom. Increase the richness of the classroom community by drawing on individuals and families. Help children appreciate their own strengths and talents as well as those of others in the class community with the "Class Expert" chart.

1. On a big piece of chart paper, print the names of all community members down the left side of the paper. You can add small snapshots of the children and adults, if you like.
2. Help each member identify a strength or talent, and print that talent on the right side of the chart. Enhance with a photo of the child doing the behavior or clip art if you like. Some examples are ties shoes, pumps on the swing,

knows the day of the week, knows the names of dinosaurs, dances, can print letters, and so on.

3. As often as possible, call upon children to contribute to the class using their unique skill. Also, get into the habit of referring children to each other for expertise. For example, if Lara asks you for help to draw a dog, help her refer to the expert chart to find that Lee is the class drawing expert, and have her ask Lee for help.

4. Periodically, redo the expert chart to reflect new skills or to find experts to fill a need in the classroom. For example, if many children are asking for help with zippers, try to find a child who is a zipper expert to help.

We All Have Goals

We all come with areas of strength and expertise. And we all come with areas of challenge. Part of the excitement of life is to use our talents and work on our more challenging areas. Help children identify their own personal goals and give them the practice and support that they need to reach those goals.

1. Make a goal chart using the same directions as the expert chart. Make sure goals are stated in the positive.

2. Work with each child to find a way that the community can provide support with instruction, coaching, practice, or cheerleading.

3. Weave a reminder of goals into the daily schedule. At morning meeting or transition time, you might want to quickly go around the circle for children to state their goal. You can also do this at the lunch table or when patting children's backs at rest time. However it is done, it is important to help children focus on their goal every day.

4. Periodically, check in with each member to evaluate where they stand.

5. Goals are personal, and evaluation of goals should be an exercise in self-reflection, not a "grade" from others. One teacher meets with children one-on-one periodically and says, "So, how are you doing with your goal?" Another checks in randomly during morning meeting.

6. All adults in the classroom should have goals as well. Make the goals challenging and realistic. Model for children the frustration of meeting goals, the persistence in pursuing goals, and the feeling of achievement when one has reached a goal.

Together We Are Better

Help children appreciate that it sometimes takes the talents of many to achieve a goal or complete a task. Provide children with activities that depend on each child's skills and contributions to be successful.

- Cooperative classroom activities, projects, and games.
- Act out a book.
- Put on a puppet show. Ask some children to be players and others to be the audience. Switch roles.
- Make a class garden. Rotate gardening chores such as watering and weeding. Make sure everyone plants and harvests. Take photos of all stages of the project, making sure that all children are represented in the pictures.
- Plan and execute a party or celebration. Help children make decisions about the decorations, food, and activities. Make sure each child has an important role in executing the plans. During the celebration, help children recognize that it took the efforts of everyone to make the vision a reality.
- Play "everybody wins" games such as those from chapter 3.

Cooperation and Competition

Focus children on the delicate task of balancing needs of self with the needs of the community. At the same time you guide children in the art of cooperation, stay aware that part of the job of being a preschool child is to explore personal power. Provide many opportunities for children to personally strive and shine.

- For cooperative activities, explain to the children that "You win the game by playing the same." This is a new concept for some very competitive children who are used to winning by standing out from the crowd. Try using this singsong reminder: "Not louder, not lower, not faster, not slower. You win this game by playing the same."
- Give clear cues when it is time to match the others. Motivate children to match others by letting them know that matching others is a very tricky skill. These children already know that faster is tricky. They know climbing higher is tricky. And it helps them to reframe cooperation as being equally tricky, which in reality it is. It is very tricky to curb one's own impulses to conform to group norms. Sometimes the trick is to be the same; the trick is not to be different.

Consensus

Majority voting is not the best decision-making strategy to teach young kids. Preschool is an opportunity to help children move from being egocentric toward caring about the wants and needs of others. What happens when we use majority voting? "Raise your hand if you want to eat outside. Raise your hand if you want to eat inside. Okay. Everybody except Louisa and Brandon voted to eat outside so we're all eating outside." What have we just taught the children about the needs and feelings of the minority? How did this process help children to practice inclusion of those who see the world in a different way? How does it support our problem-solving process, in which we teach children that for a solution to work, it has to meet everyone's needs?

Instead of using a majority vote to make class decisions, try using a process of consensus building. Consensus takes more time than majority voting. But the payoff is that the process of consensus building promotes mutual respect, problem-solving skills, and inclusion. Help children in your care learn that might doesn't necessarily make right.

How can that outside/inside episode be handled with consensus instead of majority voting?

Sarah said to the children, "Raise your hand if you want to eat outside. Raise your hand if you want to eat inside. Uh-oh, not everybody agrees. Some people want to eat outside and some want to eat inside. How can we work it so everybody feels okay? Who has some ideas?"

"I know," volunteered Gloria. "We can eat outside today and inside tomorrow."

The teacher posed this solution to the group. "Let's see if this will work for everyone. The idea is to eat outside today and inside tomorrow. Raise your hand if that's okay. William, I see you don't agree with this. Do you have another idea that might work?"

"Maybe some of us can eat outside with you and some of us can eat inside with Miss Laura," suggested William.

"That would work for me. Miss Laura, would that work for you too? Oh good. Let's see if the kids are okay with that. William suggested that some of you can eat outside with me, and some can stay inside with Miss Laura. Raise your hand if that will work for you. Okay, I think we found a solution that works for everybody."

What did this process teach the children about the needs and feelings of the minority? How did this process help children to practice inclusion of those who see the world in a different way? Working toward consensus reinforces that it is possible to resolve differences of opinion and that everyone's needs are met.

Activities to Support Respect

The Important Book

This activity is based on *The Important Book* by Margaret Wise Brown. Here a class-made book helps children celebrate what they identify as their unique and special qualities.

1. Have each child make one page of this book.
2. Work with the child to help them complete this template. Prompt them if necessary, but make sure that the child is the one to identify his qualities and that he is the one to select which is the most important.

   The most important thing about (name) is ____________.

   He also ____________________ and _________________________ and _________________.

   But the *most* important thing about (name) is (whatever was said on the first line).

   For example: The most important thing about Tyesha is that she loves her brother.

   She also has red hair ribbons and likes to play "Hungry Hippo" and eats ice cream.

   But the *most* important thing about Tyesha is that she loves her brother.

3. Have each child illustrate their page. Then put together the pages with a cover to make "The Important Book." Put a parent response page on the back.
4. Read the book to the class. After the first few times, children will enjoy guessing who wrote each page of the book. Circulate the book among the families and invite them to respond on the response page.
5. Keep the book in your classroom library.

Community Work

Community work is different than a group project. In a group project, the members work together for the benefit of the classroom. Community work is intended to benefit those outside the immediate classroom. Research has shown that children who participate in projects to benefit others are more successful in school and in life than children who don't have those opportunities. Participation in community work helps children value "strength in numbers." Together, they are able to do far more than one child can do alone.

1. When doing community projects, it is important that every member play an essential role in getting the work done.

Some ideas for community work include these:

- Wash a staff member's car.
- Pick up trash around the play yard.
- Build a gingerbread house for a children's ward in a hospital or for a retirement village.
- Put on a play for another class.
- Paint a mural on an inside wall of the play yard.
- Grow vegetables, which then get donated to a children's shelter.

2. Reflection on community work after the project is completed is an important component of helping children visualize the process. Document the progress of the project with photos of the children participating in the project, and if possible take photos of those who benefited from the work. Have the children dictate captions. Display the work on posterboard or in a Big Book or scrapbook with a title such as "We Grew Vegetables for the Children's Shelter," or "We Made a Gingerbread House for the Senior Volunteers."

Same and Different book

Guide children to recognize and celebrate diversity with a "Same and Different Book."

1. Help children find partners.
2. Work together with the pair to help them find a way they are the same and a way they are different. Avoid using clothing as same/different characteristics.
3. Take dictation from the children to complete sentences such as "We are the same because we both_______________. We are different because (name of one child)(how child is different) and (name of other child)(how child is different)." For example, "We are the same because we both like to play computer games. We are different because Jeremiah has a dog at his house and Monte has a goat at his house."
4. Take a photo of the two children together that they can mount on the page, or have the children work together to illustrate their page.
5. Bind pages together into a book with a front and back cover. Put the title on the front and label the back as a parent response page.
6. Read the book to the class and have children take the book home to share with families. Encourage families to comment on the back cover.

Picture Graphing

As children learn about each other, they tend to form best friends and small friendship cliques. This is a normal stage of development for young children, but at the same time, we want to make sure that children don't form cliques. Some clues that this might be happening are comments such as, "She can't play with us because she wears pants like a boy," or "He can't play with us because he can't run fast."

Help children learn that while they have some things in common with one group of children, they have something else in common with a different group of children. Picture graphing is a visual way to represent this to children. One way to use picture graphing is to change the theme of the graph on a weekly basis. Help children notice that they are with a different group of children each time the topic changes.

1. Mount photos of children on individual pieces of posterboard and cover with clear Con-Tact paper. Photos that are 2 by 2 inches seem to work well for this. Attach Velcro fastener tabs to the back of each photo.
2. To make a reusable graph, divide a plain piece of posterboard with a bold horizontal line. Either laminate the board or cover with clear Con-Tact paper. Attach Velcro fastener bits or strips on both halves of the paper. Make sure there is enough Velcro fastener on each half to hold all of the children's photos.
3. Decide on a theme, and label each half of the graph with a "choice." Use both words and pictures to label choices. Some ideas include the following:
    - Which food I like better: hamburger (top half), pizza (bottom half)
    - Which I am: boy (top half), girl (bottom half)
    - Which I like to do more: water table (top half), sand table (bottom half)
4. Have each child affix their picture to indicate their choice.
5. Point out to children that children in each section are similar to each other and different from the children on the other half of the graph. Each time the theme of the graph is changed, children will be grouped with different kids. Help them notice that the groups change, depending on the topic.

Shared Problems

Sometimes it takes more than one person to get a job done. Pose these situations to children so small groups are encouraged to work together toward a common goal. Make sure to give the children reflective feedback after the activity to reinforce the value of teamwork.

- Help organize small groups of children to play rescue squad or chasing the dog out of the kitchen. At the end of the activity, say something like, "We all worked together to get the job done," or "I'm so glad we had so many helpers for this big job."
- Look for real-life opportunities during the day when many hands are better than one. Invite children to help move a heavy table or carry five or six balls out to the play yard. Make sure that your feedback encourages children to focus on the group and not on you. Instead of saying, "Thank you for helping me move the table," (teacher focused) say, "We all moved that table together. It's good to have so many hands."

Discussion/Reflection Questions

1. How might you respond to each of these comments from children to acknowledge differences and generalize sameness?
    - Boys can't play dolls with the girls.
    - Rudy is soooooo fat. We don't like her, huh?
    - Xiaozheng talks funny words. He don't know how to talk regular.
2. Why is it important to involve children's families and cultures in the classroom community? What about children who live in poverty, children's shelters, or homeless shelters? How would you represent their home life in the classroom?
3. How does the expert chart support children from homes that value independence? How does it support children from homes that value interdependence? Can you think of other strategies to support children from both kinds of cultural backgrounds?

Exercises

1. How does your classroom honor each child's family and culture? What strategies will you implement to increase family visibility in your program?
2. Make an "Expert Chart" with your class. Find a way to use the chart as a living document by using it at least twice a day. What impact does the chart have on your class?

Reflection/Journal Assignment

What unique qualities, gifts, and talents do you bring to this world? How are you using those gifts and talents? Are you using your unique gifts in your work?

If you were to put something on a goal chart, what would it be? Why did you choose that?

Resources

Covey, Stephen R. 1997. *The seven habits of highly effective families: Building a beautiful family culture in a turbulent world.* New York: Golden Books.

Gestwicki, Carol. 1999. *Developmentally appropriate practice: Curriculum and development in early education.* Albany, NY: Delmar Publishers.

Levin, Diane E. 1994. *Teaching young children in violent times. Building a peaceable classroom: A preschool–grade three violence prevention and conflict resolution guide.* Cambridge, MA: Educators for Social Responsibility.

Marston, Stephanie. 1990. *The magic of encouragement: Nurturing your child's self-esteem.* New York: William Morrow and Company, Inc.

Sparks, Louise Derman, and the ABC Task Force. 1989. *Anti-bias curriculum: Tools for empowering young children.* Washington DC: National Association for the Education of Young Children.

York, Stacey. 2003. *Roots and wings: Affirming culture in early childhood programs.* Rev. ed. St. Paul: Redleaf Press.

A Few Last Words

"Change has a considerable psychological impact on the human mind. To the fearful it is threatening because it means that things may get worse. To the hopeful it is encouraging because things may get better. To the confident it is inspiring because the challenge exists to make things better."

—King Whitney Jr.

Now, with a sack full of new tricks and ideas, I hope you feel ready to go try them out. Remember: this information is just a starting point, it is not a cure-all. Some children are going to be a challenge. They'll make you cry and break your heart. They'll make you want to just give up. Keep in mind, though, that growth and healing may be going on so far under the surface that any progress may be invisible to you.

Domingo brought this lesson home to me many years ago. Socially and emotionally, he had so far to go. At five years old, he had been "asked to leave" his previous four preschools. For months it seemed that Domingo resisted all our attempts to build nurturing relationships and mutual respect. Establishing even the most rudimentary level of trust with him seemed impossible.

And then a new boy joined our group—a child with a similar history and similar challenges. Fear washed over me as I saw those two conspiring that first day at the lunch table. I edged over close enough to hear the conversation, certain that Domingo was coaching Christopher on how to make my life miserable. But I couldn't have been more wrong.

I got there just in time to see Domingo gently pat Christopher's hand. "Don't worry," he said quietly as he leaned in. "The teachers here won't kick you out. They're here to teach you how to be good and how to do good at school."

Remember why you picked up this book and what is at stake. There is nothing to lose, but there is oh, so much to be gained.

Jenna
www.kidsfromtheinsideout.com

Appendices

Getting to Know You

Child's name____________________________________ **Date**____________________

1. Use the following list as a starting point to identifying a child's strengths and challenges. Put a mark along the continuum for each item set. The mark can be anywhere along the range.

Attachment

Has little use for the adults in his/her world ←→ Seeks out adults for love, comfort, company

Does not respond to comforting ←→ Calms down when adults comfort

Affiliation

Only plays alone ←→ Seeks play with others

No interest in what others are doing ←→ Shows interest in what others are doing

Self-regulation

Falls apart when frustrated, disappointed, hurt ←→ Manages frustration, disappointment, hurt

Impatient and impulsive ←→ Thinks before acting, patient

Hurts self, people, or property when upset ←→ Stays safe when upset

Easily distracted ←→ Can stay on a task

Initiative

Acts hopeless and discouraged ⟷ Acts optimistic

Quits easily ⟷ Keeps trying

Can't make decisions ⟷ Makes decisions for self

Problem solving and conflict resolution

Doesn't know how to solve problems ⟷ Tries different ways to solve problems

Uses hurtful strategies to resolve conflict ⟷ Resolves conflicts with adult help

Respects self and others

I am worthless and can't do anything ⟷ I have value, skills, and talents

Totally egocentric ⟷ Recognizes value of others

2. What are this child's interests and areas of expertise?
What does this child choose to play with?

1. ______________________________

____

2. ______________________________

____

3. ______________________________

____

Figure out the child's highest level of independent play

Observe the child to identify which of the five levels below describes the highest level of play the child can participate in without adult intervention or support. Circle the one highest level in the left-hand column that seems to describe this child.

LEVEL OF PLAY	LOOKS LIKE...
SOLO	Child plays alone. For example, Patrice builds a block tower in the block area.
PARALLEL	Child plays next to another child with similar materials and themes, but does not interact with the other child. For example, Paley and Quentin play side by side at the water table, but don't play with each other.
DYAD	Looks a lot like parallel play, but in dyad play, the children interact with each other. For example, Davon and Rebecca are dressing up in the dramatic play area. Davon hands a hat to Rebecca and says, "Here, you can wear this hat, and I will wear the green one." Rebecca says, "Okay, and I will be the grandma and you have to sit at the table and eat your lunch."
SMALL GROUP	Looks a lot like dyad play, but instead of just two children, there are three to five children in the play.
LARGE GROUP	Looks a lot like small group, but there are more than five children in the play.

Figure out the child's preferred learning style

Most children will use a combination of many styles. Observe the child during the day and focus in on the two most preferred styles. A "preferred" style is the way a child learns when she has a free choice. For example, a child who is cooperative in large group instruction may be compliant, but prefer to work alone. Another child might eagerly look forward to large group activities and tend to drift toward large groups even when it isn't a mandatory activity.

SEEING	Learns best when he can see what he is learning. Likes photos, pictures, posters, books, and watching puppet shows and dramatic plays. Loses interest when activities are "talk heavy," but focuses in when there is something to look at.
DOING	Learns best from hands-on activities, playacting, opportunities to practice, journal writing, experience charts, and field trips. Enjoys getting actively involved in special projects.
TOUCHING	Learns best by touching things such as artifacts and books. Likes to make things. Finds it hard to "look with no touching."
MOVING	Learns best through dramatic play, puppets, dance and movement, and learning centers. Doesn't sit still for more than a few minutes.
CHATTING	Learns best with discussions, buddy work, group work, and scripts. Finds it hard to keep quiet.
WORKING WITH OTHERS	Learns best working with a partner, in a small group, or in larger groups. Most often finds others to work with.
EXPLORING ALONE	Learns best when she can explore by herself or with an adult partner. Goes off often to work alone.
INDIVIDUAL CULTURES, INTERESTS, AND CHALLENGES	Consider culture, family, language, and individual abilities or challenges that influence the best learning situations for children.

What are the family's goals for their child this year?

____

____

____

What are the family's long-term goals for their child?

____

____

____

Where along the continuum would you put the family's overall cultural emphasis?

INDEPENDENCE	INTERDEPENDENCE
Focus on individual	Focus on part of group/family
Independence	Helpfulness
Self esteem	Conforming to expectation
Exploring and questioning	Listening and obeying
Personal property and space	Sharing
Respect for individual	Respect for authority
Parents teach their children	Teachers teach the children
Babyhood is short	Babyhood lasts longer
Nuclear family	Extended family

Making a Plan

Child's name____ **Date**____________________

Chronological age _______________ **Teacher**____

This child needs work on (circle the most basic *one* needed):

self-regulation initiative problem solving respecting self and others

This child's two preferred styles of learning are:

____

This child's highest independent level of play is:

____

This child is interested in or likes playing with:

____

The family's cultural emphasis is independence or interdependence (circle one).

As I make this plan, I will use the information above to help me tailor strategies to this particular child. I will strengthen my bond with this child by:

____

Right now, this child is at a ________________________ stage of relating to peers. I will help move the child to the next stage by:

____

This child needs help to develop the additional strength circled above. I will help this child develop this strength by adding these strategies:

____

____

____

Chapter 3 scripts

Get Close

INSTEAD OF . . .	TRY . . .
Calling across the room, "Lavone, is this your coat on the floor?"	Bringing the coat over to Lavone, squatting down, and gently saying, "Lavone, is this your coat? Put it in your cubby to keep it clean."
Calling across the room, "Frederick, did you wash your hands after you went potty?"	Walking over to Frederick, squatting down, taking his hands in yours, and gently saying, "Frederick, your hands are dry. I think you might have forgotten to wash. Scoot back in there and clean them up real quick."

Play with Children

INSTEAD OF SAYING . . .	TRY . . .
"How many rectangles did you use to build that farm?"	"How can I play?"
"Let's match up the mommy animals and the baby animals."	"Here's some food for the cows. Eat, cows."
"Oh no. Elephants don't belong in a farm. Where do elephants go?"	"Oh no. My chicken is scared of the elephant. He's running to try to get under the fence."

Sportscasting

INSTEAD OF SAYING . . .	TRY . . .
"What do you think will happen if you pour the water into the funnel?"	"Lulu is picking up the large bottle of water. It looks like she's going to pour it into the funnel."
"The boat is upside down. Turn it over and see how it works."	"Stephano has the boat upside down and is riding it in the water. He let go and the boat went right down to the bottom. Now he's picking it up. He turned it over. He let go. It is staying on top this time."
"What color is that water?"	"Tito has a pitcher of red water. He's filling little cups. Now he's filling the big cup."

Be a Pillar of Safety

WHEN	INSTEAD OF . . .	TRY
Tyesha cries to you because Jaylyn hit her back	"That's what happens when you hurt. You get hurt back. See?"	"This is a safe place. Let's find a way to keep you safe and a way to keep Jaylyn safe."
Mazen uses profanity toward you	"Do you want to get kicked out of this school like you got kicked out of your last school?"	"Let's figure out school words you can use to tell me when you are angry with me."
Sovannary gets anxious during transitions and starts to toss things around the classroom	"Go sit over there by yourself in the Thinking Chair. I'm tired of you breaking our things."	"Sovannary, come on over here with me so I can help you feel safe."
Matthew bites Amina	"Nobody likes bad boys, Matthew."	"Let's get ice for Amina and then you can stay by me so everyone stays safe here this morning."

Children's Feelings

YOU MIGHT WANT TO . . .	SOUNDS LIKE . . .
Ask how the child is feeling.	"Are you upset about that?"
Guess how the child is feeling.	"Your face and voice tell me you are very happy about your grandpa visiting you."
Mirror what you hear.	"So you tried to tie your shoes and you couldn't get it?"
Validate feelings.	"I can see why you feel frustrated."
Empathize.	"You must feel so frustrated."
Let the child know that her feelings are a reaction to a trigger.	"You got scared when the fire alarm went off, huh?"
Reassure the child that his reaction is normal.	"A lot of kids are scared of loud noises."

Feelings or Information?

WHEN A CHILD SAYS . . .	FEELING OR INFORMATION	TRY SAYING . . .
"Nobody will play with me."	Feeling	"You sound lonely to me."
"Where does this block go?"	Information	"Look on the shelf and find the shapes that match."
"I can't draw a horse."	Feeling	"You aren't happy with how your horse looks?"
"How many crackers can we take?"	Information	"The sign shows that you can take two crackers."

Use a Magic Word: *Come*

INSTEAD OF SAYING . . .	APPROACH THE CHILD, TAKE HER HAND, AND GENTLY SAY . . .
"Go wash your hands."	"Come. Let's wash hands."
"Go put on your shoes before we go out."	"Come. Let's get your shoes."
"Sit down while you eat."	"Come. Let's sit down."

Chapter 4 Scripts

Friendly Solutions

INSTEAD OF SAYING . . .	TRY . . .
"Give Amit some of the blocks."	"Find a way for Amit to play blocks."
"Stacy needs a doll too. Paul, give her one of yours."	"Find a way for Stacy to play babies with you."
"Stanley, move over so Albert can sit at circle."	"Let's make room for Albert." (Then just wait.)
"LeBron, Abby is crying because her mama just left. Can you paint with her at the easel please?"	"Abby feels sad because her mama just left. How can we help her feel better?"

Use Peers As Resources

WHEN YOU SAY . . .	THE CHILD LEARNS . . .
"____knows how to____. Go ask him/her." For example, "Brandon knows how to open the jar. Go ask him for help."	Peers are valuable resources.
"That was a heavy table. It was good to have two kids work together to move it."	Sometimes it takes more than one person to reach a goal.
"I saw you guys playing catch outside. It's good to have another kid to play with."	Interacting with others can be fun.

Chapter 4 Sentence Templates

Comment on Friendly Behavior

Examples:

- "I see two kids working together."
- "You guys look like you are having fun playing superheroes together."
- "Did the two of you set that table together?"

Name Friendly Actions

Template: "You [action] so that [impact]. That was friendly."
Examples:

- "You *moved over* so that *Emilia could sit down.* That was friendly."
- "You *got off the bike* to *give Stephan a turn.* That was friendly."
- "You *found Dexter's car in the yard and gave it back to him. Look how happy he is now.* That was friendly."

Notice Friendly Overtures

Template: "I saw [child's name, behavior]. [He or she] was being friendly to you."
Examples:

- "I saw *Raymond share his cookie with you.* He was being friendly to you."
- "I saw *CJ give you a turn with the easel.* She was being friendly to you."

Chapter 5 Scripts

How I Feel

INSTEAD OF USING THE WORD *MAKE* . . .	TRY "WHEN YOU___, I FEEL____."
"Tell Raymond how he made you feel."	"Tell Raymond that you don't like it when he calls you names."
"Don't make me call your mother."	"When I call and you don't come in, I feel very frustrated."
"Look at his face. How did you make him feel?"	"When you told Benjamin he couldn't play, he felt bad."

At School We . . .

AT SCHOOL WE . . . (RULE)	BECAUSE . . . (GUIDING PRINCIPLE OF BEHAVIOR)
At school we walk on the step	because we take care of ourselves.
At school we use words not hands	because we take care of each other.
At school we throw away our snack trash	because we take care of our stuff.

First, Then

INSTEAD OF SAYING . . .	TRY . . .
"If you don't pick up the blocks, you won't go outside."	"First pick up the blocks, then you can go outside."
"You're not going to get snack if you don't come inside right now."	"First come inside, then you can have snack."
"If you finish your job, I'll let you have a turn at the cooking table."	"First finish your job, then you can cook."
"If you lie quietly at rest for ten minutes, I'll give you a sticker."	"First rest quietly for ten minutes, then you can get up and play."

Feelings Are Responses

WHEN . . .	TEMPLATE . . .	EXAMPLE . . .
Outside events have an impact on their feelings	You feel (emotion) because (event).	"You feel excited because March is coming for supper," or "You feel tired because you worked so hard on the climber."
Other people's actions have an impact on their feelings	When (person) (action), you felt (emotion).	"When Margaret said you couldn't go to her birthday, you felt sad," or "David shared his blocks and you felt good."
Their actions have an impact on other people's feelings	When you (action), (other person) felt (feeling).	"When you pushed Denise, she felt angry," or "Jose liked it when you asked him to sit by you at circle."

Label and Validate Feelings

INSTEAD OF SAYING . . .	TRY . . .
"What's that face supposed to be all about?"	"I wonder if you are feeling frustrated (hurt, scared, disappointed)."
"Pouting isn't going to get you anywhere."	"It looks like you want to use the soccer ball first."
"There's no reason to be angry."	"You're angry and that's okay."
"There's nothing to be upset about."	"I can see you're upset and I understand."
"Don't feel that way."	"I'm sorry you feel that way."
"Go sit on the beanbag chair until you're ready to stop crying."	"What do you need? What do you want?"

What's Underneath Angry?

INSTEAD OF SAYING . . .	TRY . . .
"You seem angry that you have to wait for a turn."	"You seem frustrated that you have to wait for a turn."
"I bet you're angry that it isn't your 'Show and Tell' day."	"I bet you're disappointed that it isn't your 'Show and Tell' day."
"When Emmaline said your shoes are ugly, you felt angry."	"When Emmaline said your shoes are ugly, you felt hurt."
"You're angry that we have a new teacher-helper today."	"You're scared about the new teacher-helper today."

Validate Feeling, Then Guide Behavior

INSTEAD OF . . .	VALIDATE FEELING BY SAYING . . .	GUIDE BEHAVIOR BY SAYING . . .
"Stop grabbing that doll. Arsenio is using it."	"Do you want to use that doll?"	"You can ask Arsenio for a turn or I will help you find another one."
"Quit kicking Jarvis's block tower."	"Do you want to play with Jarvis?"	"At school we don't kick blocks. You can ask Jarvis if you can play with him."
"Move away from the sink. Sophia has been waiting a long time."	"It looks like you are having fun in the water."	"This sink is for washing. Let's find a different place to play in water."
"No throwing shoes."	"Are you frustrated with those shoes?"	"We need to keep kids safe, so no throwing. I can help you tie if you like."

Change Self-Talk

INSTEAD OF . . .	SUGGEST . . .
I can't stop.	I am the boss of me.
I hate her.	I'm angry.
I'm gonna punch you.	I need to walk away.
I can't do this. I'm dumb.	I can do this. I'm a smart kid.

Chapter 5 Sentence Templates

Reflect Cause and Effect

Template: "You [action] and [result]."
Examples:

- "You *turned the crank* and *the clown popped up*."
- "You *mixed red and yellow* and *look what happened*."
- "You *wiped up that spill* and *now the table is all clean again*."

Where Are You?

Template: "Look around you. Where are you right now?"
Examples:

- When Shea gets up during circle time and starts twirling around, bumping into others, say, "Shea, stop a minute. Look around. Where are you right now?"
- When Santo is on the loft tossing baby dolls over the railing, say, "Santo. Look around. Where are you right now?"

Reflective Feedback

Template: "You [action] because [principle]."
Examples:

- "You *washed your hands before you ate* because *we take care of ourselves*."
- "You *waited for a turn at the slide* because *we take care of each other*."
- "You *put all the blocks back on the shelf* because *we take care of our stuff*."

Feelings Change

Template: "You felt [feeling] and now you feel [feeling]. Feelings change."

Examples:

- "This morning you were angry with Jhon and now you two are having fun with the police cars. Feelings change."
- "You used to not like to eat salad and now you do! Feelings change."
- "You were so sad this morning when your nana left. Then you played with your friends and you felt better! Feelings change."

Chapter 6 Scripts

One More Thing

WHEN YOU ARE PLAYING WITH A CHILD . . .	TRY SAYING . . .
in blocks	"One more thing. Can we add three more blocks to the tower?"
in home living	"One more thing. Would you get me some pretend supper before you go?"
at the water table	"One more thing. Would you hold this funnel a minute so I can pour this big pitcher?"
at the writing table	"One more thing. Would you find me Orson's name card?"
in the book center	"One more thing. Before you go, would you find me a fun book that I can read from our bookshelf?"

Instead of "Doing For"

INSTEAD OF SOLVING . . .	TRY TEACHING AND COACHING . . .
"Nakita, don't hit Faith. Hitting hurts. She doesn't like that."	"Faith, you can tell Nakita you want her to stop hitting you. Say, 'Stop hitting me.' I'll stand by you to help."
"Oops. You spilled some milk. Move over and let me wipe it up before it gets all over the place."	"Oops. You spilled some milk. Do you need help to get some towels to wipe it up?"
"The red marker is broken? Here, let me get you another one."	"The red marker is broken? I wonder where you can find another one."

Descriptive Feedback

DESCRIPTIVE FEEDBACK	FOCUS ON PROCESS	ENCOURAGE SELF-REFLECTION
"I see you made it all swirly up here on top."	"Tell me how you made this swirly part up here."	"What's your favorite part of this painting?"
"Look how many different colors you used."	"How did you decide what colors to use in this?"	"Do you like the colors you used for this painting?"
"That tower is almost as high as you are."	"That must have been tricky to build a tower so high."	"What do you think of that tower?"
"You got all the way across the monkey bars."	"You worked hard to learn how to get across those monkey bars."	"How do you feel about getting all the way across the monkey bars?"

Strive Up

INSTEAD OF SAYING . . .	TRY . . .
"Get out from under that table right now."	"I wonder if you're a kid who knows how to get out from under the table all by herself."
"I'm counting to three and you had better get yourself inside this door."	"I wonder if you can get all the way into the classroom by the time I reach blast off. Here I go . . . five-four-three-two-one-blast off."
"You took all those puzzles out, so you need to put them all back on the shelf."	"Do you think you're a kid who can put all seven puzzles back on the shelf with no help?"
"Why do I have to keep reminding you to put your shoes in your cubby?"	"Pretty soon you'll be a kid who can put his shoes in his cubby all by himself."

Problems As Opportunities

INSTEAD OF FOCUSING ON THE PROBLEM	TRY TO FOCUS ON WHAT HAPPENS NEXT
"Do you want to stay in from recess?"	"How can we solve the problem?"
"I warned you about that, didn't I?"	"Let's figure out a way to fix this."
"You should know not to do that. Go pull a color card."	"Everyone makes mistakes. Let's figure out a way to fix this."
"Why did you do that?"	"What can you do differently next time?"

Recognize Positive Intent

WHEN A CHILD . . .	SAY . . .
has been working on being quiet at story but had a hard time today	"I know you are working hard to stay quiet during story time."
has been working to come inside at the signal but continued to play today instead	"Pretty soon, you'll be a kid who can come inside when the chime rings."
is learning to share supplies and refused to share the markers today	"Pretty soon, your brain will be strong enough to tell your body to share the markers."
is learning to stop using profanity and slipped today	"It takes a long time to learn how to use new strong words."

Chapter 7 Scripts

Model Cooperative Language

INSTEAD OF SAYING . . .	TRY SAYING . . .
"Do it because I said so."	"Let's figure this out together."
"Whoever cleans up fastest gets to be line leader."	"Let's see how fast we can work together to get the room cleaned up."
"You took them out so you put them back or you don't get to use them again."	"Let's help Bianca put the blocks away. She needed to use so many for the airport she made, and she needs some help."

That's A Problem

WHEN A CHILD SAYS . . .	TRY SAYING . . .
"I can't find my shoe."	"Wow. That's a real problem."
"The paintbrush fell on the floor and there's paint all over the place."	"Uh, oh. You have a real problem."
"Is it my job to be snack helper?"	"Hmmm. You don't remember your job. That's a problem. I wonder how you might find out what your job is?"

Assume the Child's Responsibility

INSTEAD OF SAYING . . .	TRY SAYING . . .
"Did you grab that toy from Connie?"	"Tell me what happened about the toy."
"Did you spill that water?"	"Uh, oh. I see the water spilled. Let's find the paper towels to clean it up."
"Did you finish cleaning the home living area?"	"Let's go to the home living area to check it out."
"Did you knock over the bookshelf?"	"I see you knocked over the bookshelf. You must have been pretty angry."

Coach Assertive Language

WHEN . . .	CHILDREN CAN SAY . . .
A child is being controlled by another child	"I don't want you to help. I'll do it myself."
A child is the object of name-calling or profanity	"I don't like those words. Stop it."
A child is being bullied	"I don't like that. I'm going to play with somebody else."
Someone is grabbing a toy from them	"Stop it. Ask for a turn."

Scaffold Assertive Language

	TEACH	INCLUDES . . .	FOR EXAMPLE
FIRST	"Stop" or "No."	A single word to set a boundary	"Stop."
SECOND	"I don't like that."	Expression of a feeling	"I don't like that."
THIRD	"I don't like it when you (behavior)."	Expression of feeling as a result of the action of another	"I don't like when you call me names."
FOURTH	"I don't like it when you (behavior). I want you to (suggestion for change)," or "I don't like it when you (behavior). I'm going to (action)."	Expression of feelings, the action of another, and a suggestion for change or action	"I don't like when you call me names. I'm going to play with somebody else."

Model Assertive Language

WHEN A CHILD . . .	INSTEAD OF . . .	TRY SAYING . . .
Calls you a name	Sending the child to time out	"I don't like those words. I'm going to walk away right now."
Talks while you are trying to read a story	Saying, "That's so rude to talk while I'm reading."	"When you talk I have trouble reading. I wish you could be more quiet."
Calls another child a rude name	Saying, "Be nice."	"When you call Passion names, I wonder what you are trying to say. Let's see what's wrong and find another way to say that."
Grabs a toy from another child	Grabbing the toy back and returning it to the child	"I don't like it when you grab toys. We take care of people in our classroom. I want you to give the squirter back to Dana."

Reword Profanity

INSTEAD OF USING . . .	TEACH THEM TO SAY . . .
Profanity for frustration	"This is too hard for me."
Profanity for disappointment	"I wanted to do that."
Profanity for hurt feelings	"I didn't like when he said that."

Define Solution Parameters

ACCEPT THE FEELING . . .	SET THE PARAMETERS . . .
"You wish you could take that bike from Kyrha."	"Kyrha is going to use that bike for now. Let's find another way to solve the problem."
"I know you want to be with your Mommy."	"It's Mommy's time to go to work and your time to go to school. Let's figure out something for you to do while you are here."
"Drawing a dog is hard for you right now."	"Markers need to stay on the table. Is there something I can do to help you with your drawing?"

At School We . . . Redux

WHEN . . .	"AT SCHOOL . . ."
Children physically fight over a bike.	"At school we use words, not hands, to solve problems."
Children cry to intimidate adults into meeting their demands.	"At school, the rules stay the same, even when children cry."
Children act helpless to get adults to do tasks for them.	"At school, (zipping, flushing, drawing, pouring, and so on) is a kid job."

Model Guiding Principles

WHEN THE CHILD . . .	WEAVE IN THE GUIDING PRINCIPLE . . .
Wants to grab a bike from another child	"You wish you had that bike. At school, we can't just grab things because we take care of others. Let's find another way to solve this."
Cries for his mama	"You miss your mama so much. Let's see how we can help you because at school we take care of ourselves."
"Borrows" things from school without asking	"You would love to take this toy to your house. We take care of our stuff at school, so we'll leave it here to play with tomorrow. Let's find something that you can take home with you."
Hits a child to get she wants	"We take care of others at school. If the kids won't listen to your words, come get me and I'll help you."
Throws markers on the floor because he's frustrated by not being able to draw a dog	"You can't draw that dog the way you want. At school, we keep markers on the table because we take care of our stuff. Let's see if there is some way to help you."

Brainstorm Solutions

IF . . .	TRY . . .	SOUNDS LIKE . . .
The child is very new at brainstorming solutions	Give a choice between two acceptable solutions.	"You have a choice. You can get another book or find another area to play in right now. What will you choose?" "Would you rather do (this) or (that)?" "What would be better for you? (This) or (that)?"
	If the dispute is over space or stuff, common preschool solutions are to share or take turns. When children are first practicing solutions, propose one or both of these strategies whenever you can.	"Some kids decide to take turns with the shovel. Other kids like to find a way to play with shovels together."
When a child has had ample experience brainstorming solutions	Encourage the child to find a peer to help.	"Would you like to find another friend to help you think?" "Who might know?" "Who can you ask?"
	Help the child break through their block.	"Pretend you're a kid who has an idea. What would you say?"

Chapter 8 Scripts

Recognize "Insides"

INSTEAD OF SAYING . . .	TRY SAYING . . .
"Good morning. I like your new tennis shoes."	"Good morning. I feel happy when I see your big smile."
"What pretty hair ribbons."	"Tell me about your visit with your grandma."
"Aren't you a handsome boy today."	"I'm so happy to see you this morning."

Validate Observations

WHEN A CHILD SAYS . . .	ACKNOWLEDGE THE DIFFERENCE	GENERALIZE THE SAMENESS
"Dharma's lunch looks yucky."	"Dharma's lunch is different than yours."	"But everybody's lunch is yummy food."
"Karen's skin is all pasty white."	"Karen has light skin and you have dark skin."	"All people have skin on the outside of their bodies."
"Passion don't have no mama."	"Passion lives with her grandma and you live with your mama."	"All kids live with grown-ups who take care of them."

Index